PassKey EA Review
WORKBOOK

Six Complete Enrolled Agent Practice Exams
2016-2017 Edition

Authors:
Richard Gramkow, EA
Christy Pinheiro, EA, ABA®
Kolleen Wells, EA
Joel Busch, CPA, JD

PassKey
Learning Systems

Editor: Joel Busch, CPA, JD

This study guide is designed for test-takers who will take their exams in the current EA Exam testing window (May 1, 2016, to February 28, 2017).

PassKey EA Review Workbook: Six Complete Enrolled Agent Practice Exams, 2016-2017 Edition

ISBN: 978-1-935664-47-5

Second Printing. 2016 PassKey EA Review
PassKey EA Review® is a U.S. Registered Trademark

All Rights Reserved ©2016, PassKey Publications Licensing Corp. dba PassKey EA Review. Revised and updated every year based on updated IRS EA exam specifications. United States laws and regulations are public domain and not subject to copyright. The editorial arrangement, analysis, and professional commentary are subject to this copyright notice. No portion of this book may be copied, retransmitted, reposted, duplicated, or otherwise used without the express written approval of the publisher. Questions for this study guide have been adapted from previous IRS Special Enrollment Examinations and from current IRS publications. The authors have also drafted new questions.

All the names used in this book are fictitious and any resemblance to real people, companies, or events is purely coincidental.

PassKey Publications, Elk Grove, CA.
www.PassKeyPublications.com

Table of Contents

Introduction _____ *5*

Essential Figures for Tax Year 2015 _____ *9*

Part 1: Individuals Practice Exams _____ *21*

   #1 Sample Exam: Individuals _____ 23

   #2 Sample Exam: Individuals _____ 52

Part 2: Business Practice Exams _____ *81*

   #3 Sample Exam: Businesses _____ 83

   #4 Sample Exam: Businesses _____ 111

Part 3: Representation Sample Exams _____ *137*

   #5 Sample Exam: Representation _____ 139

   #6 Sample Exam: Representation _____ 163

Test Answers _____ *185*

   Answers to Exam #1: Individuals _____ 187

   Answers to Exam #2: Individuals _____ 205

   Answers to Exam #3: Businesses _____ 221

   Answers to Exam #4: Businesses _____ 238

   Answers to Exam #5: Representation _____ 256

   Answers to Exam #6: Representation _____ 271

About the Authors _____ 289

Introduction

PassKey EA Review Workbook is designed to accompany the PassKey EA Review study guides, which present a comprehensive overview of the material you must learn to pass the IRS Special Enrollment Exam (SEE), commonly called the EA exam. This workbook features six complete enrolled agent practice exams, specifically created for the EA exam cycle that runs from May 1, 2016, to February 28, 2017.

Each sample exam has 100 questions similar to the ones you will encounter when you take your actual exam. These test questions are all unique and not found in the PassKey study guides. This is intentional, so EA candidates can have a more true-to-life test-taking experience when they go through the workbook questions.

Any EA exam candidate will benefit from the exam questions and detailed answers in this workbook. We suggest that you use it as a study tool to prepare for the exam in a realistic setting. Set aside an uninterrupted block of time and test yourself just as you would if you were actually taking the EA exam at a testing center.

Score yourself at the end, and then review the answers carefully. Unlike the Prometric exam, you will have a complete, clear answer for each question. If you miss a question, you will know why. Use this workbook to uncover your weak points and concentrate on improving in those areas. You should answer at least 80% of the questions correctly. Any score below 80% means you need to study more.

All of the questions in the workbook are based on 2015 tax law, which corresponds with the 2016-2017 EA exam cycle. If you have any questions about the actual exam or if you want to sign up for it, contact Prometric directly at 1-800-306-3926 or on the internet at www.prometric.com/IRS.

If you would like to find out more about the Complete EA Review study guides and other learning products by PassKey Publications, visit our website at *www.passkeypublications.com*.

Successfully passing the EA exam can launch you into a fulfilling and lucrative new career. The exam requires intense preparation and diligence, but with the help of PassKey's EA Review, you will have the tools you need to learn how to become an enrolled agent. As the authors of the PassKey EA Review, we wish you much success.

Recent Praise for the PassKey EA Review Series

You will pass with PassKey. I did!
Anne Stone (New Jersey)
I can't overemphasize how useful it is to do all the tests in the Workbook and to study the explanations in the answers. I have the highest praise for the books and the folks at PassKey.

Outstanding!
Derrell L. Chastain
Outstanding! Helped me pass the EA exam...I used all three books!

Highly recommend these materials
Tosha H. Knelangeon
Using only this book and the workbook, I passed all three EA exams on my first try. I highly recommend these materials. As long as you put in the time to read and study all the information provided, you should be well-prepared.

PassKey was the only study aid that I used
Stephen J Woodard, CFP, CLU, ChFC
The guides were an invaluable resource. They were concise and covered the subject matter succinctly with spot-on end of chapter questions that were very similar to what I encountered on the exams.

Very useful, I passed 1st and 2nd exams by reading only PassKey!
Shixiong Feng
Very useful, I passed the 1st and 2nd exams by only reading the PassKey EA Review. If you are willing to spend some time to read the whole book thoroughly, then this book is the only thing you need to pass the EA exams.

PassKey is the way to go!
Alaina Crowell
I passed all three of my exams on the first try in ten weeks! Each unit is explained so clearly, and I was completely prepared for each SEE. Wonderful books!

Worked like a charm!
Brian Lang (New York, New York)
I passed on my first try.

This review is the best on the market.
Yaw Asiante-Asamoah
I passed on all three parts on one attempt. The questions in the Review and Workbook are similar to the real exams. I got a big raise and my bonus went up at my seasonal job. It's worth the money, trust me.

Excellent explanations!
Janet Briggs
The best thing about these books is that each answer has a comprehensive explanation about why the answer is correct. I passed all three EA exams on the first attempt.

This book is worth the money.
Bridgette Holzapple
I passed Part 2 on my first try. The questions on the test were very similar to the questions in the workbook. You will pass, no doubt!

I passed!
Ismail Osman
The book is excellent to pass the EA exam. I passed Part 1 on my first attempt. These are great study resources. I love PassKey!

Michelle D. Stroschen
I passed all three parts on my first attempt. I would definitely recommend! These books are reasonably priced and have up-to-date information.

A great EA review book
William Highfield (Lafayette, Colorado)
I used the Complete EA Review book as a study guide and passed all my tests the first time. Don't get the idea the tests were easy, but the book was so well-organized and inclusive that the memorization and familiarization processes went very well.

Amazing!
Sopio Svanishvilion
PassKey helped me pass all three parts of the Enrolled Agent exam. They are a "must have" if you want to pass your EA exams.

Essential Figures for Tax Year 2015
Part One: Individuals

Here is a quick summary of some of the important tax figures for the current enrolled agent exam cycle (May 1, 2016, to February 28, 2017):

Income Tax Return Filing Deadline: April 18, 2016

Note: The normal filing deadline for individual taxpayers is April 15. However, April 15, 2016, is Emancipation Day, a legal holiday, so 2015 returns are due Monday, April 18, 2016. Taxpayers living in Maine and Massachusetts observe Patriots' Day on April 18, 2016, so they have until Tuesday, April 19, 2016, to file their 2015 tax returns.

Personal Exemption: $4,000

Personal Exemption Phaseout Thresholds:
- Single: $258,250 - $380,750
- Head of Household: $284,050 - $406,550
- Married Filing Jointly or Qualifying Widow(er): $309,900 - $432,400
- Married Filing Separately: $154,950 - $216,200

Standard Deduction Amounts:
- Single: $6,300
- Married Filing Jointly: $12,600
- Married Filing Separately: $6,300
- Head of Household: $9,250
- Qualifying Widow(er): $12,600
- Dependents filing their own return: $1,050
- Blind taxpayers and taxpayers age 65 or over qualify for an increased standard deduction. Additional amounts per taxpayer are:
    - $1,550: Single or Head of Household
    - $1,250: Married Filing Jointly or Qualifying Widow(er)

Gross Income Filing Thresholds for U.S. Citizens and U.S. Residents:
- Single: $10,300
- Married Filing Jointly: $20,600
- Head of Household: $13,250
- Married Filing Separately (any age): $4,000
- Qualifying Widow(er) with dependent child: $16,600

Gross Filing Thresholds for Taxpayers 65 or Over:
- Single and 65 or older: $11,850
- Married Filing Jointly (one spouse 65 or older): $21,850
- Married Filing Jointly (both spouses 65 or older): $23,100
- Head of Household, 65 or older: $14,800
- Qualifying Widow(er) with dependent child, 65 or older: $17,850

2015 Mileage Rates:
- Business: 57.5¢ per mile
- Charitable purposes: 14¢ per mile
- Medical and moving: 23¢ per mile

Retirement Contribution Thresholds:
- Roth and traditional IRA contribution limit: $5,500
- Roth and traditional IRA catch-up contribution limit (age 50 or over): $6,500
- Maximum 401(k) elective deferrals: $18,000
- Maximum 401(k) elective deferrals (age 50 or over): $24,000 (an additional $6,000)
- Maximum SIMPLE elective contributions: $12,500
- Maximum SIMPLE elective contributions (age 50 or over): $15,500 (an additional $3,000)

Traditional IRA Phaseout (Participants in Employer Plans):
- Married Filing Jointly: $98,000 - $118,000
- Married Filing Separately: $0 - $10,000
- All other filing statuses: $61,000 - $71,000
- Nonparticipant married to a participant: $183,000 - $193,000

*If neither spouse is a participant in an employer plan, the traditional IRA contribution is fully deductible.

Social Security Taxable Wage Base: $118,500
FUTA Wage Base: $7,000
Medicare Taxable Wage Base: No limit

Health Savings Accounts (HSAs) Annual Contribution Limits:
- HSA for self-only coverage: $3,350
- HSA for family coverage: $6,650

Estate and Gift Tax Exclusion Amount: $5,430,000
Annual Exclusion for Gifts: $14,000
Marital Threshold for Gift Tax for Non-Citizens: $147,000

Maximum Education Credits and Deductions:
- American Opportunity Credit: $2,500 per student
- Lifetime Learning Credit: $2,000 per return
- Coverdell Education Savings Account (amount per beneficiary): $2,000
- Tuition and fees deduction: $4,000
- Student loan interest deduction: $2,500

Maximum Earned Income Credit (EITC):
- Taxpayers with no children: $503
- Taxpayers with one child: $3,359
- Taxpayers with two children: $5,548
- Taxpayers with three or more children: $6,242

*Investment income must be $3,400 or less for the year in order to qualify for the EITC.

Earned Income Credit (EITC) Phaseout Ranges:
To be eligible for the EITC, the taxpayer must have earned income less than:
- $14,820 ($20,330 if MFJ) with no qualifying child
- $39,131 ($44,651 if MFJ) with one qualifying child
- $44,454 ($49,974 if MFJ) with two qualifying children
- $47,747 ($53,267 if MFJ) with three or more qualifying children

Foreign Earned Income and Housing Exclusions:
- Maximum foreign earned income exclusion: $100,800
- Base housing amount: $16,128

Maximum Credit Amounts:
- Adoption Credit: $13,400 per child
- Child Tax Credit: $1,000 per child (unchanged from the previous year)
- Credit for Child and Dependent Care Expenses: $3,000 (one child); $6,000 (two or more)
- Retirement Savings Contributions Credit: $1,000 ($2,000 if MFJ)
- Nonbusiness Energy Property Credit: the credit equals up to 10% of the purchase price of qualified purchases, up to a maximum amount of $500 (a maximum of $200 for windows)

Withholding Threshold for "Nanny Tax" or Household Employees: $1,900

"Kiddie Tax" Unearned Income Threshold: $2,100

Alternative Minimum Tax (AMT) Exemption:
- Married Filing Jointly or Qualifying Widow(er): $83,400
- Single or Head of Household: $53,600
- Married Filing Separately: $41,700

New Tax Laws Affecting Individuals in 2015

PATH Act Late Tax Extenders: On December 18, 2015, the President signed into law the "Protecting Americans from Tax Hikes (PATH) Act", commonly known as the "2015 Tax Extenders" bill. The law made permanent many of the more than 50 tax breaks that had expired and retroactively extended many others. This legislation made several changes to existing tax provisions and made many more permanent. Provisions related to individuals that were extended for tax year 2015 include the following:

- The qualified charitable distribution (QCD) option for charitable contributions from an IRA for those over age 70 ½ was extended for 2015. The contribution limit is $100,000 per taxpayer.
- American Opportunity Tax Credit was extended and made permanent.
- The tuition and fees deduction was extended through 2016.
- The deduction for state and local sales taxes was extended.
- The enhanced Child Tax Credit was made permanent.
- The enhanced Earned Income Tax Credit was made permanent.
- The Teacher Credit ($250 deduction) was made permanent.
- The charitable deduction allowed for conservation property was made permanent at a 50% of adjusted gross income (with a special 100% allowance for farmers and ranchers), rather than normal 30%-of-AGI limit. This provision is now permanent.
- The PATH Act permanently extended the 100% exclusion from gain for Qualified Small Business Stock. It also eliminates the gain as an AMT preference item.
- The exclusion from gross income of forgiven debt of qualified principal residence indebtedness was extended for 2015.
- The deductibility of mortgage insurance premiums was extended for 2015.

Surface Transportation Act of 2015: A number of tax law changes were also included in the *Surface Transportation and Veterans Health Care Choice Improvement Act of 2015*, which was signed into law on July 31, 2015. Provisions related to individuals include the following:

- **New Estate Reporting Requirements:** The estate executor is required to furnish a statement identifying the value of each interest in that property as reported on the estate tax return. The statement must be provided to the IRS and each beneficiary. Penalties will be assessed if a taxpayer reports a higher basis in the inherited property than the value reported on the estate tax return. The provision applies to any estate tax returns filed after July 31, 2015.
- **New Form 8971:** On December 18, 2015, the IRS released draft Form 8971, *Information Regarding Beneficiaries Acquiring Property from a Decedent*. Once this IRS form is finalized, executors who file estate tax returns will complete it and provide it to the IRS and beneficiaries in compliance with the new reporting laws passed in 2015.
- **Overstatements of Basis:** The statute of limitations for examination is extended to six years in the case of "overstatements of basis". The extended statute will apply when an overstatement of basis results in an understatement of income of greater than 25% on a return.

New Forms for the Affordable Care Act: Taxpayers may receive the new Form 1095-B, *Health Coverage,* or Form 1095-C, *Employer-Provided Health Insurance Offer and Coverage*, from their insurance provider or employer, reflecting the dollar amounts of their health coverage and any Advanced Premium Tax Credit they received during the year.

ACA Forms Delayed: On December 28, 2015, the IRS issued a notice delaying the reporting requirement for ACA forms. The due date for employers to provide Forms 1095-B and 1095-C statements to individuals was extended from February 1, 2015, to March 31, 2015, and the due date for filing the forms was also extended. The IRS recognized that many individual taxpayers would be affected by this delay.

Retirement Savings Contribution Credit Limits Increased: The Retirement Savings Contribution Credit income limits increased in 2015. In order to claim this credit, a taxpayer's MAGI must not exceed $30,500 ($61,000 if MFJ; $45,750 if HOH). These increased thresholds mean that more taxpayers will qualify for this credit in 2015. The maximum credit is still $1,000 ($2,000 for MFJ taxpayers).

The ABLE Act: The ABLE Act establishes a new type of tax-advantaged savings program designed specifically for disabled individuals. ABLE accounts function similarly to an education savings account, but contributions may be used for qualified expenses of a disabled individual. Up to $14,000 in yearly contributions can be made to an ABLE account, and distributions are tax-free if used to pay qualified disability expenses. Two new IRS forms were introduced for reporting ABLE account programs. Form 1099-QA is used for distributions and Form 5498-QA is used for contributions to these accounts. Contributions to an ABLE account are not deductible on the taxpayer's return. Qualified distributions are tax-free to the beneficiary.

MyRA® accounts: This is a new type of "starter" retirement savings account developed by the Department of the Treasury for people without access to a retirement savings plan at work. The IRS will allow direct deposits of a taxpayer's refund into a myRA® account. A taxpayer can start a myRA® with as little as $25. However, when the account reaches $15,000, the taxpayer must rollover into a private-sector Roth IRA.

Additional Child Tax Credit Restrictions: A taxpayer can no longer claim the additional child tax credit if he files Form 2555, *Foreign Earned Income Exclusion*.

IRA Rollover Limits: Starting in 2015, a taxpayer can make only one IRA rollover per year. However, the taxpayer can continue to make unlimited trustee-to-trustee transfers between IRAs, because this type of transfer is not considered a rollover. There is also no limit to the number of IRA conversions (a conversion from a traditional IRA to a Roth IRA).

Shared Responsibility Provision (Health Insurance Penalty) Increase: In 2015, taxpayers who do not have health insurance or qualify for an exemption must pay $325 per person, or 2% of their household income, whichever is greater. The maximum penalty in 2015 is $975 per family. The penalty has more than tripled from the previous year (it was $95 per person in 2014), and is set to increase again in 2016.

New Requirements for ITINs: New regulations state that ITINs will automatically expire in three years if tax returns are not filed. Also, taxpayers who were issued ITINs before 2003 are now required to have them renewed. The ITIN renewals will occur on a staggered schedule between 2017 and 2020. Documentation proving identity, foreign status, and residency is required for ITIN renewal.

Prevention of Certain Retroactive Claims: Effective immediately, retroactive claims for the Earned Income Credit, Child Tax Credit, and American Opportunity Credit are prohibited after the issuance of a valid Social Security number. This new law prohibits individual taxpayers from retroactively claiming these credits by amending a return (or filing an original return if they failed to file on time) for any prior year in which the taxpayer did not have a valid SSN. In previous years, taxpayers were allowed to amend past returns to take these refundable credits after a valid SSN had been issued.

Section 529 Accounts and Qualified Education Expenses: The definition of "qualified higher education expenses" for distributions from 529 accounts now includes the purchases of computer equipment and technology.

Compensation for Wrongfully Incarcerated Individuals: Civil damages, restitution, or other monetary awards that the taxpayer received as compensation for a wrongful incarceration are no longer taxable income.

Essential Figures for Tax Year 2015
Part Two: Businesses

Here is a quick summary of some of the important business tax figures for the current enrolled agent exam cycle (May 1, 2016, to February 28, 2017).

2015 Social Security Taxable Wage Base: $118,500. A combined tax rate of 12.4% applies up to this limit, consisting of employee and employer portions of 6.2% each. The Social Security tax rate for self-employed persons is 12.4%.

2015 Medicare Taxable Wage Base: No limit. A combined tax rate of 2.9% applies, consisting of employee and employer portions of 1.45% each. The Medicare rate for self-employed persons is 2.9%.

2015 FUTA Wage Base: $7,000

2015 Mileage Rates:
- Business: 57.5¢ per mile
- Charitable purposes: 14¢ per mile
- Medical and moving: 23¢ per mile

Retirement Plans:
- SIMPLE Plan maximum employee deferrals: $12,500 (age 50 and over: $15,500)
- SEP annual contribution limit: $53,000
- Traditional and Roth IRA Contribution Limit: $5,500 (age 50 and over: $6,500)

Traditional IRA Phaseout (Participants in Employer Plans):
- Married Filing Jointly: $98,000 - $118,000
- Married Filing Separately: $0 - $10,000
- All other filing statuses: $61,000 - $71,000
- Nonparticipant married to a participant: $183,000 - $193,000

*If neither spouse is a participant in an employer plan, the traditional IRA contribution is fully deductible.

Roth IRA Phaseout based on MAGI:
- Married Filing Jointly: $183,000 - $193,000
- Married Filing Separately: $0 - $10,000
- All other filing statuses: $116,000 - $131,000

*Roth conversions (the "backdoor" Roth IRA) are still allowable in tax year 2015.

401, 403, and 457 Plans:
- Maximum employee elective deferral: $18,000
- Employee catch-up contribution (age 50 or older): $6,000
- Defined contribution maximum limit from all sources: $53,000. This maximum amount includes employee deferrals, employer contributions, and catch-up contributions.

Gift and Estate Tax Thresholds:
- Combined Estate and Gift Tax Exclusion: $5.43 million
- Annual Gift exclusion: $14,000
- Gift to non-citizen spouse: $147,000
- Highest estate tax bracket: 40%

Generation-Skipping Transfer (GST) Tax:
- GST Tax Rate: 40%
- GST Tax Exemption: $5.43 million

AMTI phaseout for Trusts and Estates: $ 79,450 - $174,650

New Tax Laws Affecting Businesses in 2015

The PATH Act of 2015: On December 18, 2015, Congress passed legislation that retroactively extended multiple provisions which were set to expire at the end of the year. Provisions related to businesses that were extended for tax year 2015 include the following:

- Section 179 expense deduction of $500,000, with a dollar-for-dollar phaseout between $2 million and $2.5 million of Sect. 179 purchases for the year.
- A Section 179 expense deduction of $250,000 is also allowable for retail improvements, as well as qualified leasehold and restaurant property. The limitation for qualified real property remains $250,000 in 2015. This cap on qualified leasehold property will be removed in 2016.
- Section 179 expensing for computer software was permanently extended, as well as the ability of a taxpayer to revoke a Section 179 election without prior IRS consent.
- Bonus depreciation extended and enhanced for 2015 (explained below).
- The Work Opportunity Tax Credit was retroactively reinstated and extended through 2019. The credit was also modified by adding an additional target group for qualified long-term unemployment recipients.
- The 100% exclusion for gain on qualified small business stock is now permanent.

Charitable Contribution of Food Inventory: The PATH Act permanently extended the enhanced deduction for charitable contributions of food inventory to pass-through entities (S-corporations, sole proprietorships, and partnerships). The new provisions also provide special rules for valuing food inventory.

Extensions of Charitable Contributions for Conservation Easements: The PATH Act included a special provision for contributions of capital gain real property (real estate) made for conservation purposes. Contributions of easements have a 50% limit with a 15-year carryover. Farmers and ranchers are allowed a special allowance of 100%.

Parity for Employer-Provided Transportation Benefits: The PATH Act made retroactive parity provisions to transit pass and parking pass fringe benefits to employees. For 2015, the monthly limit on the exclusion for combined transit pass and parking benefits is $250. The parity applies retroactively for 2015. Congress made this parity permanent in 2015.

Bonus Depreciation Extended and Enhanced: The PATH Act extends 50% bonus depreciation, but not permanently. Bonus depreciation only applies to new property. The law also modifies bonus depreciation to include certain trees, vines, and plants bearing fruit or nuts. This is a new provision for growers and farmers.

Research and Development Credit: This valuable credit is based on qualified research and experimental costs related to the development or improvement of a product. The credit was retroactively reinstated and made permanent by the PATH Act.

S-Corporation Built-in Gains: The PATH Act permanently extended the S-corporation recognition period for built-in gains tax (the BIG tax) to five years. The previous recognition period was ten years. In 2015, this five-year recognition period also applies to real estate investment trusts (REITs) and regulated investment companies that do not elect "deemed sale" treatment.

ACA Employer Provisions: Starting in 2015, employers with at least 50 full-time employees (or full-time equivalent employees) will be subject to an Employer Shared Responsibility Payment.

Forms 1095-C and 1094-C: These ACA reporting forms became mandatory with the 2015 tax year. All employees eligible for employer-provided health coverage will get a Form 1095-C, regardless of whether they actually participate in the employer's health plan. Employers would normally need to provide these forms to their employees by January 31st, but the IRS announced transitional relief in late 2015 to allow businesses provide the 2015 forms to employees by March 31, 2016.

S Corporation Charitable Gifts: The PATH Act permanently extends the basis adjustment in stock when an S corporation makes charitable donations of appreciated stock or property to charity.

TEFRA Repealed: The *Bipartisan Budget Act of 2015* included major changes to the way the IRS will audit partnerships. The budget act repeals the current TEFRA partnership audit rules, replacing them with a new procedure that will make it easier for the IRS to audit partnerships. The new rules generally apply after December 31, 2017. However, partnerships may elect for these changes to apply to any partnership return filed after November 2, 2015.

SIMPLE Plan: Taxpayers may now roll over amounts from employer-sponsored retirement plans into a SIMPLE IRA.

501(c)(4) Exempt Entities: The PATH Act contained several key provisions affecting exempt entities. There is now a mandatory application process for 501(c)(4) entities. In the past, 501(c)(4) organizations were not required to file an exemption application. The organization was allowed to "self-declare" exemption or complete IRS Form 1024 to receive an IRS determination at a later date. The PATH Act added a new provision that requires all 501(c)(4) organizations to file a notice of registration with the IRS within 60 days of formation. In addition, any 501(c)(4) organizations already in existence that have never filed a Form 1024 or a Form 990 must file a one-page notice of registration with the IRS within 180 days of December 18, 2015 (the date of passage of the PATH Act).

Gift Taxes and Exempt Entities: The PATH Act confirmed that gift taxes do not apply to contributions to 501(c)(4), 501(c)(5), and 501(c)(6) exempt organizations.

New Information for Part 3: Representation, Practices, and Procedures

Here is a quick summary of some of the important tax legislation for the current enrolled agent exam cycle (May 1, 2016 to February 28, 2017).

The FAST ACT: Fixing America's Surface Transportation Act (the FAST Act) instituted a number of major changes that affect tax professionals. This new bill included new provisions for IRS collection, requires the IRS to use private debt collectors, and allows the IRS to have passports suspended for taxpayers with large delinquent balances.

Private Debt Collectors: The FAST Act Amends IRC §6306 to require that the IRS use private debt collectors to try and collect older receivables. Under the new law, the IRS is required to use private debt collection companies to collect debts that are classified as "inactive tax receivables".

Revocation or denial of Passports: The FAST Act provides that having a "seriously delinquent tax debt" is, unless an exception applies, grounds for denial or revocation of a U.S. passport.

AFSP Representation Rights Clarified: Beginning with the 2016 tax season, only Annual Filing Season Program participants have limited practice rights before the IRS. Unenrolled preparers who do not participate in this annual program will have no authority to represent clients before the IRS after December 31, 2015.

Annual Filing Season Program Record of Completion: Unenrolled tax preparers who wish to participate in the Annual Filing Season Program (AFSP) must complete the required continuing education from IRS-approved CE providers by Dec. 31, 2015, in order to receive a 2016 Annual Filing Season Program Record of Completion.

Directory of Federal Tax Return Preparers: On February 5, 2015, the IRS launched an online preparer directory for the 2015 filing season. The database contains: the name, city, state and zip code of attorneys, CPAs, enrolled agents, enrolled retirement plan agents, enrolled actuaries and Annual Filing Season Program (AFSP) participants with valid PTINs for the current filing season.

Repeal of Post-Appeals Mediation: On September 21, 2015, the IRS announced that it would discontinue the process of post-appeals mediation. This decision is outlined in Revenue Procedure 2015-44, which announced the cancellation of the option of binding arbitration for taxpayers that could not reach a settlement with IRS Appeals.

New measures to combat identity theft: On August 12, 2015, the IRS issued temporary regulations which eliminated an automatic deadline extension that had been available to companies filing employees' Form W-2s. This new measure is intended to help combat rising identity theft.

Identity theft protection services are not taxable: In August 2015, the IRS announced that individuals who receive identity protection services because their personal information may have been compromised do not need to include the value of the services in their taxable income.

The New ITIN Procedures: In 2015, the IRS instituted stricter procedures for obtaining an ITIN. Another provision of the *PATH Act of 2015* requires that taxpayers who were issued ITINs before 2013 renew their ITINs on a staggered schedule between 2017 and 2020. ITINs will automatically expire after three years of non-use.

Changes to the ITIN Fraud Detection Program: Fraud detection in the ITIN program was originally run by the IRS Criminal Investigation Division. This program is now handled by the Accounts Management function of the IRS.

Preparer penalty increases: Two preparer penalties increased in 2015. The penalty for tax preparers who negotiate a client's refund check, and the penalty for failure to use due diligence in determining eligibility for the earned income tax credit both increased to $505 per failure (from $500 from the previous year). Unlike previous years, these penalties will be increased and adjusted for inflation every year. However, the yearly maximum that can be imposed on preparers remains $25,000 per year.

Due Diligence Expanded: The PATH Act legislation enacted in December 2015 extended tax preparer Due Diligence requirements to several refundable credits, including the American Opportunity Credit and the Child Tax Credit. At the time of this book's printing, the IRS indicated that it was seeking IRS Counsel guidance on this issue.

Contingent fees: The IRS has long prohibited the use of contingent fees in connection with the preparation of original tax returns. Recent revisions to Circular 230 permitted limited contingent fee arrangements for the preparation of certain amended returns and refund claims. In 2014, in the landmark case of *Ridgely v. Lew*, the U.S. District Court issued a permanent injunction preventing the IRS from regulating contingent fee arrangements. As a result of this case, in June 2015, the IRS issued Fact Sheet FS-2015-19, conceding that "tax return preparation is not *'practice [before the IRS]'* as currently defined by case law," conceding that the IRS Office of Professional Responsibility does not have the authority to regulate the preparation of tax returns.

PTIN Fee Revised: Effective Nov. 1, 2015, the annual fee for PTINs will be $50 for both new applications and renewals. In 2015, a lawsuit over the IRS's PTIN fees received class-action status.

TEFRA and ELP Audit Procedures Repealed: The *Bipartisan Budget Act* of 2015 repealed the TEFRA and Electing Large Partnership (ELP) audit provisions. In repealing the TEFRA rules, Congress also eliminated the role of the "tax matters partner" in partnership audits and replaced it with a "partnership representative" who does not have to be a partner. Although the repeal applies to tax years beginning after December 31, 2017, partnerships can elect to apply the new audit procedures earlier.

Part 1: Individuals Practice Exams

Sample Exam #1
Sample Exam #2

Test Tip: Time yourself. Set up a watch or other digital timer while you read and answer the questions. You will have 3.5 hours to take the EA exam, with approximately two minutes to answer each question. Don't spend an inordinate amount of time on any one question and make sure to answer each one, even if you're not sure of the right answer. All questions left blank are counted as wrong.

#1 Sample Exam: Individuals

1. Polly is 72. She was supposed to take required minimum distributions (RMD) on her traditional IRA in 2015, but forgot to do so. What is the percentage of excise tax that will be assessed on the amount she neglected to withdraw?

A. 6%
B. 10%
C. 50%
D. 100%

2. Benedict and his wife Emma both attend graduate school, having both received four-year undergraduate degrees. They file jointly, and their combined AGI is $45,000. In 2015, they had the following expenses paid to their university for tuition and required books and materials:

- Benedict: $4,800
- Emma: $6,900

Based on the information given, what is the maximum amount of education credits they may they claim on their joint return?

A. A $960 Lifetime Learning Credit for Benedict, and a $1,380 Lifetime Learning Credit for Emma.
B. Benedict and Emma are each eligible for a $2,500 American Opportunity Credit. The maximum credit on the return will be $5,000 ($2,500 × 2).
C. Benedict and Emma are limited to a $2,000 maximum of Lifetime Learning Credits on their return.
D. Benedict and Emma are limited to a $4,000 maximum of Lifetime Learning Credits on their return.

3. Royce and Thea have a 3-year-old child. Royce and Thea file a joint return for the year. Royce's employer offered him family health coverage. The employer only covers a portion of the premiums, and the cost of the policy would have been 7% of Royce's modified adjusted gross income. Royce declines the coverage because of the cost. As a result, no one in the family has health coverage during the year. In this scenario, will the taxpayer owe a Shared Responsibility Payment (SRP)?

A. Yes, since Royce declined his employer coverage, and he does not qualify for an exemption, then Royce and Thea will owe an SRP on their jointly filed return.
B. No, Royce will not owe an SRP.
C. Royce will owe an SRP, but his wife and child will not.
D. Royce will not owe an SRP, but his wife and child will both owe an SRP for not having minimum essential coverage.

4. Herb owns several investments. He has the following transactions in 2015:

- $1,000 loss on ABC Co. stock he purchased on January 15, 2015, and sold on November 15, 2015
- $5,000 gain on the sale of an empty lot that he inherited on February 2, 2015
- $2,000 gain on the sale of XYZ Co. stock he purchased on March 15, 2014, and sold on June 15, 2015

What is the amount and nature of Herb's net gains and net losses?

A. Herb has a $1,000 short-term capital loss and a $7,000 long-term capital gain.
B. Herb has a $1,000 short-term capital loss, a $2,000 long-term capital gain, and a $5,000 short-term capital gain.
C. Herb has a net $1,000 short-term capital loss and a $5,000 long-term capital gain.
D. Herb has a net $2,000 short-term capital loss and a $5,000 long-term capital gain.

5. Sheila and Ralph are married and both have life insurance. In December 2014, Ralph dies and Sheila, as the beneficiary, is awarded the life insurance. The face amount of the policy is $270,000. Instead of a lump sum, Sheila chooses to receive 180 monthly installments of $1,800, starting on January 1, 2015. How should Sheila treat these installments on her 2015 tax return?

A. All of the payments are excluded from income.
B. $18,000 is excluded from income per year, and $3,600 must be recognized as interest income.
C. $21,600 is included in Sheila's income.
D. $18,000 is excluded from income, and the remainder is taxed as a capital gain.

6. Joe has owned his home for ten years. Cristina is his girlfriend, and they have lived together in the home for five years. She was not an owner on the title. Joe and Cristina are married on January 1, 2015, but start having marital problems immediately after the marriage, and Joe moves out. They divorce on June 1, 2015. As part of their divorce settlement, Joe transfers full ownership of the home to Cristina, who puts the house on the market and sells it for a $165,000 gain on November 30, 2015. How much of the gain is excludable on Cristina's individual tax return?

A. All of the gain is excludable.
B. All of the gain is taxable, because Cristina does not meet the ownership and use tests to exclude the gain.
C. A portion of the gain is taxable, because Cristina meets the ownership test but not the use test.
D. A prorated portion of the gain is taxable based on how long Cristina occupied and owned the property.

7. Robert and Hailey have been separated since September 2015, but they are not divorced. Their 14-year-old son, Vincent, lived with Robert the entire year. Hailey lives in her own apartment, and she sees her son Vincent on the weekends. Robert provided over half the cost of keeping up his home. Robert plans to file married filing separately, and he also plans to itemize his deductions. What are Hailey's options for filing her tax return?

A. Hailey can file as head of household, provided she does not take the dependency exemption for Vincent.
B. Hailey must file as MFS, and she may itemize deductions or take the standard deduction.
C. Hailey can file as head of household, provided she lives with her husband the last six months of the year.
D. Hailey must file as MFS, and she will also be forced to itemize. She cannot claim the dependency exemption for Vincent.

8. Lucille owns a home in the Lake Tahoe ski area. She stays at the ski home most weekends and spends the entire months of December, January, and February there. When she is not at the ski home, she lives in a four-room apartment that she rents in Denver. She does not own the home in Denver. She works primarily online, from her computer. What is Lucille's primary residence for purposes of the section 121 exclusion?

A. Her ski home in Vail.
B. Her apartment in Denver.
C. She is considered a transient for tax purposes.
D. None of the above.

9. Anya is 21 and a full-time student. Her parents claim her as a dependent and provide more than half of her financial support. She had a part-time waitressing job in 2015, where she earned $4,250. She also had $3,600 of capital gains from the sale of stock. Which of the following statements is correct?

A. Her income will be taxed at her own tax rate, rather than her parents'.
B. A portion of her income will be taxed at her parents' tax rate.
C. Anya's parents will not owe the kiddie tax because she is over age 18.
D. Anya's parents will owe the kiddie tax because her wages are over the threshold amount.

10. Which of the following taxes is deductible on Schedule A as an itemized deduction?

A. State inheritance tax.
B. Qualified foreign income taxes.
C. Employment taxes.
D. Federal income taxes.

11. Carlos moves to another city in 2015, and he decides to convert his home into a residential rental property. Three years ago, Carlos bought his home for $182,000. At the time of the purchase, the value of the land was assessed at $20,000. On the date the home was converted to a rental, Carlos's property had a fair market value of $168,000, of which $21,000 was allocated to the land value, and $147,000 was for the house. What is Carlos's basis of depreciation for the rental property?

A. $134,000
B. $147,000
C. $162,000
D. $182,000

12. Genevieve and Lester are divorced. They have one child who is 13 years old. The child lives with Genevieve most of the time and stays with Lester on weekends. Genevieve has physical custody, but Lester provides more than half of the child's support. If Lester receives permission from Genevieve, the custodial parent, to claim the child on his tax return, is Lester eligible for the Earned Income Credit based on the dependent child?

A. Yes.
B. No.
C. Only if Lester provides over half of his child's overall support.
D. Only if Lester provides over half of his child's overall support and also obtains a signed Form 8332, *Release and Revocation of Release of Claim to Exemption for Child by Custodial Parent*.

13. Immanuel received 200 shares of stock as an inheritance from his grandmother, who died on January 2, 2015. His grandmother's adjusted basis in the stock was $18,000. The stock's fair market value on the date of her death was $24,500. The executor of the estate elects the alternate valuation date for valuing the gross estate. Immanuel received the stock on February 26, 2015, when its fair market value was $26,000. On July 2, 2015, the stock's fair market value was $21,500. Immanuel sells the stock two weeks later. What is Immanuel's basis in the inherited stock, and what is his holding period?

A. $26,000 is his basis, and his holding period is long-term.
B. $24,500 is his basis, and his holding period is long-term.
C. $21,500 is his basis, and his holding period is long-term.
D. $18,000 is his basis, and his holding period is short-term.

14. Jordana owes thousands of dollars of unpaid student loans. She was not married to her husband, Peter, when she incurred the debt. The two file a joint return in 2015, which shows a refund of $5,000. Which of the following is a correct statement?

A. Since he filed a joint return with his wife, Peter has no recourse to claim a portion of the refund. The entire $5,000 refund will be used toward Jordana's unpaid student loan debt.
B. Peter should apply for innocent spouse relief to request his portion of the refund be allocated to him.
C. Peter should apply for equitable relief to request his portion of the refund be allocated to him.
D. Peter should apply for injured spouse relief to request his portion of the refund be allocated to him.

15. Bianca, who is married, gave a vase worth $40,000 to her brother. Bianca's basis in the vase is $10,000. What amount will she report as the value of the gift on Form 709?

A. $10,000
B. $26,000
C. $30,000
D. $40,000

16. A taxpayer may be eligible for the Premium Tax Credit if he:

A. Has qualifying health coverage from an employer.
B. Has qualifying health coverage from an employer or through the Health Insurance Marketplace for all 12 months of the year and meets income requirements.
C. Has qualifying health coverage from an employer or through the Health Insurance Marketplace for at least one month of the year and meets income requirements.
D. Has qualifying health coverage through the Health Insurance Marketplace for at least one month of the year and meets income requirements.

17. Which of the following would be a qualified charitable contribution?

A. Direct donation to a homeless individual.
B. Cost of raffle tickets at a church fundraiser.
C. Value of blood given to a blood bank.
D. Expenses paid for a foreign exchange student living with the taxpayer, if the student is sponsored by a qualified organization.

18. Carlton dies in 2015. Carlton's will dictates that each of his ten grandchildren shall receive $1 million. Assuming that none of his GST exemption amount has previously been used in connection with gifts to the grandchildren or other skip persons, what portion of the total amount distributed to the grandchildren after his death in 2015 would be subject to GST?

A. $0
B. $4.57 million
C. $5.34 million
D. $10 million

19. Alejandro's house was burglarized, with losses totaling $5,000. His insurance company reimbursed him $3,500. Alejandro's adjusted gross income for the year is $20,500. What is Alejandro's theft loss deduction on Schedule A, after applying the $100 rule and the 10% rule?

A. $0
B. $1,400
C. $1,550
D. $1,950

20. Mai Lin is single. In 2015, she has $120,000 in wage income. She also owns a residential rental property that has a $28,000 loss for the year. Mai Lin actively participated in the rental activity, but is not considered a real estate professional. How much of her rental loss is deductible in the current year?

A. $0
B. $15,000
C. $25,000
D. $28,000

21. Gianna has four dependents. Which of the following dependents would qualify for the Child Tax Credit?

A. Larkin, 22 years old and a full-time college student.
B. Danica, 21 years old and disabled.
C. Enoch, 16 years old and a full-time student.
D. Susan, 65 years old, Gianna's dependent parent.

22. Mitchell is 63. In November 2015, he marries Linda, age 66, and they decide to file jointly. Their AGI is $28,000. The two have the following medical expenses in 2015:

Mitchell	Cost	Linda	Cost
Cataract surgery	$3,000	Facelift	$5,000
Prescription eyeglasses	$500	Prescription contact lenses	$400
Cholesterol pills (prescription)	$480	Aspirin purchased over the counter	$20

What is their allowable medical expense deduction for 2015?

A. $0
B. $2,100
C. $2,280
D. $4,380

23. Mavis has group health coverage through her husband's employer. The employer pays 100% of her husband's insurance premiums, and 50% of her insurance premiums as part of the company's fringe benefits program. Mavis and her husband do not file jointly. Does Mavis have minimum essential coverage (MEC), and if so, where is she required to report it?

A. Yes, Mavis has minimum essential coverage. She is not required to report anything to the IRS.
B. No, Mavis does not have minimum essential coverage. She is not required to report anything to the IRS.
C. Yes, Mavis has minimum essential coverage. She is required to report her enrollment in MEC on her separate Form 1040.
D. No, Mavis does not meet the requirements for having minimum essential coverage, because she is filing a separate tax return from her spouse, and her health coverage is through her husband's group policy.

24. Britta, age 42, is single and has no dependents. She has significant medical expenses in 2015 and would like to roll over a portion of funds from her traditional IRA to her high deductible health savings account (HSA). She has not yet contributed to her HSA for the year. Which of the following statements is correct?

A. This is a prohibited transaction.
B. This transaction is allowed, but Britta will have to pay tax on the withdrawal from her IRA.
C. This transaction is allowed up to $3,350 in 2015 and is tax-free. Britta may make a similar tax-free rollover from her IRA to her HSA each year.
D. This transaction is allowed up to $3,350 in 2015 and is tax-free. Britta may make this kind of rollover only once in her lifetime.

25. Valentina works in New York. She travels to New Orleans to attend a one-week conference at the suggestion of her employer. The conference is educational and is designed to supplement her current job requirements. While in New Orleans, she does some sightseeing and visits friends. On the last day of the conference, Valentina flies home. Valentina has the following expenses during her trip:

Roundtrip airfare to the conference	$360
Parking at the airport	24
Meals while at the conference	220
Meals while sightseeing	72
Hotel costs during the conference	450

How much of these expenses are deductible, before consideration of any AGI limitations?

A. $1,054
B. $980
C. $944
D. $360

26. Zheng spends two years working in China as a private consultant. He is an American citizen and a legal resident of China. He has qualified foreign earned income and earns $190,000 in 2015. What is the maximum amount he can exclude from his income?

A. $0; American citizens cannot exclude foreign earned income.
B. $99,200
C. $100,800
D. Zheng may exclude the full amount of his salary, with no income threshold.

27. Quinn sold all his shares in a mutual fund. The sale resulted in a capital loss of $7,000. Quinn has wages of $32,000 in 2015. He has no other income or losses. What is Quinn's adjusted gross income in 2015?

A. $25,000
B. $29,000
C. $32,000
D. $39,000

28. In 2007, Josiah received 10 shares of Rust Valley Corporation stock as a gift from his father. His father had originally paid $10 per share for this stock, and it was trading for $20 per share at the time of the gift. In 2012, Josiah purchased an additional 20 shares of Rust Valley stock for a price of $30 per share, and paid a $20 transaction fee on this purchase. In October 2015, Josiah sold 20 shares of his Rust Valley stock. He cannot specifically identify the shares he disposed of. What is Josiah's basis in the Rust Valley Corporation shares he still owns?

A. $100
B. $200
C. $310
D. $360

29. Under the simplified home office deduction calculation, the maximum amount a taxpayer can claim per year is:

A. $300
B. $500
C. $1,500
D. $3,000

30. Katrina is single and a software designer for a large company. She is also the sole proprietor of a vintage clothing store. Katrina received the following in 2015:

Regular wages	$188,000
Bonus	10,000
Self-employment income	56,000
Interest income	3,000
Inheritance	5,000

What amount does Katrina owe for the <u>additional</u> Medicare tax in 2015? (The threshold is $200,000 for single filers.)

A. $486
B. $558
C. $2,286
D. $9,652

31. What type of income is reported on Line 21 of Form 1040?

A. Wages
B. Capital gains and losses
C. Farm income or (loss)
D. Other income (miscellaneous taxable income)

32. Pastor Gregory Green is a full-time minister. The church allows him to use a parsonage that has an annual fair rental value of $24,000. The church also pays him an annual salary of $67,000, of which $7,500 is designated for his home utility costs. His actual utility costs during the year were $7,000. What is Pastor Green's income for self-employment tax purposes?

A. $500
B. $60,000
C. $67,000
D. $91,000

33. Reggie is a U.S. Army veteran who recently returned to college for his first undergraduate degree. He receives educational assistance from the GI Bill. The GI Bill paid $4,750 toward his tuition, which was paid directly to the college. Reggie's total tuition cost for the year was $6,800. Reggie also paid the following additional educational costs during the year:

Required textbooks	$450
Mandatory student health fees	186
Required lab equipment	1,260
Commuting costs	340
Parking at the college	80

Reggie wants to claim the American Opportunity Credit (AOC) on his tax return. Of the items listed above, what are his qualifying educational expenses for purposes of the credit?

A. $3,946
B. $3,760
C. $8,510
D. $2,050

34. Brittany is 25 years old and single. In 2015, she was covered by a retirement plan at work, but she also has a traditional IRA set up through her bank. Her wages in 2015 were $68,000 and her modified AGI was $78,000. Based on this information, is she allowed to make a contribution to her traditional IRA?

A. No, she is not allowed to make a contribution.
B. Yes, she is allowed to make a contribution, and it will be partially deductible.
C. Yes, she is allowed to make a contribution, and it will be fully deductible.
D. Yes, she is allowed to make a contribution, but she must designate the contribution as nondeductible.

35. Brock agrees to sell his vacation property to a buyer under an installment sale. He sells the property at a contract price of $120,000, and his gross profit is $15,000. Brock will receive four payments (one payment per year) of principal and interest until the note is paid off. He receives the first payment of $30,000 in 2015. The first payment does not include any interest. He wants to use the installment method to report income from the sale. What is the amount of installment sale income that Brock must report in 2015?

A. $0
B. $3,750
C. $7,500
D. $15,000

36. Brice is 34, and has several investment accounts. During the year, his car breaks down and he must pay for an expensive repair. He withdraws money from various accounts in order to pay for the repair, and in the process, he is charged penalties. Which of the following penalties would be deductible on his Form 1040?

A. A penalty for early withdrawal of funds from a certificate of deposit.
B. A 10% penalty for early withdrawal from a traditional IRA account.
C. A 10% penalty for early withdrawal from a 401(k) plan
D. None of the above. Penalties are never deductible.

37. John and Dianne are married, but have lived apart since April 2015. They do not have a formal separation agreement. They have one daughter, Simone, who lived with Dianne all year. Dianne provided over half of Simone's support. John refuses to file jointly with Dianne. What is the best filing status for Dianne?

A. Single.
B. Head of household.
C. Married filing separately.
D. Married filing jointly.

38. Which of the following taxpayers would not be considered self-employed and therefore would not be subject to self-employment tax?

A. An independent contractor.
B. A general partner of a partnership.
C. The estate of a deceased taxpayer that carries on a trade or business.
D. A person who works full-time and also has a part-time business.

39. Tristan buys a residential rental property for $35,000 of cash and assumes a mortgage of $80,000 on the property. He also pays $2,300 in settlement fees to close the deal. Of those settlement fees, $800 was for title insurance on the property. Based on this information, what is Tristan's basis in the property?

A. $35,000
B. $115,000
C. $117,300
D. $116,500

40. During the year, Lupe received ordinary dividends in the amount of $175. She also had a $700 capital gain from the sale of stock. How should these items of income be reported?

A. Both amounts should be reported on Form 1040, Schedule B.
B. Lupe's ordinary dividends should be reported on Form 1040, and the capital gain from the stock sale should be reported on Schedule D.
C. Lupe's ordinary dividends should be reported on Schedule B, and the capital gain from the stock sale should be reported on Schedule D.
D. Both amounts should be reported on Form 1040, Schedule D.

41. Amelia died in 2015. Which of the following assets would be included in the calculation of her gross estate?

A. Life insurance proceeds payable to Amelia's beneficiaries.
B. Property owned solely by Amelia's spouse.
C. Lifetime gifts that are complete.
D. All of the items above would be included in Amelia's gross estate.

42. A fire destroyed Chelsea's vacation home. The home had an adjusted basis of $80,000, and the insurance company paid her $130,000 for the loss. Chelsea bought a replacement vacation home for $100,000. How much is her taxable gain, and what is her basis in the new vacation home?

A. No taxable gain; basis of $130,000.
B. Taxable gain of $30,000; basis of $80,000.
C. Taxable gain of $50,000; basis of $80,000.
D. Taxable gain of $30,000; basis of $100,000.

43. Andy donated to his church several times during the year. Which of the following charitable gifts does not meet IRS substantiation (recordkeeping) requirements?

A. A $210 donation paid by check. Andy has a copy of the canceled check, but no receipt from the church.
B. A $340 donation made in cash. Andy has a contemporaneous receipt from the church.
C. A contribution of noncash property worth $5,200. Andy has a receipt from the church, but no appraisal.
D. Charitable mileage totaling $50 that was incurred while Andy was volunteering. Andy does not have a receipt, but he has a written mileage log.

44. Araceli used 25% of her home exclusively as an office for business. She owned and used the home as her principal residence for eight years before she sold it. She realizes a $40,000 gain on the sale. She had claimed $14,000 in depreciation deductions on her home. How would Araceli treat this transaction on her tax return?

A. $14,000 of ordinary income; $16,000 gain qualifies for section 121 exclusion.
B. $14,000 of ordinary income; $26,000 gain qualifies for section 121 exclusion.
C. $30,000 gain qualifies for section 121 exclusion.
D. $26,000 gain qualifies for section 121 exclusion.

45. Leslie files as single and has no refundable credits. Based on the amounts below, is Leslie required to pay estimated tax in the current year?

AGI for prior year	$73,700
Total tax on prior year return	9,224
Anticipated AGI for current year	82,800
Total current year estimated tax	11,270
Tax expected to be withheld in current year	$10,250

A. Yes, she is required to make estimated tax payments.
B. No, she is not required to make estimated tax payments.
C. She is not required to make estimated tax payments, but she must increase her withholding at her job.
D. None of the above is correct.

46. Charlene is a tax preparer who reports her business income on Schedule C. She prepares the tax return for JAMS Corporation, and charges the company $1,200 for the tax return preparation and bookkeeping. JAMS Corporation is having financial difficulties, so it offers Charlene computer equipment worth $2,000 in lieu of paying the debt. Charlene agrees to accept the equipment in full payment of her invoice. Based on this information, how much business income would Charlene report on Schedule C as a result of this transaction?

A. $1,200
B. $2,000
C. $1,200 in business income, $800 in passive income.
D. $0, since the amount was not paid in legal tender.

47. In 2015, Elizabeth gave the following gifts:
- $14,000 to her sister, Marjorie
- $16,000 for her grandson Tim's tuition, which was paid directly to the college
- $15,000 to her uncle Clyde
- $18,000 to the Democratic Party

How should these gifts be reported under the gift tax rules?

A. Marjorie and Clyde are required to file gift tax returns and pay tax on their gifts.
B. Elizabeth must file a gift tax return and report the $15,000 gift to Clyde.
C. Elizabeth must file a gift tax return and report the gift to Clyde and the Democratic Party.
D. A gift tax return must be filed for each gift, because the gross amount exceeds the yearly maximum.

48. Paloma bought her home two years ago, but later began having trouble making her mortgage payments. In 2015, Paloma's mortgage lender agreed to reduce the principal balance on her home loan and refinance it with a better interest rate and lower monthly payments. The principal balance before the refinance was $230,000, and the lender reduced the balance to $200,000. The home has never been used for business or as rental property, and Paloma has not filed for bankruptcy. She continued to live in the home as her primary residence. Based on this information, how should Paloma report this transaction?

A. Report the $30,000 as nontaxable canceled debt on Form 982.
B. Report the $30,000 as a reduction in the basis of the home on line 10b of Form 982.
C. Report the $30,000 as a loss on Schedule D.
D. Include $30,000 of debt cancellation in taxable income on Form 1040.

49. Which of the following events would NOT provide for a valid exemption from the shared individual responsibility provision for 2015?

A. Not having access to affordable coverage based on projected household income.
B. Having a short coverage gap of four consecutive months.
C. Foreclosure.
D. Belonging to a religious sect that is conscientiously opposed to accepting health insurance.

50. Several years ago, Mandy bought an old painting from a thrift store for $20. In 2015, Mandy discovers the painting is an expensive original work of art. She takes the painting to an auction house and sells it for $6,000. The auction house takes a 30% commission. What amount must Mandy report as taxable gain?

A. $4,180
B. $5,000
C. $5,880
D. $6,000

51. What is the due date for Form 706 for a decedent who died in 2015?

A. Six months after the date of death.
B. Nine months after the date of death.
C. Twelve months after the date of death.
D. April 15, 2016

52. Gregory and Florence are married, but file separately (MFS). In 2015, Gregory sells 300 shares of Hallberg Company stock. The stock value had fallen, and he has a $4,000 long-term capital loss on the sale. He has no other capital gains or losses. Within 15 days after Gregory sells his stock, Florence purchases 500 shares of stock in Hallberg Company. How should the stock sale be reported on Gregory's separate tax return?

A. Gregory can deduct the $4,000 on his tax return as a long-term capital loss.
B. Gregory can deduct $3,000 of the loss on his tax return, and the remaining $1,000 must be carried over to the next year.
C. Gregory can deduct the loss only if he files jointly with Florence. Otherwise, the entire loss is treated as a carryover.
D. Gregory has a wash sale, and he cannot deduct the loss.

53. Which of the following statements is correct regarding the filing of Form 4868?

A. Form 4868 provides a taxpayer with an automatic six-month extension to file and pay.
B. Even though a taxpayer files Form 4868, he will owe interest and may be charged a late payment penalty on the amount owed if the tax is not paid by the regular due date.
C. Interest is not assessed on any income tax due if Form 4868 is filed.
D. A U.S. citizen who is out of the country on vacation on the due date will be allowed an additional twelve months to file when "Out of the Country" is written across the top of Form 1040.

54. Howard is an engineer who works for Amtrak and is subject to the Department of Transportation's hours of service rules. He incurs $3,080 in meal expenses while away from home on business during 2015. Without applying the 2%-of-AGI threshold, what amount, if any, can Howard deduct for meal expenses on his Schedule A?

A. $0
B. $1,540
C. $2,464
D. $3,080

55. Angela and Donald are married and file jointly. On December 22, 2015, Donald dies. For filing status purposes, the IRS considers Angela to have been _____ all year.

A. Married.
B. Unmarried.
C. Single.
D. Legally separated.

56. Hugh and Nicole are married and file jointly. They owned and lived in a home as their primary residence for 22 years. They had purchased it for $273,000 and sold it for $805,000 in 2015. Also in 2015, the couple sold a vacation home, which they had purchased for $195,000 18 months ago. They sold it for $192,000. What amounts of taxable gain (or loss) result from these transactions?

A. $0 taxable gain; $3,000 of capital loss
B. $32,000 of capital gain
C. $32,000 of capital gain; $3,000 of ordinary loss
D. $529,000 of capital gain

57. Ted is a seventh-grade science teacher. He spent $800 of his own money on books, computer software, and other supplementary materials for his classroom in 2015. His wife, Maya, is an adjunct professor at a community college. She spent $200 of her own money on books and other supplies for the courses she teaches. The couple files jointly. What amount can they claim for an educator expense deduction in 2015?

A. $250
B. $500
C. $800
D. $1,000

58. Theresa died in 2015. At the time of her death, she had the following assets:

Traditional IRA	$150,000
Automobile titled in her name	15,000
Life insurance proceeds payable to her beneficiaries	750,000
Brokerage account held jointly with her spouse	100,000
Checking account held in her name	30,000
Property held jointly with her spouse	500,000

Theresa also had $50,000 of unreimbursed medical expenses at the time of her death. What is the amount of her gross estate?

A. $1,545,000
B. $1,245,000
C. $1,195,000
D. $795,000

59. Dante has 200 shares of Global Marine Corporation stock he purchased three years ago. On January 10, 2014, Dante gives his son, Ryan, 200 shares of Global Marine stock. Dante's adjusted basis in the stock immediately before the gift is $950. On the date of the transfer, the fair market value of the stock was $1,100. Ryan sells all 200 shares for $1,320 on November 16, 2015. What is the amount and nature of Ryan's gain?

A. $370 short-term capital gain
B. $150 long-term capital gain
C. $370 long-term capital gain
D. $220 short-term capital gain

60. For the purposes of a taxpayer claiming the Earned Income Credit, which is not a type of qualifying income?

A. Nontaxable combat pay.
B. Union strike benefits.
C. Tips.
D. Legal gambling income.

61. Kelsey owns a residential rental duplex. Both units were vacant at the beginning of the year. On April 1, 2015, Kelsey begins renting the first unit for $1,300 per month. She also collects a $1,000 refundable cleaning deposit from the first tenant. The second unit is being advertised in the local newspaper, but Kelsey is having trouble finding a responsible tenant. On October 1, 2015, Kelsey is finally able to rent the second unit for $600 per month. Kelsey obtains a $300 refundable cleaning deposit from the second tenant. On December 12, 2015, Kelsey's second tenant leaves on vacation and pays his January 2016 rent in advance. Kelsey accepts the check for $600, but does not cash it until January. Based on this information, how much rental income should Kelsey report on her Schedule E for 2015?

A. $13,500
B. $15,400
C. $14,800
D. $14,100

62. Which of the following items is taxable income to the recipient?

A. Life insurance proceeds.
B. Traditional IRA distributions to a beneficiary after the death of the IRA owner.
C. Accelerated death benefits for a terminally ill individual under a life insurance contract.
D. Canceled debt from qualified principal residence indebtedness.

63. Irene owns a residential rental condo with an adjusted basis of $17,000 and a fair market value of $50,000. In 2015, she trades her existing property for a new condo with an FMV of $68,000. As part of the exchange, she pays $20,000 to the owner of the other property. This is a qualified section 1031 exchange. What is Irene's basis in her new rental property?

A. $37,000
B. $68,000
C. $70,000
D. $51,000

64. Donna received the following income during the year:

Source	Taxable?
Wages	$26,200
Interest	5,400
Child support	6,200
Alimony income	7,400
Inheritance	12,600
Worker's compensation	2,300
Unemployment compensation	5,300

Based on the amounts above, what is Donna's gross income before adjustments and deductions are applied?

A. $52,800
B. $63,100
C. $41,300
D. $44,300

65. Inez's unmarried son, Zeke, lived with her all year. Zeke was 27 years old at the end of the year, and his gross income from wages was $5,200. Zeke is not disabled. Inez paid all the costs of keeping up the home. Can Inez claim Zeke as a dependent and also file as head of household?

A. Inez can claim Zeke as a dependent and file as head of household.
B. Inez can claim Zeke as a dependent, but she cannot file as head of household.
C. Inez cannot claim Zeke as a dependent, but she can file as head of household.
D. Inez cannot claim Zeke as a dependent, and she does not qualify for head of household filing status.

66. In 2014, Judy, age 42, had gross medical expenses of $1,400, but could deduct only $300 on Schedule A due to the 10%-of-AGI limit. In 2015, Judy received a $900 reimbursement from her insurance company for a portion of the medical expenses. How much of this recovery must be included on her 2015 return?

A. $0
B. $300
C. $600
D. $900

67. Larry owns a U.S. Series EE savings bond. He paid $250 for the bond earlier in the year. When the bond matures, Larry will receive $500. At the end of the first year, the bond is worth $257. How should Larry report the interest income on his tax return?

A. Larry must report the bond interest as it is being earned. Therefore, on his current year return, he would report $7 of taxable interest income.
B. U.S. Series EE savings bonds are exempt from federal income tax.
C. Larry may report $250 of interest income when the bond matures, or he may choose to report $7 of interest income at the end of the year.
D. Larry is required to report the interest when the bond reaches maturity, regardless of the redemption date.

68. Victoria and Pete divorced five years ago. Under her divorce settlement, she must pay her ex-husband $15,000 a year, which she has paid in equal installments each month. She is also required to pay his ongoing medical expenses for a condition he acquired during their marriage. In 2015, Pete's medical expenses were $11,400. She paid $10,000 of the medical expenses directly to the hospital. The other $1,400 she gave directly to Pete after getting a copy of the doctor's bill. How much of these payments can be properly deducted by Victoria as alimony?

A. Victoria can claim $25,000 in alimony paid as an adjustment to income.
B. Victoria can claim $15,000 in alimony paid as an adjustment to income and $10,000 as a medical expense on Schedule A of her own return.
C. Victoria can claim $26,400 in alimony paid as an adjustment to income.
D. Victoria can claim $26,400 in alimony paid as a deduction on Schedule A.

69. Rayna pays $500 a month for after-school care for her daughter Melanie. On May 1, Melanie turned 13. How much of Rayna's expenses are qualifying expenses for purposes of the Child and Dependent Care Credit?

A. $0
B. $2,000
C. $3,000
D. $6,000

70. Mason is single and 32. He does not have any dependents. In 2015, Mason wins $12,000 at a casino. The casino withholds $1,300 in federal income taxes on the winnings. He also has $14,500 in gambling losses during the year. Mason itemizes deductions. How should this be reported on his return?

A. Mason must report $12,000 of gambling winnings. He should also report the $1,300 withholding on his return. He cannot deduct his gambling losses.
B. Mason must report $12,000 of gambling winnings. He should also report the $1,300 withholding on his return. Mason can deduct $14,500 in gambling losses as a miscellaneous itemized deduction.
C. Mason should report his net gambling losses of $2,500 ($14,500 - $12,000). He should also report the $1,300 withholding on his return.
D. Mason must report $12,000 of gambling winnings. He should also report the $1,300 withholding on his return. Mason can deduct up to $12,000 of gambling losses as an itemized deduction.

71. Reiko is 32, unmarried, and files as head of household. Her modified AGI was $120,000 in 2015. Is she allowed to contribute to a Roth IRA?

A. No, she cannot contribute to a Roth.
B. Yes, she can contribute to a Roth, but her contribution is limited by MAGI.
C. Yes, she can contribute to a Roth, and her contribution is not limited by MAGI.
D. Insufficient information to answer.

72. Which of the following taxpayers is the most likely to be required to pay estimated taxes?

A. A household employee.
B. A nonresident alien with U.S. investments, who is subject to backup withholding.
C. A statutory employee.
D. A statutory nonemployee.

73. Gary has three kids in college. They are all his dependents:
   1. Brianna, age 22, a college sophomore working on her first bachelor's degree
   2. Devon, age 19, a college freshman working on his first bachelor's degree
   3. Keisha, age 23, a college graduate working on her first master's degree after having completed and graduated from a four-year undergraduate program.

Based on the above scenario, what is the maximum amount in American Opportunity Credits (AOC) Gary can claim on his 2015 return?

A. $2,500
B. $6,000
C. $5,000
D. $7,500

74. Ellie and Timothy are married and file jointly. In 2015, they have the following items of income and loss:

W-2 wages for Ellie	$60,000
W-2 wages for Timothy	105,000
Income from a passive investment partnership	4,000
Rental losses from residential real estate	(4,500)

They actively participated in the rental activity, but neither can be classified as a real estate professional. Based on this information, what amount of rental losses can they deduct in 2015?

A. $12,500
B. $4,500
C. $25,000
D. $4,000

75. Whitney refinanced her main home in 2015. As part of the refinance, she paid $1,800 in mortgage points, which was reflected on her closing statement. The new mortgage was a 30-year loan starting on November 1, 2015. How much of the points would be deductible as mortgage interest in 2015?

A. $10
B. $12
C. $60
D. $1,800

76. Martina works as a secretary during the week and as a hairdresser on the weekends. Based on the amounts below, what will Martina show as wage income on her individual Form 1040?

Secretary, Form W-2 wages	$25,600
Hairdresser, Form W-2 wages	4,950
Hairdresser, unreported tips	300
Unemployment compensation	3,700
State income tax refund	2,000

A. $36,550
B. $30,850
C. $30,550
D. $34,250

77. Which of the following are qualified adoption expenses for purposes of the Adoption Credit?

A. Expenses paid in an unsuccessful attempt to adopt an eligible child.
B. Expenses for adopting a spouse's child.
C. A surrogate parenting arrangement.
D. Adoption expenses reimbursed by an employer.

78. Jae Hwa is a nonresident alien working as a consultant for an American company. He is present in the U.S. on a J-1 Visa and must file Form 1040-NR. Which of the following deductions is he not allowed to claim?

A. Deduction to a qualified U.S. charity.
B. Ordinary and necessary business expenses connected with his job.
C. Deduction for state income tax paid.
D. Mortgage deduction for a home he owns in the United States.

79. In 2015, Audrey discovers that her housekeeper stole an expensive gold necklace from her. The necklace had a basis of $4,000 and a fair market value of $10,000. Audrey's adjusted gross income in 2015 is $24,000. What is Audrey's casualty loss deduction?

A. $1,500
B. $2,400
C. $7,500
D. $8,910

80. Larissa has an 18-year-old dependent son named Braden. Braden has a part-time job, and he files his return on March 1, mistakenly claiming his own exemption on the return. Larissa tries to e-file her return and receives an e-file rejection when she tries to claim Braden on her return and files as head of household. What should a tax practitioner advise in this situation?

A. Advise Braden to amend his tax return using Form 1040X, removing his personal exemption from the return. Once the amended return is processed, Larissa can file her tax return normally, claiming her son as a dependent.
B. Larissa cannot claim Braden, because he has already filed his own return claiming himself.
C. Larissa should use Form 1040X (instead of Form 1040), explaining the situation and reporting Braden's error.
D. Larissa cannot claim Braden as a dependent this year, but she is allowed to claim head of household on her tax return.

81. Theo works as an independent bookkeeper and has several business clients. His biggest client, Danville Construction Company, sends Theo a Form 1099-MISC to report he received $12,400 for bookkeeping work in 2015. Theo also received other cash payments of $2,500 from several different individuals for the work he completed. He did not receive Forms 1099-MISC for the $2,500. Based on this information, how much of his income is subject to regular income tax, and how much is subject to self-employment tax?

A. $12,400 is subject to income tax and self-employment tax. The remaining $2,500 is only subject to regular income tax.
B. $12,400 is subject only to income tax. The other $2,500 is subject to income tax and self-employment tax.
C. $14,900 is subject to income tax. None of the amounts is subject to self-employment tax, because Theo qualifies as a statutory employee.
D. $14,900 is subject to self-employment tax and income tax.

82. Veronica is 26 and single. She purchased her first home in 2008. She applied for the $7,500 First-Time Homebuyer Credit in 2008. How could this now-expired tax credit affect her individual tax return in 2015?

A. It cannot. Expired credits have no effect on current-year returns.
B. In 2008, this credit was in the form of a loan that must be repaid. Veronica must pay a portion of this loan back on her tax return in 2015.
C. This credit is a refundable credit and does not need to be repaid unless Veronica sells or disposes of the property.
D. This past credit will only affect Veronica's current year return if she purchases a second home. In that case, the credit would be prorated.

83. Allie converted her home to a residential rental several years ago. On the date she converted the property, her cost basis was $375,000 and the fair market value was $230,000. She had claimed $18,000 of depreciation when she sold the property for $205,000 in 2015. What is the amount of Allie's deductible loss?

A. $152,000 loss
B. $43,000 loss
C. $25,000 loss
D. $7,000 loss

84. Which of the following corporate distributions must be reported on Form 1040 as taxable income?

A. Capital gain distributions.
B. A return of capital.
C. Stock dividends.
D. Dividends paid to cash-value life insurance policyholders.

85. Harvey, 73, and Cindy, 66, are married and live together. They both work and each has a traditional IRA. In 2015, Harvey earned $4,000 in wages, and Cindy earned $30,000. If they file separate returns, what is the maximum that Harvey can contribute to his IRA for 2015?

A. $0
B. $4,000
C. $5,500
D. $6,500

86. In 2015, James had a number of stock sales. His investment transactions were:

Activity	Bought	Sold
Sold 1400 shares of Davis stock for $3,000 (basis: $1,400)	1/3/2013	12/1/2015
Sold 200 shares of Moore for $500 (basis: $1,000)	1/3/2012	12/25/2015
Sold 50 shares of Harris stock for $1,700 (basis: $1,500)	2/1/2015	9/12/2015

Based on all the transactions listed above, what is James's net long-term capital gain (or loss) in 2015?

A. $1,000 long-term capital loss
B. $1,200 long-term capital loss
C. $1,100 long-term capital gain
D. $1,600 long-term capital gain

87. Tamara and Bill are married and file jointly in a non-community property state. In 2015, they decide to give Tamara's nephew, Jared, $25,000. Both consent to the gift. What are the tax consequences of this gift?

A. The gift is taxable to Jared on his individual return.
B. The gift is taxable to Tamara and Bill on their joint return.
C. The gift is not taxable, but it must be reported on Form 709.
D. The gift is neither taxable nor reportable.

88. In 2015, Mariko spent time searching for a new job as a dental assistant. She was a dental assistant in her previous job before being laid off. She also applied for several jobs in other industries. At the end of the year, she is still unemployed. Which of the following job search expenses are deductible on Schedule A as an itemized deduction?

A. Mariko cannot deduct her job search expenses because she is still unemployed.
B. Only job search expenses for Mariko's current occupation as a dental assistant are deductible.
C. Mariko's job search expenses are all deductible, whether they are in her current occupation or in a new occupation.
D. None of the above. Job search expenses are never deductible, regardless of the situation or outcome.

89. Two years ago, Harold loaned his neighbor, Trish, $10,000 in a bona-fide loan. In 2015, Trish files for personal bankruptcy, and she permanently settles her debt with Harold by paying $2,000. Which of the following statements is correct?

A. Harold must report $2,000 of income, and Trish must report $8,000 of canceled debt.
B. Trish must report $10,000 of canceled debt. Harold is not required to report any income.
C. Trish must report $8,000 of canceled debt. Harold is not required to report any income.
D. Neither Harold nor Trish has taxable income from this transaction.

90. To meet the substantial presence test in determining residency for IRS purposes, an individual must be physically present in the United States for at least _____ days over a three-year period.

A. 214
B. 183
C. 120
D. 365

91. Marcel and Anna are U.S. citizens who file a joint return. They have a bank account in Switzerland with $168,000 in funds that they deposited in several years ago, when they were trying to purchase a home overseas. The home sale fell through and the money remained in the account. They did not deposit any additional funds in 2015. What is their reporting requirement to United States authorities in 2015?

A. None, because they made no new deposits in 2015.
B. They must file an FBAR by the due date (including extensions) of their tax return.
C. They must file an FBAR by June 30, 2016, with the Treasury Department and Form 8938 with the IRS by the due date (including extensions) of their tax return.
D. They must file an FBAR with the Treasury Department and Form 8938 with the IRS. Both must be filed by the due date (including extensions) of their tax return.

92. Aaron is a self-employed appliance repairman. His business has two employees. Which of the following insurance expenses is not deductible on Aaron's Schedule C?

A. Health insurance for Aaron.
B. Health insurance for Aaron's employees.
C. Liability insurance for Aaron's business.
D. Auto insurance on Aaron's work truck.

93. Jerome is age 32 and single. His AGI for 2015 was $33,200. Of this amount, $3,000 was from gambling winnings. He had the following itemized deductions:

Medical expenses (gross amount)	$10,400
Mortgage interest paid on his main home	6,700
Property tax on his main home	2,300
Miscellaneous unreimbursed work expenses	1,200
Charitable donation to his church	1,600
Gambling losses	4,600

After applying AGI limitations, what amount can he deduct on his Schedule A?

A. $20,680
B. $21,216
C. $22,046
D. $22,816

94. In 2015, an estate has distributable net income of $3,000, consisting of $1,800 of rents and $1,200 of taxable interest. The executor distributes $1,500 each to the two beneficiaries, Emily and Olivia. How should they report this income on their individual tax returns?

A. Each will be treated as having received $900 of rents and $600 of taxable interest.
B. Each will be treated as having received $1,500 of ordinary income.
C. Each will be treated as having received $1,800 of rents and $1,200 of taxable interest.
D. This income does not need to be reported by the taxpayers, because it has already been taxed at the estate level.

95. You are an enrolled agent. You have a new client named Monique who received a bill from the IRS regarding a joint return she filed with her ex-husband, Steve. During the course of your interview, you learn that Steve was a gambling addict. Upon further examination of the client's IRS transcripts, you discover several items of income that were left off the original return, and all of them were related to Steve's gambling habit. Monique had no idea that the return she filed had underreported income. Does your client have any recourse in this case?

A. No, Monique and her ex-husband are both jointly and severally liable for the tax on the return, and she has no recourse in this case.
B. Monique may qualify for relief as an innocent spouse.
C. Monique may qualify as an injured spouse.
D. Monique should request a Tax Court appearance to prove her innocence.

96. Aiden bought his primary residence on September 1, 2009. He lived in the home until March 30, 2015, when he moved in with his girlfriend. On September 15, 2015, Aiden sold the home and had a $23,000 gain. Is Aiden required to report any of the gain, and, if so, what is the nature of the gain?

A. He must report $23,000 of long-term capital gain.
B. He must report $23,000 of short-term capital gain.
C. He must report $23,000 of ordinary income.
D. All the gain can be excluded from income.

97. For purposes of the Child Tax Credit, a qualifying child is a child who:

A. Is under the age of 18 and a full-time student (or disabled of any age).
B. Is the taxpayer's daughter, under the age of 17, and claimed as a dependent on the taxpayer's return.
C. Lived with the taxpayer for the entire year, regardless of age.
D. Supplies more than half of his own support.

98. Claudia has a minimum tax credit carryforward of $1,600 available from the prior year. In 2015, her regular tax is $4,750 and her tentative minimum tax is $4,000. What amount of the minimum tax credit carryforward can Claudia use, if any, to reduce her regular tax in 2015?

A. $0
B. $750
C. $1,600
D. $4,000

99. Which of the following is a prohibited transaction relating to a traditional IRA?

A. Early withdrawal of IRA funds.
B. Using the IRA as security for a loan.
C. Making excess contributions.
D. Failing to take required minimum distributions.

100. Stephanie is 26 and unmarried. She and her 4-year-old daughter, Hannah, lived with Stephanie's father, Fred, all year. Fred paid all the costs of keeping up the home. Stephanie provides all her own support, but Fred helps support Hannah, his granddaughter. Stephanie's AGI is $19,000. Fred's AGI is $45,000. Based on these facts, which of the following statements is correct?

A. Stephanie can file head of household, claim her daughter as a dependent, and claim the Earned Income Credit.
B. Stephanie can file as single, claim her daughter as a dependent, and claim the Earned Income Credit.
C. Stephanie can file as head of household and claim her daughter as a dependent, but she cannot claim the Earned Income Credit.
D. Stephanie cannot claim her daughter as a dependent because she did not pay the costs of keeping up the home.

Please review your answer choices with the correct answers in the back.

#2 Sample Exam: Individuals

1. Angelo is age 25 and unmarried. He does not have any dependents. In 2014, he earned $6,700 in wages and had no other income. He did not have to pay income tax because his gross income was less than the filing requirement. He filed a return only to have his withheld income tax refunded to him. In 2015, Angelo began work as a self-employed plumber. He expects to earn $30,000 in 2015. Based on his income and expenses, Angelo expects his tax liability for the year to be $3,684. Angelo made no estimated tax payments in 2015. Will he owe an underpayment penalty for failure to pay estimated tax?

A. He will owe an underpayment penalty.
B. He will not owe an underpayment penalty.
C. He will owe a failure-to-pay penalty, not an underpayment penalty.
D. He will owe an underpayment penalty, but in this case, assessment of the penalty will be at the IRS's discretion.

2. Kris owns a vacation home by the lake. In 2015, she rented the home for two weeks (14 days), earning $1,200. She also lived in the home for four months. Kris paid $5,000 in mortgage interest on the home in 2015. The remainder of the year, the home was vacant. What is the proper treatment of this activity?

A. Kris does not have to report the rental income. The mortgage interest is deductible on Schedule A as an itemized deduction.
B. The rental income should be reported on Schedule E, and the mortgage interest is deductible on Schedule A as an itemized deduction.
C. The rental income and mortgage interest should be reported on Schedule E.
D. The rental income should be reported as other income on Form 1040. The mortgage interest is not deductible, since it is a vacation home.

3. Starting in 2015, what is the maximum number of IRA rollovers a taxpayer can make in a single year?

A. One IRA rollover per year is permitted, *including* trustee-to-trustee transfers.
B. One IRA rollover per year is permitted, *excluding* trustee-to-trustee transfers.
C. Two rollovers per year are permitted.
D. Unlimited rollovers are permitted, as long as the taxpayer completes the rollover within the 60 day required window.

4. Monica and Dale are married and file separately (MFS). In 2015, each had minimum essential health coverage through the state exchange where they live. Monica had qualifying health coverage for six months and Dale had qualifying coverage for all 12 months. Their household income was 300% of the federal poverty line. Do either, or both, qualify for the Premium Tax Credit?

A. Yes, they both qualify for the credit.
B. Only Dale qualifies because he had coverage for all 12 months of the year.
C. Neither qualifies because their household income is above the threshold for eligibility.
D. Neither qualifies because of their filing status.

5. Gabriel has a part-time nanny who works in his home. Gabriel paid his nanny $1,850 in wages during 2015. Which of the following statements is correct?

A. Gabriel does not have to report and pay Social Security and Medicare taxes on the nanny's 2015 wages.
B. The income is not taxable to the nanny, because it is under the reporting threshold for household employees.
C. No reporting is required by either party if the wages are paid in cash.
D. Gabriel can deduct the nanny's wages on Schedule C-EZ, since she is his employee.

6. Collette is single and is required to file a tax return in 2015. She is a U.S. citizen and legal resident of Bermuda. As of December 31, 2015, she had the following funds held in bank accounts in Bermuda:

- Account #1: $8,000
- Account #2: $9,000
- Account #3: $35,000

What are Collette's federal tax filing requirements for these funds?

A. None. Funds held in offshore accounts are not taxable by the U.S. government.
B. She must file an FBAR.
C. She must file Form 8938.
D. She must file both an FBAR and Form 8938.

7. Mike's cost basis was $2,400 for 900 shares of Devalle Corporation stock he purchased in June 2005. Mike sold the 900 shares on December 12, 2015, for $4,400 and paid an additional $100 commission. The gross proceeds from the sale were $4,400 on Form 1099-B. What was the amount of his capital gain?

A. $2,000 gain
B. $1,900 gain
C. $2,100 gain
D. $2,200 gain

8. Tracy and Kevin are married and file jointly. They had the following income in 2015:

Kevin	Amount	Tracy	Amount
Wages:	$155,000	Wages	$176,000
Commissions:	$18,000	Court Settlement	$56,000

Neither of their employers withheld the additional Medicare tax from their wages. Tracy's court settlement was from a car accident where she suffered a broken leg. What amount, if any, do Tracy and Kevin owe for the additional Medicare tax in 2015 (the threshold is $250,000 for couples filing jointly)?

A. $0
B. $729
C. $891
D. $3,141

9. Otto is 38 and has a dependent son who is 15 years old. Otto is single and qualifies for head of household filing status. In 2015, his income was $22,000 in wages, and he also had investment income. What is the maximum amount of investment income that Otto can have before he is disqualified from claiming the Earned Income Credit (EITC) in 2015?

A. $1,250
B. $2,900
C. $3,400
D. $3,950

10. Shane, who had not given taxable gifts in any prior year, gave his five children the following gifts in 2015:

- A new car to his daughter, Patricia: $16,500
- Cash to his daughter, Lizzie: $12,000
- Stock to his son, Adam: $10,500
- Stock to his son, Ben: $9,500
- Cash to his daughter, Christy: $5,000

From the information above, determine the amount, if any, of taxable gifts given by Shane.

A. $0
B. $2,500
C. $37,000
D. $52,000

11. Jenni has lived apart from her husband for three years and files separately. In 2015, Jenni has $48,000 in wages and $26,500 of passive losses from a rental real estate activity in which she actively participated. How much of her rental losses are allowable on her MFS return?

A. $0; all the losses must be carried forward.
B. $12,500
C. $25,000
D. $26,500

12. Pearl paid $280 for six tickets to a fundraising dinner at her church. The value of the dinner (printed on the ticket) was $20 per person. All the proceeds from the dinner will go to the church. How much can Pearl deduct as a charitable gift on Schedule A?

A. $0
B. $280
C. $120
D. $160

13. Mateo received two Forms W-2: one showing wages of $5,000 and another showing wages of $18,500. He also had $4,000 in long-term capital losses from a stock sale, and a $130 early-withdrawal penalty from a certificate of deposit. He had no other items of gain or loss during the year. What is his adjusted gross income (AGI) on Form 1040?

A. $20,370
B. $20,500
C. $21,500
D. $19,500

14. Tanner has a health FSA (flexible spending arrangement) through his employer. In 2015, he contributes $2,000 to his FSA to pay for his medical expenses. Which of the following statements is correct?

A. Amounts contributed to an FSA must be reported on the taxpayer's individual return.
B. Amounts contributed to an FSA are not subject to federal income taxes, but the full amount is subject to Social Security tax.
C. Amounts contributed to an FSA are not subject to employment or federal income taxes.
D. Employers cannot contribute to an employee's FSA. The amounts must be fully funded by employee salary reduction in order to be qualifying contributions.

15. Bernhard is a nonresident alien from Germany who is required to file a US Tax Return in 2015. He is unmarried and has three dependent children. He can claim _____ exemption(s) on his Form 1040NR.

A. Zero.
B. One.
C. Three.
D. Four.

16. Darryl wants to contribute to his traditional IRA for 2015. He requests an extension to file his 2015 tax return. What is the latest that Darryl can contribute to his traditional IRA and still take a deduction on his 2015 tax return?

A. October 15, 2016
B. October 15, 2015
C. April 18, 2016
D. December 31, 2015

17. Virgil gave his granddaughter, Savannah, $30,000 in cash. Savannah is 14 years old and lives with her parents. Which of the following statements is correct regarding the generation-skipping transfer tax?

A. Because the gift is subject to the generation-skipping transfer tax, it is not subject to the gift tax.
B. The gift is subject to both the gift tax and the generation-skipping transfer tax.
C. The gift is not subject to the generation-skipping transfer tax because Savannah's parents are still alive.
D. If Virgil had transferred the funds into a trust solely for his granddaughter's benefit, the gift would not be subject to the generation-skipping transfer tax.

18. In 2015, Laetitia rolled over funds from her traditional IRA to a Roth IRA. However, she changed her mind and wanted to move the funds back to the traditional IRA. Which of the following statements is correct?

A. It is not possible to convert a Roth IRA to a traditional IRA.
B. Laetitia can reverse the conversion, but must do so by April 15, 2016.
C. Laetitia can undo the conversion through a recharacterization.
D. Laetitia can convert the Roth IRA to a traditional IRA, but must pay an excise tax on the conversion.

19. Phil is single and is not a real estate professional. He owns one rental property. In 2015, he had the following income:

Wages	$210,000
IRA distribution	25,000
Capital gains from the sale of stock	12,000
Rental income	15,000
Dividends	9,000
Total MAGI	$271,000

What amount does Phil owe for the Net Investment Income Tax in 2015? (The threshold for single filers is $200,000.)

A. $0
B. $1,368
C. $2,318
D. $2,698

20. Kaia is 22 years old and attending college full-time. She lives with her parents, but she also works to support herself. Kaia provides over half of her own support. In this scenario, who is responsible for Kaia's health insurance under the Affordable Care Act?

A. Kaia's parents are responsible for providing her health coverage, because she is under 26 years of age
B. Kaia's parents are responsible for providing her health coverage, because she is under 24 years of age and a full-time student.
C. Kaia is responsible for her own health coverage.
D. The school is responsible for offering Kaia minimum essential coverage through their on-campus health center.

21. Which credit from a previous year may affect a taxpayer's income for the current year?

A. Earned Income Tax Credit.
B. Child and Dependent Care Credit.
C. Retirement Savings Contribution Credit.
D. Credit for Prior Year Alternative Minimum Tax.

22. Leonard, who was single, died of a heart attack in March 2015. He had used $2 million of his basic exclusion during his lifetime to offset gift taxes. Leonard's estate included the following items, determined either as of the date of his death or determined later:

Self-employment income earned but not received before he died	$50,000
Cash and investments	700,000
Burial expenses	40,000
Administration expenses	30,000
State death tax	20,000
Life insurance proceeds payable to his beneficiaries	1,000,000
Other property transferred to his beneficiaries	5,000,000

What amount of Leonard's estate is subject to estate tax in 2015?

A. $6.66 million
B. $3.76 million
C. $3.23 million
D. $1.33 million

23. Ling, age 36, and Bao, age 35, are married and file jointly. Bao had major medical issues in 2015, and they incurred $19,500 in qualified medical expenses. Their AGI is $68,000. What amount, if any, can they claim for their medical expense deduction in 2015?

A. $0
B. $12,700
C. $14,400
D. $19,500

24. Eddie is a police officer. In 2015, he pays $450 for new uniforms and $300 for dry cleaning the uniforms. How much of this expense is deductible, and how would the expense be reported?

A. $0; none of the costs are deductible.
B. $450 (the cost of the uniforms) is deductible as a miscellaneous itemized deduction, subject to the 2% floor. No other expenses are allowable.
C. $750 is deductible as a miscellaneous itemized deduction, not subject to the 2% floor.
D. $750 is deductible as a miscellaneous itemized deduction, subject to the 2% floor.

25. A taxpayer dies on March 18, 2015. For estate tax purposes, what is the alternate valuation date for the taxpayer's estate?

A. September 18, 2015
B. December 31, 2015
C. March 18, 2016
D. April 15, 2016

26. Kaitlyn is now divorced from her husband, but two years ago, she signed a joint return with him. She knew then that he was claiming fraudulent business expenses, but she signed the return anyway, because she was afraid he would beat her if she refused. Last year, Kaitlyn moved into a battered women's shelter with her children. The IRS has now audited their joint return and is recommending stiff penalties against Kaitlyn and her husband for the fraudulent items. Given her particular set of circumstances, Kaitlyn may be eligible for:

A. Innocent spouse relief.
B. Injured spouse relief.
C. Equitable relief.
D. Relief from separation of liability.

27. Wilson rents a two-bedroom apartment. He is a self-employed enrolled agent and works exclusively out of a home office. In 2015, Wilson paid $1,000 a month in rent for his apartment. He also paid $50 a month in utilities. His home office is 240 square feet (12 feet × 20 feet). The total square footage of his apartment is 1,200 square feet. Ignoring any income limitations, what is Wilson's allowable deduction for home office expense?

A. $1,050
B. $1,200
C. $2,520
D. $12,600

28. Melissa had a difficult year financially. In 2015, she stopped paying her credit card bills and other obligations, and she received a 1099-C reporting canceled debt. In which case must canceled debt be included in Melissa's gross income?

A. If the debt was discharged before Melissa filed for bankruptcy.
B. If Melissa was insolvent at the time of cancellation.
C. If the cancellation is qualified principal residence debt.
D. If the canceled debt was forgiven as a gift from a family member.

29. Kayla, age eight, has a small role in a television series. She made $65,000 during the tax year, but her parents put all the money in a trust fund to pay for her college. Her parents have a joint AGI of $41,000. Kayla lived at home with her parents all year. Does Kayla meet the support test in order for her parents to claim her as a dependent?

A. Yes, Kayla meets the support test, and her parents can claim her as a dependent.
B. No, Kayla does not meet the support test, and her parents cannot claim her as a dependent.
C. Since Kayla made the most money in the household, she can legally file her own tax return as single and claim her parents as dependents.
D. Kayla can file her own tax return and claim head of household filing status.

30. Five years ago, Keith and Tiffany obtained home equity loans totaling $91,000. The couple used the loans to pay off gambling debts, overdue credit payments, and some other expenses. The current balance of their home equity loan is $72,000. The fair market value of their home is $230,000, and they carry $30,000 of outstanding acquisition debt on the home. If Keith and Tiffany file jointly, can they deduct the interest they pay on these loans?

A. Yes, they can deduct the interest on all their mortgage loans.
B. No, they cannot deduct the interest on their mortgage loans.
C. The interest on the loans is only partially deductible and must be prorated to the amount of acquisition debt on their home.
D. They may deduct the mortgage interest on the home equity loan, but only as a miscellaneous itemized deduction, subject to the 2% floor.

31. Which of the following persons can claim the Earned Income Tax Credit?

A. A taxpayer with a valid Social Security number and a foster child.
B. A disabled taxpayer who is a dependent of another person.
C. A taxpayer with a qualifying child who files married filing separately.
D. A 66-year-old single taxpayer who meets the income thresholds for the credit, but does not have a qualifying child.

32. Josh, a full-time student with no compensation, marries Heather during the year. Both are age 28. For the year, Heather has taxable wages of $50,000. She plans to contribute the maximum to her traditional IRA. If Josh and Heather file jointly, how much can each contribute to a traditional IRA?

A. Heather can contribute $5,500 to her traditional IRA.
B. Heather and Josh can each contribute $5,500 to their respective traditional IRAs.
C. Heather and Josh can each contribute $6,500 to their respective traditional IRAs.
D. Heather can contribute $6,500 to her traditional IRA.

33. On the one-year anniversary at her new job, Faith's employer gave her restricted stock in the company with the condition that it would be forfeited if she did not complete five years of service with the company. The stock's FMV is $30,000. How much should she include in her income for the current year, and what would be her basis in the stock?

A. Income of $30,000; no basis.
B. No income; basis of $30,000.
C. Income of $30,000; basis of $30,000.
D. Faith would not report any income or have any basis in the stock until she has completed five years of service.

34. Dylan is a nurse in Dallas who attends a continuing education course in Los Angeles. His expenses related to the trip were as follows:

Lodging	$300
Airfare to the event	245
Meals	60
Fees for the course	150

His employer did not reimburse any of his expenses. What amount, if any, is Dylan's deductible expense for the trip (before the application of any AGI limits)?

A. $0
B. $150
C. $725
D. $755

35. Chuck purchased his main home five years ago. He sells his home in June 2015. Chuck marries Julie in September 2015. For purposes of the section 121 exclusion, Chuck meets the ownership and use tests, but Julie does not. On their jointly filed return, how would Chuck report the sale of his home?

A. Chuck cannot exclude any of the gain from the sale of his home, because Julie does not meet the ownership and use tests.
B. Chuck and Julie can exclude up to $500,000 of gain on their joint return for 2015, because they are legally married.
C. Chuck can exclude up to $250,000 of gain on their joint return for 2015.
D. Chuck must file separately from Julie to exclude any of the gain.

36. Vanessa has $11,000 in adoption expenses for an adoption that became final in December 2015. Her tax liability for the year is $9,500, and she claims the Adoption Credit, which reduces her tax to zero. What happens to the unused portion of the Adoption Credit?

A. The Adoption Credit is refundable. Therefore, Vanessa will receive a refund of $1,500.
B. The Adoption Credit is nonrefundable. Therefore, Vanessa will receive a carryover of $1,500 that she can use in the following year.
C. The Adoption Credit is nonrefundable. Therefore, Vanessa will lose the remaining $1,500 in unused adoption expenses.
D. Adoption expenses are not deductible.

37. Income in respect of a decedent (IRD):

A. Is taxed on the final return of the deceased taxpayer.
B. Is not included in the decedent's estate.
C. Is taxable income that was received by the decedent before death.
D. May be subject to estate tax.

38. Which of the following deductions is not allowed as an adjustment to income on Form 1040?

A. Long-term care expenses.
B. Self-employed health insurance deduction.
C. Student loan interest deduction.
D. Penalty on the early withdrawal of a certificate of deposit.

39. For the past year, Sarah has designed custom tutus and hair accessories for her friends' daughters. She gives the items as presents for birthdays and other special occasions. Sarah has also sold some of her custom items to a local children's boutique. In 2015, Sarah had $2,400 in expenses for fabric and other supplies. She received income of $950 from selling her items. How should Sarah treat this income and expense on her Form 1040?

A. Report $950 of income on Form 1040 and $2,400 of expenses on Schedule C.
B. Report $950 of income on Form 1040 and $2,400 of expenses on Schedule A.
C. Report $950 of income on Form 1040 and $950 of expenses on Schedule A.
D. Sarah does not have to report the income since it is a hobby. She also cannot deduct the expenses.

40. Jennifer paid the following taxes and fees in 2015:

State income tax	$2,000
Real estate taxes	1,900
Personal property fee on DMV auto license	100
Homeowners' association fee	250

What is Jennifer's total deduction for taxes on Schedule A?

A. $1,900
B. $3,900
C. $4,000
D. $4,150

41. All of the following statements are correct about section 529 plans except:

A. Contributions are deductible.
B. The taxpayer may designate an unrelated person as a beneficiary.
C. Distributions representing the amounts contributed to a plan are not included in income.
D. Section 529 plans are designed to help pay for students' qualified educational expenses at colleges or other postsecondary educational institutions.

42. Jean owns a business office. She allows her church to use the building rent-free for six months. Jean normally rents the office for $600 a month. However, other offices are renting for $700 a month in the same building. How much can Jean deduct as a charitable deduction?

A. $0
B. $3,600
C. $4,200
D. $7,200

43. The Lifetime Learning Credit is limited to $2,000 per:

A. Qualifying student.
B. Tax return.
C. College.
D. Dependent.

44. Madison is a beneficiary of her uncle's estate. In 2015, she receives a distribution of nonpassive income from the estate. How will this distribution be reported to Madison, and how should she report the income on her own return?

A. The distribution from the estate would be reported to Madison on Schedule K-1 (Form 1041). The amounts would be reported on Schedule E (Form 1040).
B. The distribution from the estate would be reported to Madison on Schedule K-1 (Form 1041). The amounts would be reported as other income on Line 21 on page 1 of Form 1040.
C. The distribution from the estate would be reported to Madison on Schedule K-1 (Form 1041). The amounts would be reported on Schedule D (Form 1040).
D. A distribution from an estate is never taxable to the beneficiary, only to the estate.

45. Which of the following could never be considered a taxable recovery?

A. Insurance reimbursement.
B. State income tax refund.
C. Rebate of a deduction itemized the prior year on Schedule A.
D. Federal income tax refund.

46. Three years ago, Lenny bought 500 shares of Erickson Corporation stock for $1,500, including his broker's commission. On April 6, 2015, Erickson distributed a 2% nontaxable stock dividend (10 shares). Three months later, on July 6, 2015, Lenny sold all 510 shares of his Erickson stock for $2,030. What is the nature of Lenny's gain?

A. Long-term capital gain.
B. Short-term capital gain.
C. Ordinary income.
D. Lenny must prorate his gain between the short-term gains and long-term gains. Five hundred shares will have long-term capital gain treatment, and the remainder will have short-term capital gain treatment 29.

47. Raymond has a traditional IRA. Rollover rules allow Raymond to do which one of the following without incurring any income tax or penalty?

A. Roll over funds from his traditional IRA plan to a Roth IRA account.
B. Roll over his traditional IRA into the IRA of a spouse.
C. Roll over funds into a government deferred-compensation plan.
D. Roll over into an educational savings plan.

48. When can the IRS reclassify alimony payments defined in a divorce decree as child support?

A. If the alimony payments are to a nonresident alien spouse.
B. If the alimony is decreased because of a contingency related to the child.
C. If one spouse refuses to cash the alimony checks.
D. If one spouse contests a prenuptial agreement.

49. Roxanne makes the following donations to nonprofit organizations in 2015:

Temple Israel	$22,000
SPCA Animal Shelter	8,000
University of California	7,000
Veterans of Foreign Wars	6,000

Roxanne's adjusted gross income is $60,000. What amount can she deduct in charitable contributions in 2015?

A. $43,000
B. $34,000
C. $30,000
D. $20,300

50. In January 2015, Lawrence received an acre of land as a gift from his Uncle Barry. At the time of the gift, the land had an FMV of $58,000. Barry's adjusted basis in the land was $50,000. Lawrence then spent $1,500 of his own funds to clear stumps from the land. On September 1, 2015, Lawrence sells the property for $53,000. How should he report this transaction on his tax return?

A. $1,500 gain
B. $3,000 gain
C. $5,000 loss
D. $6,500 loss

51. Which of the following statements regarding Roth IRAs is incorrect?

A. A Roth IRA requires minimum distributions at age 70½.
B. A Roth IRA does not permit a tax deduction in the year of contribution.
C. Married taxpayers who file separate returns (MFS) may contribute to a Roth IRA.
D. Compensation for purposes of a Roth IRA does not include earnings and profits from rental property.

52. Walter estimated his household income for 2015 when he enrolled in the federal health insurance marketplace. Based upon this projection, he qualified for the Premium Tax Credit (PTC). He chose to have all of the credit paid in advance to his insurance company. When Walter does the calculations for his tax return, he discovers the actual amount of the credit earned is less than the amount of the advance premium tax credit payments. Which of the following statements is correct?

A. Walter will receive a refund on his 2015 tax return.
B. The excess advance payments will be applied to Walter's PTC in the next tax year.
C. Walter must repay the excess amount of the advance payments on his 2015 tax return.
D. Because he did not project his income accurately, Walter will not be eligible to claim the PTC in subsequent tax years.

53. Clark received a scholarship to attend San Francisco State University. He decides to take three classes, but he is not a degree candidate. The scholarship is for $5,000. Clark's tuition was $3,000 and his books were $900. He had no other education expenses. How much of the scholarship is taxable to Clark?

A. $0
B. $2,000
C. $1,100
D. $5,000

54. Giselle's main home was destroyed by a tornado. The area where the home was located was later declared a disaster area. Giselle receives an insurance reimbursement that exceeds her basis in the home. How many years does Giselle have to replace the home before she will have to pay tax on the gain?

A. Two years.
B. Three years.
C. Four years.
D. There is no gain on the involuntary conversion of a primary residence.

55. Rebecca works as a real estate agent for Veranda Fine Realty. She visits Veranda's offices at least once a day to check her mail. She manages dozens of listings and splits her real estate commissions with Veranda, her sole employer. How must Rebecca be classified by her employer?

A. Employee.
B. Statutory employee.
C. Corporate shareholder.
D. Statutory nonemployee.

56. Janice is the sole proprietor of a restaurant that had a net profit of $25,000 in 2015. Her husband, Marty, is also self-employed. Marty runs a carpentry business that had a net loss of $1,500 in 2015. Janice and Marty file jointly. How should this income and loss be reported?

A. They may file a single Schedule C netting the income and loss from both businesses. The Schedule SE will show total earnings subject to SE tax of $23,500.
B. Janice must file a Schedule C for the restaurant showing her net profit of $25,000, and Marty must file his own Schedule C for the carpentry business showing his net loss of $1,500. Their Schedule SE will show total earnings subject to SE tax of $23,500.
C. Janice must file a Schedule C for the restaurant showing her net profit of $25,000, and Marty must file his own Schedule C for the carpentry business showing his net loss of $1,500. Janice's Schedule SE will show total earnings subject to SE tax of $25,000.
D. Janice must file a Schedule C for the restaurant showing her net profit of $25,000, and Marty must file his own Schedule C for the carpentry business showing his net loss of $1,500. Janice's Schedule SE will show total earnings subject to SE tax of $25,000. Marty's Schedule SE will show a credit for $1,500 (the amount of his loss).

57. In 2015, the maximum amount taxpayers can claim for the nonrefundable Child Tax Credit is _____ for each qualifying child.

A. $500
B. $1,000
C. $3,950
D. $5,000

58. Nora has one Form W-2 for $22,000, one Form 1099-INT, and no other income. Her Form 1099-INT shows both interest income of $2,000 and an early withdrawal penalty of $450. Nora does not itemize deductions, and she cannot claim any tax credits. Which of the following statements is correct?

A. Since Nora does not itemize deductions, she cannot deduct the early withdrawal penalty of $450.
B. Nora can claim an adjustment for the penalty on early withdrawal of savings on Form 1040.
C. Nora can claim an adjustment for the penalty on early withdrawal on Form 1040-EZ.
D. Nora is precluded from claiming the penalty for early withdrawal this year, but the amount can be treated as a carryover to a future year to offset investment income.

59. Zoe worked for two different employers during the year. As a result, she had excess Social Security tax withheld by her employer. How can Zoe receive a credit for these overpaid amounts?

A. She can claim the excess as a credit against her income tax.
B. She must request a refund of her overpaid Social Security tax from her employer.
C. She can claim the excess as a credit against next year's Social Security tax liability.
D. Zoe can claim the excess Social Security tax as a carryover against her tax liability in future years.

60. Felix and Samantha sold their home on May 7, 2015. Through April 30, 2015, they made home mortgage interest payments of $12,200. The settlement sheet (HUD-1) for the sale of the home showed an additional $50 of interest for the six-day period in May up to, but not including, the date of sale. They also had a mortgage prepayment penalty of $2,000. In March, they paid $120 in late payment fees to their mortgage lender due to a missed payment. How much is their allowable mortgage interest deduction in 2015?

A. $12,200
B. $12,250
C. $12,370
D. $14,370

61. Which of the following taxpayers would not be able to file jointly in 2015?

A. A married couple with one spouse who is a nonresident alien and not eligible for a Social Security number.
B. A couple living together in a common law marriage recognized in the state where they live.
C. A married couple who are separated under an interlocutory (not final) decree of divorce.
D. A couple whose marriage was annulled on January 12, 2016.

62. Sharon has a traditional IRA. Her birthdate is February 8, 1945. When must Sharon take her first required minimum distribution from her retirement account in order to avoid the 50% excise tax?

A. February 8, 2015
B. December 31, 2015
C. April 1, 2016
D. April 15, 2016

63. A deductible nonbusiness bad debt is reported on:

A. Schedule C.
B. Form 1120.
C. Schedule D.
D. Schedule E.

64. Luke had the following items of income and loss in 2015:

Wages reported on Form W-2	$42,000
Gambling winnings	2,000
Gambling losses	4,000
Dependent care benefits (spent $3,200 on childcare)	3,000
Capital loss carryover from prior year	7,500

He does not itemize deductions. How much income must Luke report on his tax return?

A. $58,500
B. $39,000
C. $36,500
D. $41,000

65. Which of the following individuals are required to have individual taxpayer identification numbers (ITINs)?

A. All nonresident aliens.
B. All nonresident and resident aliens.
C. Anyone who does not have a Social Security number.
D. All nonresident and resident aliens who must file a tax return or who are claimed on someone else's return and are not eligible for a valid SSN.

66. Gerald dies in 2015. According to his will, $5,000 a year is to be paid to his widow, Abigail, and $2,500 a year is to be paid to his daughter out of the estate's income during the period of administration. For the year, the estate's distributable net income is $6,000. Based on this information, how much income is Abigail required to report on her individual tax return?

A. $2,500
B. $5,000
C. $4,000
D. $6,000

67. Penelope's home was damaged by a hurricane. She had $58,000 of damage and received $50,000 from her insurance company. In 2015, her AGI was $22,000. She had no other casualty losses during the year. What is her deductible casualty loss on Schedule A after applying the personal casualty loss deduction limits?

A. $8,000
B. $7,900
C. $2,200
D. $5,700

68. Which of the following items is not an adjustment to income?

A. Alimony paid.
B. Bad debt deduction.
C. Moving expenses.
D. Employee business expenses.

69. In general, royalties from copyrights, patents, and oil, gas, and mineral properties are taxable as:

A. Capital gains.
B. Ordinary income.
C. Self-employment income.
D. Exempt income.

70. Matt works as a coach and is also a part-time investor who subscribes to *Forbes* and *Kiplinger* magazines. He pays for a safe deposit box where he holds his investments and stock certificates. Which of the following statements is correct?

A. Matt can deduct these expenses on Schedule A as a miscellaneous itemized deduction, subject to the 2% floor.
B. Matt can deduct these expenses on Schedule A as a miscellaneous itemized deduction, not subject to the 2% floor.
C. Matt cannot deduct these expenses.
D. Matt can deduct these expenses on Schedule C as a business expense.

71. Jeremiah sells land with an adjusted basis of $100,000 in 2015. The buyer agrees to pay $125,000, with a cash down payment of $25,000 and $20,000 (plus 4% interest) in each of the next five years. What is Jeremiah's gross profit on the installment sale, and what amount is taxable in 2015?

A. The gross profit is $25,000, and $2,000 is taxable in 2015.
B. The gross profit is $10,000, and $10,000 is taxable in 2015.
C. The gross profit is $25,000, and $5,000 is taxable in 2015.
D. The gross profit is $5,000, and $5,000 is taxable in 2015.

72. A couple filing jointly can claim a maximum of _____ through the Saver's Credit in 2015 (depending on their AGI and retirement contributions for the year).

A. $4,000
B. $2,000
C. $1,000
D. $500

73. David moved to a new home 40 miles from his former home because he changed job locations. His old job was three miles from his former home. His new job location is 60 miles from that home. David paid $3,000 to move his belongings to his new home. He also paid $150 in storage fees during the move and had $50 in meal expenses while moving. Which of the following statements is correct?

A. David's moving expenses are not deductible because he does not meet the distance test.
B. David can deduct all his moving expenses ($3,000 + $150) except for the cost of his meals ($50).
C. David can deduct only the $3,000 in actual moving expenses. The cost of the meals and storage fees are not deductible.
D. David can deduct all the costs related to his move, including the cost of meals.

74. Bonnie, who was single, died in 2015. During her lifetime, she had used the full $2,117,800 of the applicable credit (also known as the unified credit) to avoid payment of gift taxes. What amount of Bonnie's basic exclusion amount is available to reduce her taxable estate?

A. $0
B. $2,007,800
C. $3,258,200
D. $5,340,000

75. Janet is a freelance copy editor who files a Schedule C. Janet operates her business on the cash basis. On December 14, 2015, she completed a project editing an author's novel. She billed the publisher $2,000 for the work on the same date. On December 26, 2015, the check arrived in Janet's mailbox. Her son collected it and the other mail because Janet was on vacation. Janet did not receive the check until she arrived back in town on January 5. She deposited the check on January 10, 2016. When must Janet recognize the income on her Schedule C?

A. 2015.
B. 2016.
C. Either 2015 or 2016.
D. Janet will not have to report the income if her business has a loss in 2015.

76. Paulo is an Army veteran. He was injured while serving in a combat zone and was later awarded Veterans Affairs (VA) disability severance benefits. How are these payments reported on Paulo's tax return?

A. 100% of the disability severance benefits may be excluded from income.
B. Up to 50% of the disability severance benefits may be excluded from income.
C. 100% of the disability severance benefits may be excluded from income tax, but is still subject to Social Security tax.
D. The disability severance benefits are taxable as ordinary income.

77. Alice is a self-employed graphic artist who designs custom stationery. She reports income on the cash basis. In December 2015, she gives a set of liqueurs to seven of her best clients. The sets cost $42 each, and she pays $59 to ship them. What amount can Alice deduct for the gifts on her Schedule C?

A. $25
B. $175
C. $234
D. $353

78. Which of the following amounts is not taxable income?

A. $20,000 in wages
B. $12,000 inheritance
C. $2,500 of traditional IRA distributions
D. $3,000 of alimony payments

79. Stan owns a residential rental property and actively participates in the rental activity. The cost basis of the building is $210,000. According to the property tax rolls at the time of the acquisition, the cost of the property was allocated as follows:

- $150,000 to the building
- $60,000 to the land

The building was placed into service two years ago, which was the time of its acquisition. Stan chose to depreciate the building using MACRS straight-line depreciation. Residential rental property is always depreciated over 27.5 years. Based on this information, how much depreciation expense may Stan claim in 2015?

A. $5,455
B. $5,000
C. $12,500
D. $17,500

80. Kenneth, age 60, made a traditional IRA contribution of $6,500 on March 25, 2015. Two weeks later, he lost his job. His wages for 2015 were $5,000. His unemployment benefits totaled $12,600. Which of the following statements is correct about Kenneth's IRA contribution?

A. He has made a $1,500 excess contribution to his IRA. He must correct the excess contribution, or he will have to pay an excise tax.
B. He has made a $500 excess contribution to his IRA. He must correct the excess contribution, or he will have to pay an excise tax.
C. He has made a $6,500 excess contribution to his IRA. He must correct the excess contribution, or he will have to pay an excise tax.
D. He has not made an excess contribution to his IRA, because his overall compensation for the year exceeds his IRA contribution.

81. George, age 55, and Kristin, age 48, file a joint return. They are self-employed partners in a husband-and-wife business. Their adjusted gross income is $58,000. During the year, they paid the following medical expenses:

Copayments for prescription drugs	$750
Dental fees	1,200
Health insurance premiums	8,500
Life insurance premiums	500
Orthodontia fees	1,500
Vitamins	90
Emergency room bill	7,000
Prescription eyeglasses	350
Total costs	$19,890

What amount can they deduct on their Form 1040?

A. $5,500 on their Schedule A.
B. $13,500 on their Schedule A.
C. $5,000 on their Schedule A and $8,500 as an adjustment to income.
D. $6,450 on their Schedule A and $8,500 as an adjustment to income.

82. In 2015, Laverne pays her attorney $8,000 for handling her divorce. After the divorce is final, Laverne's ex-husband refuses to pay the alimony. Laverne pays an additional fee of $4,500 for legal services to ensure the alimony is collected. How much of the legal fees are deductible on Laverne's individual tax return, and how should they be reported?

A. $0; none of the legal expenses are deductible.
B. She can deduct $4,500, subject to the 2% limit, as a miscellaneous itemized deduction.
C. She can deduct $4,500, not subject to the 2% limit, as a miscellaneous itemized deduction.
D. She can deduct $12,500, subject to the 2% limit, as a miscellaneous itemized deduction.

83. In 2014, Raul loaned his friend Kathy $10,000 so she could start a new business. They shook hands on the deal, but neither signed any paperwork. Kathy never got her business up and running, and in 2015, she left the state. Raul has not been able to find Kathy to try to collect on his debt. Which of the following statements is correct?

A. Raul can deduct $10,000 in a nonbusiness bad debt on his 2015 return.
B. Raul cannot deduct $10,000 in a nonbusiness bad debt because he does not have adequate documentation showing there was a legitimate debtor-creditor relationship.
C. Raul can deduct the debt only if he finds Kathy and she agrees to sign statement saying the debt is genuine.
D. Raul can deduct the debt only if Kathy becomes insolvent.

84. Rose is single. She received the following income in 2015:

Social Security benefits	$12,400
Wage income	42,000
Capital gains	31,000

Based on this information, what is the maximum taxable amount of Rose's Social Security benefits?

A. $6,200
B. $10,540
C. $12,400
D. $25,000

85. Benny and Arabella are married and file jointly. In 2015, a mutual fund they invest in reported they had $12,000 of capital gains. However, only $5,000 was actually distributed to them during the year. What is the correct amount of capital gain they must report on their 2015 tax joint return?

A. $0
B. $5,000
C. $7,000
D. $12,000

86. Terry is married but files separately from her husband. She has a dependent child in daycare. Terry has a flexible spending account at work and had $2,500 taken out of her wages for daycare costs. She paid $3,000 in daycare costs during the year and used the $2,500 from her FSA to pay a portion of these costs. Which of the following statements is correct?

A. Terry can exclude the $3,000 from her wages as part of the flexible spending account.
B. Terry can exclude $2,500 from income. She can take the Child and Dependent Care Credit for the remaining $500.
C. Terry can exclude a total of $2,500 from her gross income. She cannot claim the Child and Dependent Care Credit for the remaining $500.
D. Terry cannot exclude any amount because she is married filing separately. All the benefits are therefore taxable to Terry as ordinary income.

87. Sierra is 17 years old. In 2015, she had the following:

Wages	$3,000
Dividends	1,200
Taxable interest	900
Tax-exempt interest	100
Capital gains	500
Capital losses	(400)

The dividends were qualified dividends on stock given to her by her grandfather. Is Sierra subject to the kiddie tax, and what is her unearned income for 2015?

A. No. Her unearned income totals $700.
B. Yes. Her unearned income totals $1,000.
C. Yes. Her unearned income totals $2,100.
D. Yes. Her unearned income totals $2,200.

88. Joaquin, who was single, died in 2015 and left an estate valued at $8 million. During his lifetime, he had used $2 million of his basic exclusion to offset payments of gift tax. What portion of Joaquin's estate will be subject to tax?

A. $660,000
B. $3.34 million
C. $4.57 million
D. $6 million

89. Emmett was injured in a train wreck three years ago and suffered serious physical injuries. After several years of litigation, He received a settlement in 2015 that included reimbursement of his medical bills of $200,000, reimbursement of lost wages of $100,000, additional compensation of $450,000 for pain and suffering, and interest of $15,000. What portion of his settlement is taxable income in 2015?

A. None
B. $15,000
C. $450,000
D. $115,000

90. Which of the following is correct about Roth IRAs?

A. In 2015, A taxpayer can make a qualified rollover contribution to a Roth IRA, regardless of his AGI.
B. A taxpayer can participate in and contribute to a Roth IRA, regardless of the amount of the taxpayer's modified AGI.
C. A taxpayer must start making required minimum distributions at age 70½.
D. Taxpayers can contribute to a traditional IRA as well as a Roth IRA, regardless of their AGI.

91. When Francis died in 2015, his executor gathered the following information about Francis's assets and liabilities at the time of his death:
- Cash and investments of $325,000.
- Life insurance proceeds of $1,000,000 payable to his wife.
- Personal residence with FMV of $500,000, owned jointly with Francis's wife, who is a U.S. citizen.
- Debts of $200,000 owed at the time of death.

In addition, funeral expenses of $25,000 and administration expenses of $50,000 were paid out of the estate. All of Francis's assets passed to his wife according to his will. Based upon the information above, what is the amount of Francis's taxable estate?

A. $0
B. $1,625,000
C. $1,550,000
D. $1,575,000

92. Ethan claimed the Earned Income Tax Credit in 2013, 2014, and 2015. The IRS audited his returns and disallowed the EITC in 2015. The IRS also found that Ethan claimed the EITC due to reckless disregard of the EITC rules. Ethan cannot claim the EITC for:

A. One tax year.
B. Two tax years.
C. Three tax years.
D. Never. Once the IRS has disallowed a taxpayer from claiming the Earned Income Tax Credit, he can never claim it again.

93. A taxpayer may recognize income in connection with a nonstatutory stock option upon which of the following?

A. Grant of the option.
B. Exercise of the option.
C. Sale of the stock.
D. All of the above.

94. Daniel and Maria are married and file jointly. They do not have any children. However, Daniel supports his 85-year-old stepmother, who lives in an assisted living facility. Daniel's stepmother has interest income of $2,300 in 2015, and no other income. How many exemptions may Daniel and Maria claim on their tax return?

A. Zero.
B. One.
C. Two.
D. Three.

95. In which of the following instances is a taxpayer most likely to face an estimated tax penalty for taxes reported on Schedule H?

A. When he increases his federal income tax withheld by giving his employer a new Form W-4.
B. When he makes estimated tax payments by filing Form 1040-ES.
C. When he increases his federal income tax withheld by giving the payor of his pension benefits a new form W-4P.
D. When he pays the taxes and files Schedule H with his Form 1040 by April 15.

96. Ramon is a U.S. citizen serving in the Navy. He is stationed in Japan. His wife and children live with him, and he is able to claim his children as dependents. Ramon's wife is a citizen of Japan She chooses not to be treated as a U.S. resident alien for tax purposes. She does not want to file a joint return with Ramon. Which of the following statements is correct?

A. Ramon does not have to file a return until he comes back to the United States.
B. Ramon can file as head of household and claim his children as dependents.
C. Since Ramon is married and living with his spouse, he cannot claim head of household status. He must file as married filing separately.
D. Ramon can still file jointly with his wife and sign on her behalf, since his wife is a nonresident alien.

97. A nonrefundable credit can reduce tax liability to:

A. Zero.
B. Below zero.
C. The next year.
D. No more than $1,000.

98. Edward and Zelda are married, but do not file jointly. Both are 40 years old. Edward's gross income from wages is $30,150, and Zelda's wage income is $4,000. Which of the following statements is correct?

A. Only Edward is required to file.
B. Only Zelda is required to file.
C. Both Edward and Zelda are required to file.
D. Neither Edward nor Zelda must file.

99. Which of the following scenarios is considered a passive activity and subject to the passive activity rules?

A. Rental activity in which the taxpayer is a real estate professional.
B. Farming activity in which the taxpayer does not materially participate.
C. A general partner who earns income from the partnership.
D. Income earned from investments.

100. Leigh is single and 58. She has a traditional IRA retirement account valued at $79,000. On December 1, 2015, Leigh dies. Her only son, Gael, age 27, inherits his mother's retirement plan. Which of the following statements is correct?

A. Gael must start taking minimum distributions from the retirement account, which will be subject to the 10% early withdrawal penalty, since Gael is not 59½.
B. Gael can roll over the inherited retirement account into his own retirement account, essentially treating it as his own.
C. Gael can choose to take distributions from the inherited IRA in full within five years of Leigh's death or take minimum distributions from the retirement account over his life expectancy, either of which will not be subject to the 10% early withdrawal penalty. He cannot roll over the inherited retirement account into his own account.
D. Gael cannot start taking distributions from his inherited retirement account until he reaches age 59½.

Please review your answer choices with the correct answers in the back.

Part 2: Business Practice Exams

Sample Exam #3

Sample Exam #4

#3 Sample Exam: Businesses

1. Structim Company is a calendar-year C corporation that uses the accrual method. As of December 20, 2015, Structim had earned and was entitled to receive $22,000 in connection with a service contract. Structim received payment for half of the contract ($11,000) on December 29, 2015. However, Structim did not receive payment for the remainder of the contract from its customer until January 2, 2016. Structim did not cash either check until January 3, 2016. When should Structim report this revenue on its tax returns?

A. $22,000 in 2015
B. $22,000 in 2016
C. $11,000 in 2015 and $11,000 in 2016
D. None of the above is correct.

2. Meadows Partnership has four employees. During the year, Meadows pays one of its employees, Constanta, various fringe benefits. Which of the following would not be reported on Constanta's Form W-2?

A. The aggregate cost of employer-sponsored medical coverage.
B. Payment for sick leave.
C. Payments made under an accountable reimbursement plan.
D. The portion of group-term life insurance that exceeds the cost of $50,000 of coverage.

3. What is a closely-held corporation?

A. A small corporation with no more than 100 shareholders.
B. Another name for an S corporation.
C. A corporation with assets of less than $10 million.
D. A corporation with a small number of shareholders and no public market for its corporate stock.

4. Gabby owns a duplex. She lives in one half and rents the other. The property is condemned by the government in order to add lanes to an interstate highway, and Gabby receives a condemnation settlement of $90,000. She originally paid $75,000 for the property and spent $15,000 for improvements prior to 2015. Through 2015, Gabby had claimed allowable depreciation deductions of $20,000 on the rental half of the property. She also incurred legal fees of $2,000 in connection with the condemnation settlement process. What amount of taxable gain or loss will Gabby report in 2015 as a result of the condemnation if she elects to recognize gain that can potentially be deferred under section 1033?

A. Taxable gain of $19,000.
B. Taxable gain of $18,000.
C. Deductible loss of $2,000.
D. Deductible loss of $22,000.

5. Cotto is a self-employed building inspector who reports his income on a Schedule C. He does not have a home office. Today, Cotto travelled to three different inspection sites. He traveled 10 miles from his home to the first inspection site and 8 miles from the last inspection site back home. It is 13 miles from the first site to the second site and 5 miles from the second site to the third site. How many of Cotto's miles are deductible as business mileage on his Schedule C?

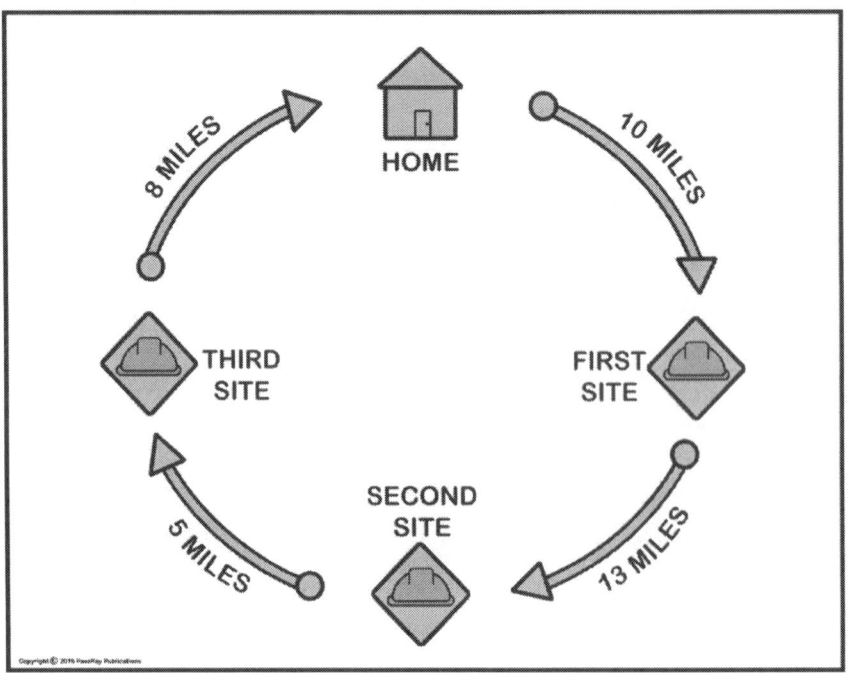

A. 33 miles
B. 31 miles
C. 18 miles
D. 15 miles

6. During the year, the Grange Partnership distributes $6,000 of cash and factory machinery with an adjusted basis of $15,000 (FMV $23,000) to Mariangel, one of the general partners. Immediately before the distribution, her adjusted basis in her partnership interest is $18,000. This was a nonliquidating distribution. What is Mariangel's basis in the factory machinery that was distributed, and what is her remaining partnership basis after the distribution?

A. $23,000 basis in machinery, $12,000 remaining partnership basis.
B. $12,000 basis in machinery, $0 partnership basis.
C. $15,000 basis in machinery, $12,000 remaining partnership basis.
D. $5,000 basis in machinery, $9,000 remaining partnership basis.

7. The Fun-ta Corporation incurred $53,000 of organizational costs in its first year of business. How should these costs be treated?

A. $5,000 can be deducted currently. The remaining $48,000 must be amortized over 180 months.
B. $2,000 can be deducted currently. The remaining $51,000 must be amortized over 180 months.
C. None of the costs are deductible currently. They must be amortized over 180 months.
D. Organizational costs are deductible only in the year prior to the official start of business for a corporation or a partnership.

8. All of the following statements are correct regarding defined benefit plans except:

A. Employees receive a fixed payout upon retirement.
B. Generally, employers, not employees, contribute to defined benefit plans.
C. Defined benefit plans can be expensive to administer and have strict reporting requirements.
D. An employee must have worked 500 hours in the prior year to be eligible for a plan.

9. The Golden Touch Partnership is formed by the following partners, two of which are corporate partners and one of whom is an individual. None of the partners are related persons or related entities.

Partner	Ownership stake	Tax year-end
Daisy Corporation (C corp.)	10%	30-April
Aster Corporation (C corp.)	45%	30-April
Lee (an individual)	45%	31-December

What is the required tax year-end for Golden Touch Partnership?

A. A partnership with corporate partners may choose to use either a fiscal year-end or a calendar year-end. Golden Touch Partnership is allowed to select any tax year-end it chooses.
B. Golden Touch Partnership is required to use a calendar year-end.
C. Golden Touch Partnership is required to use April 30 as its tax year-end.
D. Insufficient information to answer.

10. Which of the following is the IRS likely to consider an abusive trust?

A. Forming a trust that claims depreciation deductions for a taxpayer's personal residence.
B. Distributing funds to a charitable organization at the end of a period specified by the trust.
C. Creating a non-grantor trust solely for the benefit of a disabled individual under age 65.
D. Transferring assets into a trust that cannot be revoked after it is created.

11. Multitasker Corporation realized net income of $300,000 for book purposes in 2015. Included in book net income are the following:

Federal income taxes	$4,000
Excess of capital losses over capital gains	10,000
Tax-exempt interest income	5,000

What is Multitasker's taxable income?

A. $280,000
B. $290,000
C. $304,000
D. $309,000

12. Jasmine is a self-employed enrolled agent, and she files a Schedule C. In which of the following instances would Jasmine not be required to obtain an employer identification number (EIN)?

A. When she hires an employee.
B. When she forms a partnership with her husband.
C. When she operates multiple sole proprietorships.
D. When she files for bankruptcy under Chapter 7.

13. Mabel purchased a painting for her corporate office for $125,000. Mabel has taken depreciation deductions of $39,000 and her adjusted basis in the painting is $86,000 when she sells it in December 2015 for $180,000. What is the nature and amount of Mabel's gain or loss from the sale?

A. Capital gain of $94,000.
B. Ordinary income of $39,000 and capital gain of $55,000.
C. Ordinary income of $94,000.
D. Capital loss of $3,000 and ordinary income of $97,000.

14. Lori transfers machinery to Mayweather Corporation in exchange for 100% of the stock. At the time of the transfer, the machinery had a fair market value of $10,000. Lori's adjusted basis in the equipment before the transfer was $6,200, and the machinery was encumbered by an outstanding loan of $2,500, which was assumed by Mayweather. There was a bona-fide business reason for the transfer, and it qualifies for nonrecognition treatment under section 351. What is Lori's basis in her stock after the transfer?

A. $3,700
B. $3,800
C. $7,500
D. $10,000

15. Meza Trust had the following income and deductions in 2015:

Taxable interest	$13,000
Capital gain	3,000
Fiduciary fee	750

Per the trust instrument, capital gains are allocated to income. What is the trust's distributable net income (DNI) in 2015?

A. $12,250
B. $13,000
C. $15,250
D. $16,000

16. In February, Lillian and Ignacio formed the Econ Timber Corporation. Lillian contributed $500,000 of cash, and Ignacio contributed land and a building with a fair market value of $700,000 and an adjusted basis of $450,000. Ignacio also received $200,000 of cash from the corporation when the land and building were contributed. Lillian and Ignacio each receive 50% of the corporate stock after these contributions. What is the tax basis of the land and building to the Corporation?

A. $250,000
B. $650,000
C. $500,000
D. $700,000

17. Scott is a software programmer and computer repairman who reports his business income and loss on Schedule C. He creates a new software program for one of his clients, an auto dealership, to use at its business location. The cost of Scott's services is $14,000. Rather than paying the invoice, the dealership gives Scott a new van with an FMV of $14,500. Scott agrees to accept the van in lieu of a cash payment. The dealership's basis in the van is $12,300. At the time he takes possession of the van, Scott is required to pay sales tax totaling $960. Scott plans to use the van for his computer business. Based on this information, what is Scott's depreciable basis in the van?

A. $12,300
B. $14,000
C. $14,500
D. $14,960

18. On January 1, 2015, Galveston Seafood Partnership, a calendar-year, cash-basis business, purchases a fire insurance policy for its business. The policy is for three years and is required to be paid in full the first year. Galveston Seafood pays $1,800 for the policy. How much of this policy is deductible in 2015?

A. $0
B. $600
C. $800
D. $1,800

19. Michelle formed Kato Corporation in 2015 as a wholly-owned S corporation and contributed $100,000 of capital to the business. During 2015, Kato Corporation had the following business and investment activity:

Ordinary business income	$48,000
Short-term capital loss	5,000
Tax-exempt interest income	6,000
Charitable contributions	8,000
Section 179 deduction	25,000

On June 3, Michelle received a $25,000 cash distribution from the corporation. What is the adjusted basis of her stock on December 31, 2015?

A. $85,000
B. $91,000
C. $95,000
D. $116,000

20. Rico is a veterinarian with his own practice. He is a sole proprietor with five full-time employees whose wages averaged $32,000 in 2015. He paid the health insurance premiums for his employees who are enrolled in coverage through the Small Business Health Options (SHOP) marketplace. Does Rico qualify for the Small Business Health Care Tax Credit for 2015?

A. Yes.
B. No, because of the number of his full-time employees.
C. No, because of the average wages of his employees.
D. No, because sole proprietors are not eligible for the credit.

21. The Dunne Corporation is a calendar-year C corporation. In 2015, Dunne has $4,000 in charitable contributions that it cannot use on the current year return because of income limitations. How should this unused contribution be treated?

A. The corporation can carry over unused charitable contributions for five years.
B. The corporation can carry over unused charitable contributions for 20 years.
C. The corporation can carry over unused charitable contributions for 10 years.
D. The corporation can carry back unused charitable contributions for three years, and carry them forward for five years.

22. The domestic production activities deduction (DPAD) cannot exceed _____ of W-2 wages paid that are allocable to its domestic production gross receipts.

A. 20%
B. 50%
C. 60%
D. 100%

23. Ellen started her own catering business in 2015. She paid $10,000 for a delivery van and contributed $20,000 of her own savings in cash to the business. In addition, she purchased $13,000 in equipment, glassware, and other tools on her personal credit cards. What is her at-risk amount for this business activity?

A. $0
B. $10,000
C. $30,000
D. $43,000

24. Travis is a self-employed farmer who reports income and loss on Schedule F. On February 1, 2015, a vandal destroyed a large tractor on Travis's farm with a pipe bomb. The tractor could not be repaired. After a period of negotiations, Travis's insurance company compensated him for the full amount of the loss. He received the insurance check on December 2, 2015. How long does Travis have to replace the tractor under the rules for involuntary conversions?

A. February 1, 2017
B. December 2, 2017
C. December 31, 2017
D. December 31, 2018

25. Persil Corporation is a calendar-year C corporation that makes $50,000 nonliquidating distributions to each of its two equal shareholders, April and Charles. At the time of the distributions, Persil Corporation's current and accumulated earnings and profits were $90,000. Persil's paid-in capital for tax purposes was $390,000 at the time of the distribution. Based on this information, how would this transaction affect Charles's taxable income and the basis of his stock?

A. He would recognize a taxable dividend of $45,000 and would reduce his stock basis by $5,000.
B. He would recognize a return of capital of $50,000.
C. He would reduce his stock basis by $90,000 and report a gain of $10,000.
D. He would reduce his stock basis by $45,000 and report a taxable dividend of $5,000.

26. Which of the following types of fringe benefits would be deductible by an employer but not taxable to the employee?

A. Use of an employer's vacation home or boat.
B. Membership in a country club or athletic facility.
C. A gift card.
D. De minimis fringe benefit.

27. Christian is a 50% partner in Kilduff Partnership. On January 1, Christian's partnership basis was $1,000. Kilduff Partnership had the following items of income, calculated at the end of the year:

Ordinary income	$40,000
Tax-exempt income	20,000
Rental income	4,000

There were no distributions to any of the partners during the year. Based on this information, what is Christian's partnership basis on December 31?

A. $33,000
B. $23,000
C. $21,000
D. $22,000

28. Patricia is a sole proprietor with six employees. She has been in business for six years, and she reports her business income on Schedule C. She wants to set up a new SIMPLE IRA for herself and her employees. She has never had any type of retirement plan for her business. What is the final deadline for her to set up a SIMPLE IRA for the 2015 tax year?

A. October 1, 2015
B. April 15, 2016
C. December 31, 2015
D. January 1, 2015

29. Section 1245 generally does not apply to:

A. Depreciable personal property.
B. Fruit trees held for the production of income.
C. Pieces of machinery or equipment.
D. Real property.

30. Jerry transfers a building to Hanlon Corporation in exchange for 70% of its outstanding stock. The building had an adjusted basis of $125,000 to Jerry, and an FMV of $300,000. The stock that Jerry receives in the transfer has an FMV of $300,000. How much gain (or loss) would Jerry recognize in this transfer?

A. Deductible loss of $175,000.
B. Taxable gain of $175,000.
C. Taxable gain of $300,000. Jerry's stock basis would be $125,000.
D. No gain or loss would be recognized by either the shareholder or the corporation in this transfer.

31. Which of the following is not indicative of a personal service corporation?

A. Its shareholders are also employee-owners who perform the personal services within the corporation.
B. Its principal business activity during the testing period is the performance of personal services.
C. The corporation is an S corporation.
D. The corporation's employee-shareholders own more than 10% of the FMV of the outstanding stock.

32. Unlike limited partners, general partners have _____ for a partnership's debt obligations.

A. Joint and several liability.
B. Limited responsibility.
C. Legal absolution.
D. Nonrecourse liability.

33. Which of the following events would not cause an automatic termination of an S-election?

A. One shareholder dies and the shares are now owned by the deceased shareholder's estate.
B. A nonresident alien inherits 5% of the shares.
C. The S corporation was previously a C corporation, and it has passive investment income that exceeds 25% of its gross receipts for three consecutive tax years.
D. The shareholder limit of 100 is exceeded.

34. Holly contributed an office building to the Naples Partnership in exchange for a 30% partnership interest. The fair market value of the building was $180,000, and Holly's adjusted basis in the building was $60,000. The building was encumbered by a $30,000 mortgage, which the partnership assumed. Based on this information, what is Holly's partnership basis on the date of the contribution?

A. $20,000
B. $30,000
C. $39,000
D. $150,000

35. What is the accumulated earnings tax?

A. A 15% tax that is assessed on S corporation and partnership profits.
B. A 20% tax that is assessed on the accumulated earnings and profits of a C corporation.
C. A 20% tax that is imposed upon estates.
D. A 15% payroll tax that is imposed in addition to the trust fund recovery penalty.

36. Feral Feline Rescue is a 501(c)(3) exempt entity that is organized as a calendar-year corporation. What is the normal (unextended) due date of Feral Feline Rescue's tax return, and which form number is it required to file?

Form Number	Due Date
A. Form 990	March 15
B. Form 990	May 15
C. Form 1120	March 15
D. Form 990	April 15

37. Riser Corporation is a cash-basis C corporation. During the year, Riser Corp. pays a salary to Maximiliano, its sole employee-shareholder. The following year, Riser corporation is audited by the IRS, and Maximiliano's salary is deemed excessive. In this case, the excessive part of the salary will be treated as a:

A. Constructive distribution.
B. Liquidating distribution.
C. Prohibited transaction.
D. Nontaxable distribution.

38. Brandon and Kerry form the BAKA Partnership during the year. Brandon contributes $32,000 of cash. Kerry contributes $10,000 of cash and a used delivery truck with an FMV of $40,000 and an adjusted basis of $18,000. Brandon and Kerry are equal partners in the partnership. What is Kerry's basis in her partnership interest after her contribution?

A. $10,000
B. $50,000
C. $28,000
D. $32,000

39. Helvetica Corporation liquidated during the year by distributing assets with a fair market value of $200,000 to its shareholders. The assets had an adjusted basis of $62,000. How would this transaction be treated for tax purposes?

A. The distribution is not deductible by Helvetica. No gain or loss would be recognized.
B. The distribution is treated as a sale. Helvetica would recognize income of $138,000.
C. The distribution is treated as an exchange. Helvetica would recognize a loss of $138,000.
D. The distribution is treated as a sale. Helvetica would recognize income of $200,000.

40. What is the tax rate applicable to built-in gains for an S corporation?

A. 15%
B. 25%
C. 30%
D. The highest corporate tax rate.

41. At the beginning of the year, Beatty Corporation has accumulated earnings and profits of $150,000. Christopher is the sole shareholder of Beatty, a calendar-year C corporation. On September 1, the corporation distributes $200,000 to Christopher in a nonliquidating distribution. At the time of the distribution, his stock basis is $30,000. Beatty has no additional earnings and profits during the year. How should Christopher recognize this $200,000 distribution on his return?

A. He must recognize dividend income of $150,000 and a taxable gain of $20,000. He must also reduce his stock basis to zero.
B. He must recognize dividend income of $170,000 and reduce his stock basis to zero.
C. He must recognize dividend income of $200,000. His stock basis remains the same.
D. He must recognize dividend income of $150,000 and wage income of $20,000. He must also reduce his stock basis to zero.

42. When calculating the ordinary income of a partnership, which of the following is allowed as a deduction from ordinary income?

A. Delinquent federal taxes.
B. Short-term capital losses.
C. Guaranteed payments to partners.
D. Charitable contributions to exempt entities.

43. The Saluki Partnership has a SEP-IRA plan for its six employees. What is the maximum amount the partnership can contribute to each of its employee's accounts in 2015?

A. $5,500 (or $6,500 if 50 and over).
B. 3% of an employee's compensation.
C. The lesser of $17,500, or 25% of the employee's compensation.
D. The lesser of $53,000, or 25% of the employee's compensation.

44. What does an S corporation's accumulated adjustments account include?

A. All items of income and expenses of the S corporation.
B. All items of income and expenses of the S corporation with the exception of portfolio income (and expenses related to portfolio income).
C. All items of income and expenses of the S corporation with the exception of tax-exempt income (and expenses related to tax-exempt income).
D. An accounting of each shareholder's stock basis in the corporation and related adjustments of foreign shareholders.

45. Anthony transfers a large tract of unimproved land to Runway Corporation in exchange for stock. Immediately after the transfer, Anthony has majority control of the corporation and owns 85% of the outstanding stock. The remaining 15% is owned by another individual. Runway Corporation is an investment company. Is this a qualified section 351 exchange or is the transfer a taxable event?

A. Yes, this is a qualified section 351 exchange. The exchange is not a taxable event.
B. No, it is not a qualified 351 exchange because Anthony does not own at least 90% of the outstanding stock.
C. No, it is not a qualified 351 exchange because Anthony does not own 100% of the outstanding stock.
D. No, it is not a qualified 351 exchange because Runway Corporation is an investment company.

46. Which of the following entities do not require any type of written agreement or state filing in order to be established?

A. A general partnership and a sole proprietorship.
B. An LLC and a sole proprietorship.
C. An S corporation and a sole proprietorship.
D. A general partnership, a sole proprietorship, or an LLC.

47. Distributions of stock dividends are generally tax-free to shareholders except when:

A. The distribution is made at the end of the corporation's fiscal year.
B. The distribution is only made to shareholders.
C. Some shareholders can receive cash or other property and other shareholders receive stock.
D. The distribution is made by a foreign corporation or by a member of a controlled group of corporations.

48. Apple Valley Partnership has two general partners, Douglas and Craig, who share income and losses equally. Apple Valley had $110,000 of net ordinary income in 2015. Craig received a cash distribution of $31,000 on September 12, 2015. Douglas received a distribution of $42,000 on May 1, 2015. Apple Valley is a cash-basis, calendar year partnership. How much taxable income will Apple Valley report on Craig's Schedule K-1 and on Douglas's Schedule K-1?

A. Craig: $31,000; Douglas: $42,000.
B. Craig: $55,000; Douglas: $55,000.
C. Craig: $24,000; Douglas: $13,000.
D. Craig: $79,000; Douglas: $68,000.

49. Amino Corporation trades old manufacturing equipment for new equipment in a qualified section 1031 exchange. The cost of the old equipment was $50,000 and it had $26,000 of accumulated depreciation. Amino also paid $12,000 of cash to obtain the new equipment. The new equipment has a fair market value of $48,000. What is Amino's adjusted basis in the new equipment after the 1031 exchange?

A. $24,000
B. $36,000
C. $50,000
D. $62,000

50. What will increase a shareholder's stock basis in an S corporation?

A. The shareholder's share of nondeductible expenses.
B. Contributions to capital.
C. The shareholder's share of corporate and exempt income.
D. Both B and C are correct.

51. Kathryn and Allison join together to form Orchard Farms Partnership. Allison contributes $100,000 of cash. Kathryn contributes farmland with an FMV of $90,000 and a tax basis of $10,000. Kathryn also contributes depreciable equipment that has an FMV of $50,000 and a tax basis of $75,000. Kathryn and Allison each acquire a 50% interest in the partnership. What is Orchard Farms' tax basis in the equipment and the land?

	Tax Basis	
	Land	Equipment
A.	$90,000	$75,000
B.	$90,000	$50,000
C.	$10,000	$50,000
D.	$10,000	$75,000

52. If a fisherman elects income averaging, which schedule should he use?

A. Schedule K-1.
B. Schedule E.
C. Schedule J.
D. Schedule L.

53. Pacific Property Corporation is a calendar-year, cash-basis C corporation. In 2015, Pacific has $100,000 of capital losses and $50,000 of capital gains. Its capital gains for the prior three years are:

- 2012: $0
- 2013: $24,000 capital gains
- 2014: $9,000 capital gains

Based on this information, what is Pacific Property Corporation's capital loss carryforward for 2016?

A. $50,000
B. $24,000
C. $16,000
D. $17,000

54. In general, a partnership terminates when:

A. All its operations are discontinued or at least 50% of the total interest in partnership capital and profits is sold or exchanged within a 12-month period, including a sale or exchange to another partner.
B. A partner sells his partnership interest to a corporate entity.
C. The death of a general partner occurs.
D. An ownership transfer occurs representing at least 40% interest in capital and at least 60% interest in profits.

55. Zach is a sole proprietor whose business office was damaged by flooding. The adjusted basis of the assets damaged was $200,000. He received an insurance reimbursement of $140,000 and reinvested the entire amount plus $60,000 of additional funds to repair his damaged office. How should he report his casualty loss?

A. Report a loss of $60,000 directly on Schedule C under "other expenses".
B. Report a casualty loss of $59,000 on Schedule A, but only to the extent it exceeds 10% of his AGI.
C. Report a capital loss of $60,000 on Schedule D.
D. Report a loss of $60,000 on Form 4684.

56. Which of the following best describes a controlled group?

A. A privately-held corporation that does not publicly list its financial statements or other records.
B. A type of partnership controlled by fewer than five individuals.
C. A corporation or partnership that is owned by family members.
D. A group of corporations that are related through common ownership and are subject to rules regarding related party transactions.

57. Tara paid $30,000 to acquire a 30% stake in the Harvest Breads Bakery, a new partnership she formed with two friends. Harvest Breads is a calendar-year, cash-basis partnership. Tara is a general partner and her 30% stake allows her to share in capital and profits according to her ownership percentage. In its first year, Harvest Breads earns ordinary income of $40,000. All of the profits are reinvested in the business, so no distributions are made to any of the partners during the year. How much income should Tara report on her return, and what is her partnership basis at the end of the year?

	Income	Partnership Basis Year-end Basis
A.	$0	$42,000
B.	$10,000	$36,000
C.	$12,000	$42,000
D.	$0	$30,000

58. Which of the following is not a characteristic of a simple trust?

A. A trust that distributes all of its income currently.
B. A trust that makes no distributions of principal.
C. A trust that makes distributions to charity.
D. Both A and B.

59. Which of the following would not be section 1250 property?

A. A rental duplex.
B. A greenhouse to grow orchids.
C. A factory that manufactures premium jeans.
D. An office building.

60. At the beginning of 2015, Morris Corporation has $120,000 of accumulated earning and profits. During the year, Morris has current earnings of $90,000. On December 31, 2014, Morris distributes $220,000 to Leah, one of its shareholders. At the time of the distribution, Leah's stock basis was zero. How does this distribution affect the corporation's earnings and profits, and how would Leah report this distribution?

A. The distribution reduces Morris's E&P to zero. Leah must report dividend income of $210,000 and a capital gain of $10,000.
B. The distribution reduces Morris's E&P to zero. Leah must report dividend income of $220,000.
C. The distribution reduces Morris's E&P to $120,000. Leah must report ordinary income of $210,000 and a capital gain of $10,000.
D. The distribution reduces Morris's E&P to $10,000. Leah must report dividend income of $210,000 and a capital gain of $10,000.

61. Roger is a 50% shareholder in Linden Financial, a calendar-year S corporation. His stock basis was $16,000 on January 1. At the end of the year, Linden Financial had the following income and distributions:

Ordinary income	$80,000
Municipal bond interest income	6,000
Year-end nondividend distribution to Roger	50,000

What is Roger's stock basis in Linden Financial at the end of the year after the nondividend distribution?

A. $88,000
B. $30,000
C. $12,000
D. $9,000

62. What is a disregarded entity?

A. A C corporation that is disregarded for federal tax purposes.
B. A C corporation that has chosen to elect S-status.
C. A single-member LLC that is disregarded for federal tax purposes.
D. A multi-member LLC that is disregarded for federal tax purposes.

63. Carson Corporation sets up a SIMPLE IRA plan for its employees. Employer contributions, and, in some cases, elective employee contributions, are deposited directly into each employee's individual IRA account. Regarding this type of retirement plan arrangement, all of the following statements are correct EXCEPT:

A. Participants are always 100% vested in all of the funds in their IRAs.
B. Participant loans are permitted.
C. IRA withdrawals are permitted at any time.
D. An employee may move assets from his SIMPLE IRA to another IRA provider.

64. Marsha is weighing her options as she decides on the best entity for her new business. Her primary concerns are raising capital and avoiding personal liability. Without knowing other considerations, what entity structure might you recommend as her business consultant?

A. Partnership.
B. S corporation.
C. C corporation.
D. Sole proprietorship.

65. Nicholas is a 50% partner in the Vaughn Partnership. According to the partnership agreement, Nicholas is contracted to receive a $10,000 guaranteed payment every year. At the end of 2015, Lightning Partnership has ordinary income of $42,000. Based on this information, how much partnership income will Nicholas report on his individual tax return for the year?

A. $10,000
B. $21,000
C. $31,000
D. $42,000

66. Which of the following businesses would not be subject to the uniform capitalization rules?

A. A business that produces personal property.
B. A business that produces inventory for resale.
C. A business that acquires inventory for resale to others.
D. Self-employed authors, photographers, and artists.

67. What is required before the IRS will grant an organization 501(c)(3) status?

A. Donations of at least $1,000 as start-up funds for the charity.
B. An organizing document that specifies the permanent charitable purpose of the organization and a provision for distributing funds if it dissolves.
C. The establishment of bylaws and a board of directors.
D. All of the above.

68. Alpine Ski Corporation is a cash-basis C corporation. During the year, Alpine Ski distributed property with a fair market value of $260,000 and an adjusted basis of $40,000 to one of its shareholders, Misty. The property was subject to a $100,000 outstanding loan, which Misty assumed. This was not a liquidating distribution. What is the amount of income that Misty would report from this transaction, and what is her basis in the property distributed?

A. Taxable dividend of $220,000; basis in the property is $260,000.
B. Taxable dividend of $220,000; basis in the property is $160,000.
C. Taxable dividend of $160,000; basis in the property is $260,000.
D. Misty does not have to report any taxable dividends. Her basis in the property is $220,000.

69. Randy is a partner in the Mango Fruits Partnership, which was newly-formed in 2015. On December 31, Mango Fruits reports Randy's allocable share of ordinary income as $10,000. Randy also has an allocable share of $1,500 of municipal bond interest from the partnership. No distributions were made to Randy in 2015. On January 15, 2016, Mango Partnership distributes $11,000 to Randy. What is the effect of these transactions on Randy's partnership basis? How much taxable income must Randy report and in which year is the income taxable?

A. He must report $10,000 of taxable partnership income in 2015. After the distribution, his remaining partnership basis would be $500.
B. He must report $11,500 of taxable partnership income in 2015. After the distribution, his remaining partnership basis would be $500.
C. He must report $11,000 of taxable partnership income in 2016. After the distribution, his remaining partnership basis would be $500.
D. He must report $11,000 of taxable partnership income in 2016. After the distribution, his remaining partnership basis would be $0.

70. In 2015, an S corporation's S-election was revoked, and the corporation reverted back to a C corporation. How long must the corporation wait before electing S status again?

A. One year.
B. Two years.
C. Five years.
D. A corporation cannot elect S status again after it has been revoked.

71. What is the replacement period for the sale or exchange of livestock in an area eligible for federal disaster assistance?

A. One year after the close of the first tax year in which the taxpayer realizes any part of his gain from the sale or exchange of livestock.
B. Two years after the close of the first tax year in which the taxpayer realizes any part of his gain from the sale or exchange of livestock.
C. Three years after the close of the first tax year in which the taxpayer realizes any part of his gain from the sale or exchange of livestock.
D. Four years after the close of the first tax year in which the taxpayer realizes any part of his gain from the sale or exchange of livestock.

72. In 2015, Bioresearch Corporation purchases a number of business assets, which all qualify for section 179 treatment:

Equipment	$100,000
New computer	5,000
Qualified leasehold improvements	350,000

Bioresearch Corporation is not subject to any income limitations. What is the company's maximum allowable section 179 deduction in 2015?

A. $105,000
B. $250,000
C. $355,000
D. $455,000

73. Teal Mountain Company is a calendar-year C corporation that was dissolved on July 12, 2015. When is the final tax return due for Teal Mountain?

A. March 15, 2016
B. September 12, 2015
C. September 15, 2015
D. October 15, 2015

74. Mark, Tom, Jessica, and Shannon are all equal partners in the Light Source Partnership. During the year, Light Source Partnership borrows $100,000 for the construction of a storage facility for its products. All the partners are equally liable for the debt. Before borrowing the money, Mark's partnership basis was $46,000. What effect does the construction loan have on Mark's basis, if any?

A. Mark's partnership basis is increased to $71,000.
B. Mark's partnership basis is decreased to $21,000.
C. Mark's partnership basis is increased to $146,000.
D. This transaction has no effect on partnership basis.

75. IRC section 280F sets forth rules that limit the amount of depreciation for the following types of property:

A. Cell phones.
B. Passenger cars weighing less than 6,000 pounds.
C. Rental real property.
D. Boats.

76. During the year, Apex Corporation has a $30,000 loss from business operations. Apex Corporation receives $100,000 of dividends from a 20%-owned corporation. What is the amount of Apex Corporation's dividends-received deduction and its net operating loss (if any)?

	Dividends-Received Deduction	NOL
A.	$80,000	$5,000
B.	$70,000	$10,000
C.	$80,000	$10,000
D.	$70,000	$0

77. Gram Brothers Partnership has two general partners that manage the day-to-day operations. Gram Brothers also has two employees, a receptionist and a paid intern. Which of the following taxes would not be applicable to Gram Brothers?

A. Federal income tax.
B. Excise taxes.
C. Federal unemployment (FUTA) tax.
D. Social Security and Medicare taxes (for employees' wages).

78. Which type of entity is required to file a Schedule M-3 with its tax return?

A. A partnership.
B. An LLC.
C. A corporation with less than $10 million in assets.
D. A corporation with more than $50 million in assets.

79. Jessie and Trevor are general partners in the Midway Beer Distributorship. In 2015, they drove the company van 7,000 business-related miles out of a total of 10,000 miles and had $5,500 in total gasoline expenses. They also had to pay $25 for the annual state license tags, $20 for their city registration sticker, and $235 in DMV fees. The van had been fully depreciated prior to the current year. They are claiming actual car expenses, rather than using the standard mileage rate. What amount can they deduct for automobile expenses?

A. $3,500
B. $4,046
C. $5,780
D. $8,137

80. In which of the following instances would Gabe be treated as having constructive ownership of more than 50% of the partnership?

Ownership Percentages
A. Gabe 20%; Gabe's son 20%; Gabe's brother 60%
B. Gabe 25%; Gabe's wife 10%; Gabe's aunt 65%
C. Gabe 45%; Gabe's cousin 51%; Gabe's son 4%
D. Gabe 45%; Gabe's cousin 55%

81. All of the following entities are required to use the accrual method of accounting except:

A. A C corporation with gross receipts of $10 million.
B. A tax shelter with gross receipts of $30,000.
C. A corporation with gross income of $50,000 and long-term contracts.
D. A family farming corporation with gross receipts of $24 million.

82. Gracie Development Corporation owes one of its vendors $250,000 for a delinquent invoice. The vendor threatens to sue to recover the debt. Gracie Development agrees to transfer a commercial building to the vendor in order to satisfy the debt. Gracie Development's basis in the building is $190,000. How must this transaction be reported?

A. The company must recognize a taxable gain of $60,000.
B. The company must recognize forgiven debt of $250,000.
C. The company must recognize a taxable gain of $250,000.
D. The company can recognize a loss of $60,000.

83. Brett is the sole shareholder in Mussen Corporation, a calendar-year S corporation. His stock basis is $24,000. Mussen Corporation makes a nondividend distribution of $30,000 to Brett at the end of the year. How would the distribution in excess of his stock basis ($30,000 - $24,000 = $6,000) be taxed?

A. He must report a capital gain of $6,000.
B. He must report an ordinary dividend of $6,000.
C. He must report a capital loss of $6,000.
D. This transaction would not be reported. Instead, it would reduce Brett's stock basis to ($6,000).

84. Which of the following would be eligible to claim the Disabled Access Credit?

A. An individual taxpayer who is disabled and makes modifications to his home to make it accessible.
B. A business with $1 million of assets and 30 or fewer full-time employees during the previous year.
C. A business with $10 million of assets and 100 or fewer full-time employees during the previous year.
D. Both A and B.

85. Sunway Partnership is a calendar-year, cash-basis entity. In 2015, Sunway provided services to a client, and in exchange the partnership received a used car with a fair market value of $8,000 and an adjusted basis of $7,500. The partnership also received design services with a value of $3,000. What amount must Sunway Partnership report as income in 2015?

A. $0
B. $3,000
C. $10,500
D. $11,000

86. Janelle owns a bookstore. She recently signed a contract with a vendor, which was finalized over dinner. The total cost of the dinner was $250. Janelle's own dinner was $50. The vendor ate an expensive meal and also drank liquor, so his portion of the meal was $170. The remainder of the bill was for the tip and tax. Janelle also spent $10 for a taxi ride to the dinner. How much of the evening's expense is deductible by Janelle as a business expense?

A. $25
B. $110
C. $135
D. $250

87. When using taxable income as a starting point, which of the following transactions decreases the amount of a C corporation's earnings and profits?

A. Long-term contracts reported on the completed contract method.
B. Mine exploration and development costs deducted currently.
C. Dividends-received deduction.
D. Corporate dividends.

88. Ephraim has owned an office building for 20 years. He purchased the building for $1.4 million. After taking straight-line depreciation deductions, his adjusted basis is $682,052 in 2015. He sells the building for $2,350,000. What amounts of capital gain and ordinary income should Ephraim report from this transaction?

A. $984,996 capital gain; $682,952 ordinary income.
B. $1,667,948 capital gain; $0 ordinary income.
C. $950,000 capital gain; $0 ordinary income.
D. $950,000 capital gain; $717,948 ordinary income.

89. Terries Corporation offers fringe benefits to its employees. Which of the following benefits is partially taxable to the employee?

A. Health insurance provided to an employee by the employer.
B. The value of $100,000 of life insurance coverage provided to an employee.
C. Employer-provided parking passes.
D. Employee discounts on merchandise.

90. Chavez Corporation purchases a machine to use in its business operations in July 2015. The cost of the machine is $250,000, not including $18,500 of sales tax. The entire purchase of the machine is financed with a small business loan. During 2015, Chavez Corporation pays interest of $10,500 on the loan. What is the proper treatment of this transaction?

A. Chavez Corporation must capitalize $279,000 as the total cost of the machine and record depreciation expense each year.
B. Chavez Corporation can deduct the interest paid on the loan ($10,500). The other costs, including sales tax, should be capitalized and depreciated.
C. Chavez Corporation can deduct all the costs, including the machine purchase, as current business expenses in 2015.
D. Chavez Corporation can deduct the sales tax and the loan interest as business expenses.

91. Warren died on October 18, 2015, leaving an estate valued at more than $30 million. His executor elects a calendar year for the estate. When is Form 1041 due for the estate?

A. December 31, 2015
B. March 15, 2016
C. April 18, 2016
D. September 15, 2016

92. Keller is an artist who sells his artwork at regional fairs. He does not accept credit or debit cards. A customer visiting from another state buys five of Keller's paintings at a show, paying $11,500 entirely with traveler's checks. What, if anything, is Keller's reporting responsibility for this payment?

A. He has no additional reporting requirement to the IRS.
B. He must file Form 926.
C. He must file 1099-MISC.
D. He must file Form 8300.

93. Which of the following would be a qualified like-kind exchange of property under section 1031?

A. An exchange of an apartment building in Chicago with an apartment building in Mexico City, Mexico.
B. An exchange of a vacant lot for a factory building.
C. An exchange of a primary residence for a rental duplex.
D. An exchange of shares of stock for units of bonds.

94. Which of the following entities is NOT subject to the passive activity loss rules?

A. A partnership
B. An estate
C. A closely held corporation
D. A personal service corporation

95. Ellington Corporation is a new C corporation with two equal shareholders. The corporation reports income and loss on a calendar-year basis. Valerie's beginning stock basis is $50,000. During the year, Ellington has $64,000 of current earnings and profits. The corporation allocates its profits based on stock ownership. On December 31, Ellington distributes $40,000 to each shareholder. How much gain (or loss) must Valerie recognize on this distribution, and what is her ending stock basis?

	Income	Ending stock basis
A.	$40,000 dividend	$10,000
B.	$32,000 dividend	$10,000
C.	$40,000 ordinary income	$50,000
D.	$32,000 dividend	$42,000

96. A city charges a fee for installing sidewalk curbing in front of a business. This is a type of:

A. Repair that can be deducted as a current expense.
B. Nondeductible tax.
C. Assessment that is added to the property's basis.
D. Real estate tax that can be deducted.

97. Niven Corporation is a calendar year, cash-basis C corporation. During the year, Niven Corporation has $40,000 of capital losses and $32,000 of capital gains. How should this be reported on Niven's corporate tax return?

A. Niven will have an $8,000 capital loss carryover.
B. Niven can claim $3,000 of the excess capital losses in the current year. The remaining losses will be carried over to future years.
C. A C corporation is only allowed to deduct its capital losses against its capital gains. Therefore, the $8,000 unused capital loss is disallowed.
D. Niven can carry back its net capital loss up to three years and forward up to five years. Niven should first carry back the $8,000 of net capital losses to offset any net capital gains reported within the carryback period, and then carry forward any remaining amounts.

98. Juan David owns a small grocery store that he runs as a sole-proprietorship. Juan David bought his store building ten years ago, with a down payment of $30,000 and a mortgage of $110,000. He paid off the mortgage in six years and sold the building for $205,000 in 2015 in order to expand to a larger location. Straight-line depreciation on the building through the date of sale was $22,000. What is the nature and the amount of his gain on the sale of the building?

A. $65,000 of long-term capital gain and $22,000 of ordinary income
B. $65,000 of long-term capital gain
C. $87,000 of long-term capital gain
D. $87,000 of long-term capital gain and $22,000 of ordinary income

99. Which of the following is not a benefit of electing S corporation status?

A. Avoiding double taxation on distributions.
B. Allowing corporate losses to pass through to shareholders.
C. Up to 10% of charitable contributions are deductible.
D. Corporate liability protection.

100. Pioneer Products Corporation is a manufacturing company that had the following costs in 2015:

Raw materials purchased	$5,200,000
Freight charges on raw materials purchased	175,000
Manufacturing wages and benefits	4,025,000
Selling and administrative wages and benefits	500,000
Charitable contributions	45,000
Factory depreciation and section 179 deductions	200,000
Other manufacturing costs	875,000
Administrative office depreciation expense	20,000
Costs of shipping products to customers	150,000

Pioneer's inventory (including raw materials, work in process, and finished products) was $1,200,000 and $1,575,000 on January 1, 2015, and December 31, 2015, respectively. What was its cost of goods sold for the year?

A. $10,250,000
B. $10,815,000
C. $10,100,000
D. $10,850,000

Please review your answer choices with the correct answers in the back.

#4 Sample Exam: Businesses

1. Overstreet Corporation is owned by three individuals who have more than 80% of the combined voting power for four other corporations. These three individuals also have identical common ownership within the five corporations of at least 50%. The five corporations represent an example of:

A. Personal services corporations.
B. Closely-held corporations.
C. A parent-subsidiary controlled group.
D. A brother-sister controlled group.

2. Hadiya is a managing partner of RealTime Partnership. She has a 50% partnership interest and shares profits and losses based on that percentage. At the beginning of the year, the basis of Hadiya's partnership interest is $35,000. RealTime Partnership has an $82,000 net operating loss for the year. How would RealTime Partnership report this loss on her Schedule K-1, and how would this loss be reported on Hadiya's individual return?

A. $35,000 of partnership losses and a $6,000 loss carryforward.
B. $41,000 of partnership losses a $5,000 loss carryforward.
C. $41,000 of partnership losses.
D. $6,000 of partnership losses.

3. Eugene owns a large plot of farmland. In 2015, he foregoes growing his own crops and rents the farmland to someone else. After the new tenants arrive, Eugene takes a vacation and is gone for most of the year. Eugene does not materially participate in the farming activity on his farm in 2015. How should Eugene report this income?

A. Eugene must report the income on Schedule F.
B. Eugene must report the income on Schedule E.
C. Eugene must report the income on Form 4835.
D. Eugene must report the income on Schedule C.

4. Form 3115 is used by a business to:

A. Apply for a change in accounting method.
B. Choose entity classification.
C. Report partnership income.
D. Report cash payments over $10,000.

5. Saul operates a tuna fishing boat and reports his income on Schedule F. Saul hires his 16-year-old son, Ingram, part-time to help him run the business. Saul pays his son a reasonable wage of $6,200 for the year. Which of the following statements is correct about Ingram's wages?

A. Ingram's wages are subject to the kiddie tax.
B. Saul cannot deduct the wages he paid to Ingram because of related party transaction rules.
C. Saul may deduct Ingram's wages as a business expense, and the wages are not subject to Social Security and Medicare taxes.
D. Ingram's wages are subject to backup withholding.

6. Rick wants to transfer assets to a corporation in exchange for a controlling interest in the corporation's stock. Which of the following transfers would create a taxable event for Rick under section 351?

A. Rick exchanges depreciated property in exchange for 100% of the corporation's stock.
B. The corporation assumes liabilities in excess of the basis of the assets transferred.
C. Cash is exchanged for 100% of the corporate stock.
D. Rick will not be required to recognize gain from a transfer, as long as he has ownership of over 80% of the corporation's stock after the transfer is complete.

7. Alex sold his office building to Cassandra, a real estate investor, who plans to use it as a business rental property. Alex was liable for $2,000 in delinquent real estate taxes on the property, which Cassandra agreed to pay. Which of the following statements is correct?

A. Cassandra can deduct these taxes as a business expense.
B. Cassandra cannot deduct these taxes as a current expense, but should instead add the amount to her basis in the property.
C. Alex can deduct these taxes as an expense because he was the owner of the property.
D. The expense must be divided equally between Alex and Cassandra in order to be deductible.

8. Which of the following cannot be a shareholder in an S corporation?

A. A bank.
B. A U.S. resident who is not an American citizen.
C. A nonresident alien.
D. A 501(c)(3) exempt entity that is also a corporation.

9. Lisa is the sole beneficiary of a trust that her father, Isaac, set up before his death. Given the following information related to activity following her father's death in 2015, how much income related to the trust, if any, must Lisa report on her tax return?

Taxable income	$27,000
Tax-exempt interest	3,000
Distributable net income	30,000
Required distributions	15,000
Discretionary distributions	7,500

A. $15,000
B. $22,500
C. $27,000
D. $30,000

10. Quicker Relay Corporation is going through a final liquidation and distributes property with a fair market value of $500,000 and an adjusted basis of $190,000. The property is encumbered by an existing mortgage of $620,000. How much gain (or loss) would Quicker Relay recognize in this distribution?

A. $430,000 gain
B. $120,000 loss
C. $310,000 gain
D. $180,000 loss

11. The Sutter Partnership's fiscal year-end is September 30. When is its 2015 partnership tax return due?

A. January 15, 2016
B. April 15, 2016
C. May 15, 2016
D. March 15, 2016

12. Ileana is a self-employed tax preparer who files a Schedule C to report her business income. In 2015, she has the following purchases, all of which are 100% business-use. She files on the cash basis. Ignoring any income limitations, what is her section 179 deduction for 2015?

New computer system	$4,600
New multi-line phone system	3,600
Telephone bills	1,300
Bathroom renovation for her business office	23,000

A. $8,200
B. $31,200
C. $9,500
D. $32,500

13. Talmage is a 100% shareholder in Best Builder Corporation, a calendar-year S corporation. On January 1, Talmage's stock basis in Best Builder was $95,000. Best Builder reported the following income and loss during the year:

Ordinary losses	$15,000
Long-term capital gains	4,000
Short-term capital losses	9,000
Municipal bond interest income	2,000

What was Talmage's basis in Best Builder Corporation at the end of the year?

A. $73,000
B. $77,000
C. $87,000
D. $95,000

14. Burrier Corporation sets up an HSA (Health Savings Account) for its employees during the year. Burrier Corporation will make contributions to the HSA on the employee's behalf. Which form must Burrier Corporation file in order to report contributions to an employee's HSA?

A. Form 5498-SA.
B. Form 1099-SA.
C. The HSA contributions are reported on the corporation's yearly tax return (Form 1120).
D. The employee is required to report the value of the HSA on his individual return (Form 1040). No other reporting is required.

15. Jetta is a sole proprietor who operates a shuttle service to the airport. She owns a van she drives herself for business purposes and four additional vans that her employees drive. How should she deduct her mileage for business purposes?

A. She can deduct the standard mileage rate, but cannot deduct related parking fees and tolls.
B. She can deduct the standard mileage rate in addition to related parking fees and tolls.
C. She cannot use the standard mileage rate, but she must instead deduct actual expenses of operating the vehicles.
D. She can choose whether to use the standard mileage rate or deduct actual expenses of operating the vehicles.

16. Rita transferred property to an S corporation for stock, and immediately after the transfer, she was in control of the corporation. She received stock with a fair market value of $20,000 plus cash of $15,000. The corporation also assumed a $6,000 mortgage on the property for which Rita was liable. Rita's basis in the transferred property was $25,000. What amount must she recognize as gain, if any, in this section 351 transfer?

A. $0
B. $6,000
C. $15,000
D. $16,000

17. Bruce paid $5,500 for a new commercial bandsaw for his construction business. The shipping cost was $125. When the machine arrived, it was too difficult for Bruce to assemble and install himself, so he paid a professional to set up the machine for a cost of $250. What is Bruce's adjusted basis in this asset?

A. $5,500
B. $5,625
C. $5,875
D. $5,125

18. Paul and his sister, Margaret, have formed a limited liability company (LLC). If they do not file Form 8832, *Entity Classification Election*, how will the IRS classify their business entity?

A. As a qualified family joint venture, with two separate sole proprietorships.
B. As a partnership.
C. As a C corporation.
D. As an S corporation.

19. Parcel Express Corporation is a calendar-year C corporation. In 2015, Parcel Express had taxable income of $125,000 before figuring the dividends-received deduction. The company is entitled to a $40,000 dividends-received deduction. The company also donated $30,000 to several qualified 501(c)(3) charities during the year. What is Parcel Express's allowable deduction for charitable contributions on Form 1120?

A. $30,000
B. $10,000
C. $12,500
D. $8,500

20. A company is struggling to pay its bills. The company's controller decides to pay off creditors by using amounts withheld from the employees' paychecks for income and Social Security taxes, rather than depositing them as required with the federal government. The controller would be subject to:

A. A late payment penalty.
B. A substantial understatement penalty.
C. Criminal charges for money laundering.
D. The trust fund recovery penalty.

21. Joshua is a sole proprietor who uses the cash method. In 2015, he pays $3,000 for a business insurance policy that is effective for three years, beginning on July 1, 2015. How much of the insurance policy is deductible on his 2015 tax return?

A. $250
B. $500
C. $1,750
D. $3,000

22. Anderson Architects is a cash-basis C corporation and also a personal service corporation. The corporation's net income in 2015 is $68,000 before applying a net operating loss carryover of $22,000 from the previous year. What amount of corporate tax does the company owe in 2015?

A. $10,200
B. $23,800
C. $46,000
D. $16,100

23. Lorna is the sole owner and shareholder in Mechanics Corporation, a cash-basis S corporation. In 2015, Mechanics had the following activity:

Gross income from operations	$50,000
Tax-exempt interest	1,000
Residential rental income	5,000
Charitable contribution	2,000
Deductible business expenses	20,000

How much ordinary income must Mechanics Corporation report?

A. $28,000
B. $30,000
C. $35,000
D. $55,000

24. Carey is a farmer whose crops were wiped out by a flood. He receives $100,000 of crop insurance payments in 2015 due to the disaster. What method of accounting must he use in order to postpone recognizing the gain in 2015?

A. Accrual method.
B. Cash method.
C. Hybrid method.
D. Crop method.

25. Kristy is a 10% shareholder in Bosch Corporation, a C corporation. She is not an employee of Bosch. The C corporation loans Kristy $40,000 interest-free for one year. The applicable federal rate at the time of the loan is 2%. How will this transaction be reported, and will Kristy have to recognize any income?

A. She must recognize $800 of imputed interest as dividend income. The corporation is not allowed a deduction for the dividend paid.
B. She will not be required to recognize any dividend income as long as she repays the loan within the year.
C. She must recognize $800 of imputed interest as dividend income, and the corporation will be allowed a tax deduction for the dividend paid.
D. She must recognize $800 as taxable wages. Bosch Corporation is not allowed a deduction for the wages paid.

26. Tony is a partner in the Care Heart Partnership. At the end of the year, his adjusted basis in Care Heart was $65,000. Tony received a nonliquidating distribution of land from Care Heart, as well as $15,000 of cash. The land had an adjusted basis of $65,000 to Care Heart and a fair market value of $54,000 immediately before the distribution. What is Tony's basis in the land after the distribution?

A. $44,000
B. $50,000
C. $54,000
D. $65,000

27. Which of the following statements is correct regarding a husband and wife who own and run a business together?

A. A married couple can choose to report their business as a sole proprietorship by electing to file as a qualified joint venture and filing two separate Schedules C. They must file jointly.
B. A married couple can choose to report their business as a sole proprietorship by electing to file as a qualified joint venture and filing a combined Schedule C. They must file jointly.
C. A married couple cannot operate a partnership together because of the related party transaction rules.
D. A married couple can elect to be treated as a single individual for Social Security tax purposes.

28. All of the following types of entities must be taxed as a corporation except:

A. An insurance company.
B. A joint-stock association.
C. A business owned by a local government.
D. A business with annual gross receipts of $50 million or more.

29. Cheryl is a 100% shareholder in Waterston Corporation, a cash basis C corporation. At the end of the year, Waterston has $20,000 of current and accumulated earnings and profits. Waterston makes a $30,000 cash distribution to Cheryl. At the time of the distribution, Cheryl's stock basis in the corporation was $0. What is the effect of this distribution?

A. $30,000 taxable dividend
B. $20,000 taxable dividend; $10,000 capital gain
C. $20,000 taxable dividend; $10,000 capital loss
D. $30,000 capital gain

30. Allay Corporation is an accrual-based, calendar-year C corporation. At the end of the year, Allay reported book net income of $380,000. The calculation of book net income included the following items:

Municipal bond interest income	$60,000
Federal income tax expense	120,000

In addition, $4,300 of Allay's charitable contributions resulted in a contribution carryover for tax purposes because they exceeded the deductible limit for the year. Based on this information, what is the amount of Allay Corporation's taxable income that would be reconciled and reported on Schedule M-1 of Form 1120?

A. $324,300
B. $440,000
C. $444,300
D. $500,000

31. For a business to deduct entertainment expenses, all of the following must have occurred except:

A. The main purpose of the entertainment was the conduct of business.
B. The entertainment resulted in new or expanded business.
C. Business was engaged in during the entertainment event.
D. The entertainment occurred either directly before or directly after a substantial business discussion.

32. Jorge is a 10% shareholder in Octagon Corporation with an outstanding $10,000 loan from the corporation. Jorge defaults on the loan shortly thereafter. Octagon cancels Jorge's debt in 2015. How should this cancellation of debt be reported?

A. As a $10,000 taxable distribution to Jorge.
B. As a liquidation of corporate stock.
C. The cancelled debt would be taxable as wages to Jorge, because he is a corporate shareholder.
D. As a $10,000 return of capital.

33. Which of the following statements regarding distributions from trusts and estates is not correct?

A. Distributable net income (DNI) represents taxable net income, before the income distribution deduction.
B. The income distribution deduction is limited to DNI.
C. Beneficiaries must report taxable distributions in the year they are received.
D. The amounts taxable to beneficiaries are reported to them on Schedules K-1.

34. Shania owns a small hair salon as a sole proprietor. She has the following income and expenses:

Gross receipts	$42,000
Supplies expense	3,500
Wages for part-time employee	5,000
Utility expenses	800
Section 1231 gain	800
Charitable contribution	1,200

How much business income should Shania report on her Schedule C?

A. $53,300
B. $32,700
C. $33,500
D. $32,300

35. Mario and Juan form an equal partnership. Mario contributes $30,000, and Juan contributes property with an FMV of $40,000 and an adjusted basis of $25,000. What is the basis in the partnership of each partner?

A. Mario has a $30,000 basis, and Juan has a $25,000 basis.
B. Mario has a $30,000 basis, and Juan has a $40,000 basis.
C. Mario has a $25,000 basis, and Juan has a $25,000 basis.
D. None of the above.

36. Which business is not eligible to start a SIMPLE retirement plan for its employees?

A. A business that has union employees.
B. A business that has 110 workers.
C. A business that is organized as a partnership.
D. A business that is organized as a corporation.

37. The Darby Corporation was organized on May 15. It elected the calendar year as its accounting period. When is the tax return due for this corporation?

A. October 15
B. April 15
C. March 15
D. May 31

38. Manny is an attorney. He transfers property worth $150,000 and renders legal services valued at $13,000 to the Beltway Corporation in exchange for stock valued at $138,000. After these transactions, Manny owns 85% of the outstanding corporate stock. How much gain, income, and/or loss does Manny recognize?

A. $1,000 capital loss.
B. $13,000 ordinary income.
C. $12,000 capital loss and $13,000 ordinary income.
D. No gain or loss is recognized in this transaction.

39. Which of the following is not a pass-through entity?

A. Sole proprietorship.
B. S corporation.
C. C corporation.
D. Partnership.

40. Rodolfo and Lenora formed SuperCleaners, a calendar-year partnership, to provide janitorial services to residential customers. Before they began operations in November 2015, they incurred legal fees of $2,000 and consulting expenses of $1,000 to draft the partnership agreement and file the required forms. They also paid a commission of $600 to a broker to market partnership interests to other potential partners. How much of these expenses may be either deducted or amortized?

A. $0
B. $600
C. $3,000
D. $3,600

41. In 2015, Exposition Convention Corporation made a nondividend distribution of $800 to its sole shareholder, Ned. Ned's stock basis before the distribution was $1,000. What is the effect of this transaction?

A. Ned must report a $1,000 capital gain.
B. Ned must report a $200 capital loss.
C. Ned must report an $800 capital gain.
D. Ned must reduce his stock basis by $800.

42. Doreen acquires a 20% interest in a partnership by contributing a building that had an adjusted basis to her of $800,000 and is encumbered by a $400,000 mortgage. The partnership assumes payment of the mortgage. The basis of Doreen's partnership interest is:

A. $400,000
B. $480,000
C. $640,000
D. $800,000

43. If an S corporation distributes appreciated property (rather than money) to a shareholder, what is the income effect on the corporation?

A. Gains or losses are not recognized because an S corporation is a pass-through entity.
B. Gains are recognized for distributions of appreciated property, but losses are not.
C. Gains are not recognized for distributions of appreciated property but losses are recognized.
D. Both gains and losses are recognized for distributions of appreciated property.

44. Jack is a self-employed plumber. He purchased the following equipment in 2015:

Video recorder	$195
Laptop	450
Digital camera	123
Desk chair	53
Cellular phone	75
Work tools	178
Tool belt	95
Total	$1,169

What portion of his equipment purchases is considered listed property for depreciation purposes?

A. $0
B. $768
C. $843
D. $1,041

45. Five years ago, Messenger Corporation purchased land for a cost of $90,000. In 2015, the land is condemned by the federal government for development of a new highway. The company receives a $160,000 condemnation award for the land. Within the same year, the company purchases replacement land for $80,000. How much gain, if any, should Messenger Corporation recognize on this transaction?

A. $10,000
B. $20,000
C. $70,000
D. $160,000

46. All of the following qualify for a deduction for depletion except:

A. Patents.
B. Timber.
C. Gas wells.
D. Mines and natural deposits.

47. Renee is a general partner in a partnership. Renee receives a distribution of a parcel of land from the partnership that has a fair market value of $50,000 and a basis to the partnership of $40,000. Her outside basis in the partnership was $32,000 prior to the distribution. How must Renee recognize this transaction?

A. She must recognize a capital gain of $10,000, and her basis in the land is $50,000.
B. She must recognize a capital gain of $8,000, and her basis in the land is $50,000.
C. She must reduce her partnership basis to zero, and her basis in the land is $40,000.
D. She must reduce her partnership basis to zero, and her basis in the land is $32,000.

48. The Georgia Literary Club qualifies for tax-exempt status as an animal rescue organization. Which form is used by the organization to apply for exemption under IRC section 501(c)(3)?

A. Form 990.
B. Form 1023.
C. Form 1024.
D. None of the above. Literary clubs do not qualify for tax exemption under 501(c)(3).

49. Which of the following activities qualifies for the domestic production activities deduction?

A. Selling food or beverages prepared at restaurants or dining establishments.
B. Software development in the United States.
C. Leasing items to a related party.
D. Customer service businesses.

50. What tax returns, if any, is First Community Church required to file in 2015?

- Paid $30,000 of wages to three church employees
- Received $800 of unrelated business income
- Received $300,000 of donations from parishioners

A. A church is not required to file a tax return.
B. First Community Church must file payroll tax returns and Form 990-T.
C. First Community Church must file payroll tax returns.
D. First Community Church must file Form 990, Form 941, and Form 990-T.

51. Stuart and Kara are father and daughter. Stuart is a 70% partner in the Bluerock Partnership and Kara is a 60% partner in the Sumpter Partnership. If the Bluerock Partnership sells property at a loss to the Sumpter Partnership, what is the result of the transaction?

A. Stuart can deduct his share of the loss on his Schedule K-1.
B. Stuart and Kara can each deduct his or her share of the loss according to their percentage ownership in the respective partnerships.
C. No loss is allowed in the transaction because the partnerships are considered related parties.
D. The transaction is prohibited and will be disallowed by the IRS.

52. Dermahydrate Corporation is an accrual-basis, calendar-year C corporation. On December 15, 2015, the board of directors authorizes a charitable contribution of $3,000 to a qualified charity. What is the last day that Dermahydrate can make this charitable contribution and still take the expense on its 2015 tax return?

A. December 15, 2015
B. December 31, 2015
C. January 15, 2016
D. March 15, 2016

53. Angie owns a 30% interest in the Gunter Partnership, which is in the business of selling sporting equipment. All the general partners share profit and loss according to their ownership stakes. There are no limited partners. The partnership reports $90,000 of income for 2015 and distributes $23,000 to Angie. How much income will Angie recognize on her individual return, and what is the character of the income?

A. $23,000 income, subject to self-employment tax
B. $23,000 income, not subject to self-employment tax
C. $27,000 income, subject to self-employment tax
D. $27,000 income, not subject to self-employment tax

54. Which of the following is deductible as a business expense?

A. A political contribution.
B. Lobbying expenses related to a state election.
C. Repairs to equipment that increase the useful life of an asset.
D. A prepayment penalty on a mortgage.

55. Benevolent Inc. is a fiscal year C corporation that reports income and loss on the accrual basis. Which of the following is required for Benevolent to deduct an expense?

A. Benevolent must first pay the expense in order to deduct it.
B. Benevolent must receive an invoice or other bill for an expense in order to deduct it.
C. Benevolent must meet the all events test and have economic performance in order to deduct the expense.
D. Benevolent must have received a bill for the expense and paid it before the end of its fiscal year.

56. Pascal Textiles, a qualified S corporation, has no accumulated earnings and profits. In 2015, Pascal Textiles distributed property to Lydia, its sole shareholder, with a fair market value of $75,000 and an adjusted basis of $62,000. After recognizing her share of Pascal's current year income, Lydia's adjusted basis in the company's stock at the end of the year was $60,000. What is Lydia's tax treatment for the distribution?

A. $60,000 as a return of capital and $15,000 as a nontaxable distribution
B. $73,000 as a return of capital and $15,000 as taxable capital gain
C. $60,000 as a return of capital and $15,000 as taxable capital gain
D. $75,000 as a nontaxable distribution

57. During the year, Premium Pet Food Company had the following items of income and expense:

Income from operations	$50,000
Expenses from operations	40,000
Dividends received from TAM Corp. (a 20% owned corporation)	120,000

Premium Pet Food Corporation is a calendar-year C corporation. Based on the information above, what is Premium Pet Food Corporation's dividends-received deduction?

A. $10,000
B. $96,000
C. $104,000
D. $84,000

58. Justine and Richard are equal partners in a partnership. At the end of the year, the adjusted basis of Justine's partnership interest was $60,000. She received cash of $31,000 as a year-end distribution, plus property with a fair market value of $38,000 and an adjusted basis to the partnership of $46,000. This was a nonliquidating distribution. What is Justine's basis in the property that was distributed?

A. $46,000
B. $38,000
C. $29,000
D. $9,000

59. Driveline Corporation is a calendar-year S corporation. Driveline has four shareholders. The corporation has 10,000 shares outstanding. The shareholders have the following ownership:

Shareholder	Ownership
1. Thomas	4,500 shares
2. Ashley	2,000 shares
3. Simon	2,000 shares
4. Charlotte	1,500 shares
Total Shares	**10,000 shares**

Charlotte and Thomas wish to terminate Driveline's S-election in order to become a C corporation, but Ashley and Simon do not. Which of the following statements is correct?

A. Charlotte and Thomas do not have enough stock ownership to terminate the election.
B. All of the shareholders must agree to terminate an S-election.
C. Charlotte and Thomas have enough stock ownership to terminate the election.
D. At least 75% of the shareholders with active ownership must agree to the termination.

60. Quigley Corporation rents office space from its only employee-shareholder. The fair rental value of the office space is $4,500 per month, but the corporation pays the shareholder $6,000 per month, and the corporation deducts the full amount as rent expense. Which of the following statements is correct?

A. The IRS may reclassify the excess $1,500 per month of rental payments as a constructive dividend.
B. The IRS may reclassify the $4,500 per month of rental payments as a constructive dividend.
C. The IRS may reclassify the entire $6,000 per month of rental payments as a constructive dividend.
D. The IRS may reclassify the excess $1,500 per month of rental payments as a stock dividend.

61. Lynden Corporation gives each of its traveling salespeople $1,000 a month ($12,000 a year) as a car allowance. The salespeople do not have to provide any proof of their car expenses to Lynden Corporation. How should these payments be treated?

A. The car allowances are deductible as contractor payments, and they are not taxable to the employees.
B. Lynden must include $12,000 on each salesperson's Form W-2. The amounts are not subject to Social Security or Medicare tax.
C. Lynden must include $12,000 on each salesperson's Form W-2. The amounts are subject to income tax withholding, as well as to Social Security and Medicare tax.
D. The payments can be treated as gifts.

62. Which entity does not have to use the accrual method of accounting?

A. A C corporation with average annual gross receipts of $6 million.
B. A partnership with average annual gross receipts of $7 million.
C. A PSC with average annual gross receipts of $23 million.
D. A sole proprietor with average annual gross receipts of $1,750,000. His business carries inventory valued at $200,000.

63. The Lawton Partnership has three partners: Carl, Diana, and Sherry. During the year, Carl wishes to liquidate his partnership interest. Diana and Sherry agree, and Carl receives a cash distribution of $20,000 in exchange for his entire partnership interest. Carl's partnership basis at the time of the distribution was $12,000. How would this transaction be reported by Carl?

A. $8,000 capital gain
B. $20,000 capital gain
C. $8,000 ordinary income
D. No gain or loss is recognized in this transaction.

64. Bruns Corporation is having financial trouble and liquidates in 2015. In the course of liquidation, Bruns distributes $10,000 of cash and a machine with a fair market value of $12,000 and an adjusted basis of $8,000 to Gordon, a 10% shareholder. Gordon's basis in his stock is $17,000. How much gain will Gordon recognize in this transaction?

A. $2,000
B. $5,000
C. $3,000
D. $18,000

65. Of the following examples, only a _____ would be considered section 1250 property:

A. Backhoe.
B. Welding machine.
C. Factory building.
D. Race horse.

66. Sunshine Surfwear is a new corporation that elects to amortize its organizational costs. Which of the following is considered a qualifying organizational cost?

A. State incorporation fees.
B. Costs for issuing and selling stock or securities.
C. The cost of transferring assets to the corporation.
D. All of the costs are qualifying organizational costs.

67. Philip is the sole shareholder of Leisure Crafts Corporation. In 2015, Leisure Crafts sells a utility van with an adjusted basis of $12,000 and a fair market value of $22,000 to Philip's sister, Gayle, for $11,500. Gayle plans to use the utility van in her business. How must this transaction be reported?

A. Leisure Crafts can claim a deductible loss of $500 on the sale of the asset.
B. Leisure Crafts must recognize gain of $500 on the sale of the asset.
C. Leisure Crafts will not recognize gain or loss on the sale of the asset.
D. Leisure Crafts can claim a deductible loss of $10,500 on the sale of the asset.

68. The Affordable Care Act contains responsibilities for employers. For ACA purposes, which businesses are considered Applicable Large Employers (ALEs)?

A. A large employer for ACA purposes has 50 or more full-time employees.
B. A large employer for ACA purposes has 100 or more full-time employees.
C. A large employer for ACA purposes has 25 or more full-time employees.
D. A large employer for ACA purposes has 2 or more full-time employees.

69. Gloss-X Corporation is a C corporation. Gloss-X has a net short-term capital gain of $3,000 and a net long-term capital loss of $9,000. The short-term gain offsets some of the long-term loss, leaving a net capital loss of $6,000. The corporation also has $50,000 of ordinary taxable income. Which of the following statements is correct regarding this corporation's capital loss?

A. The corporation can use $3,000 of this $6,000 loss to offset ordinary income. The remainder must be carried forward.
B. The corporation treats this $6,000 as a long-term loss that may be carried back for one year and carried forward for up to five years.
C. The corporation treats this $6,000 as a short-term loss that may be carried back for three years and carried forward for up to five years.
D. The corporation treats this $6,000 as a long-term loss that may be carried back for two years and carried forward for up to 20 years.

70. On October 1, 2015, Spillway Corporation, a cash-basis, calendar-year corporation, purchases land and a building with a $20,000 cash down payment and a mortgage of $30,000. Spillway also pays attorneys' fees of $2,300 to complete the purchase. Spillway demolishes the existing building in order to start construction of a new building. The demolition costs are $12,000. What is the basis of the land, and how much can be taken as a current expense in 2015?

A. $50,000 land basis; $14,300 current expense
B. $52,300 land basis; $12,000 current expense
C. $62,000 land basis; $2,300 current expense
D. $64,300 land basis; $0 current expense

71. Jacob is a 10% partner in Texas Tumbleweed Partnership. In 2015, his beginning partnership basis was $7,000. He received a distribution of $10,000 of cash, plus a car with a partnership basis of $3,000 and a fair market value of $4,500. What is the result of this transaction to Jacob, and how must he recognize the distributions?

A. $3,000 of capital gain; his partnership basis is zero; and his basis in the car is zero.
B. $6,000 of capital gain; his partnership basis is zero; and his basis in the car is $3,000.
C. Zero of capital gain; his partnership basis is ($3,000); and his basis in the car is $3,000.
D. $4,500 of capital gain; his partnership basis is zero; and his basis in the car is $4,500.

72. Without an extension, what is the maximum period of time allowed for a 501(c)(3) exempt entity to submit an IRS application for exemption, starting with the date of its creation?

A. Four months.
B. Six months.
C. Nine months.
D. 15 months.

73. Which of the following business-related meal expenses would not be subject to the 50% rule?

A. A meal incurred while entertaining a business client.
B. A meal while attending a business convention.
C. A meal fully reimbursed to an employee under an accountable plan.
D. A business meal that qualifies as a de minimis fringe benefit.

74. Hudson River Corporation has $260,000 of current and accumulated earnings and profits. The company distributes a parcel of land with a fair market value of $200,000 and a basis of $90,000 to one of its shareholders, Samuel. This is not a liquidating distribution. How much gain (or loss) would Hudson River Corporation realize in this transaction, and how much dividend income would Samuel report on his individual return?

A. Hudson: $200,000 gain; Samuel: $110,000 dividend.
B. Hudson: $110,000 gain; Samuel: $200,000 dividend.
C. Hudson: $110,000 gain. Samuel: $90,000 dividend.
D. Hudson: $200,000 gain. Samuel: $170,000 dividend.

75. Jaime is the sole shareholder of Nicoletta Corporation, which is a calendar-year, accrual-basis C corporation. On December 31, 2015, Nicoletta had accrued a $20,000 bonus for Jaime and $32,000 of wage expenses for other employees. The wages and the bonus were not actually paid until January 15, 2016. How much of these expenses (if any) can Nicoletta Corporation deduct on its 2015 tax return?

A. $0
B. $20,000
C. $32,000
D. $52,000

76. Which of the following businesses that otherwise qualifies for the DPAD cannot use one of two simplified calculation methods?

A. A farming business that is not required to use the accrual method.
B. A business with total trade or business assets at the end of the tax year of $20 million or less.
C. A business with average annual gross receipts of $5 million or less in the prior three years.
D. A qualifying small business taxpayer that is eligible to use the cash method.

77. With S corporations, which of the following is not a shareholder loss limitation?

A. Debt basis limitation.
B. At-risk limitation.
C. Passive activity loss limitation.
D. Casualty loss limitation.

78. Fernanda is a general partner in the Yolo Davis Partnership. The adjusted basis of her partnership interest is $165,000. During the year, she receives a cash distribution of $80,000 and property with an adjusted basis of $28,000 and a fair market value of $30,000. This is a nonliquidating distribution. What is the basis of Fernanda's partnership interest after this distribution?

A. $55,000
B. $57,000
C. $85,000
D. $113,000

79. In 2015, Jacobo decides to invest in Blue Dog Corporation, a cash-basis C corporation. In exchange for 70% of the corporation's total stock, he exchanges a business building with an adjusted basis to him of $360,000 and a fair market value of $700,000. Based on this information, what is Jacobo's stock basis and his recognized gain on the exchange?

	Jacobo's Stock Basis	Recognized gain
A.	$360,000	$0
B.	$340,000	$360,000
C.	$700,000	$238,000
D.	$700,000	$340,000

80. A two-member LLC is formed during the year. How can this entity elect to be taxed?

A. As a corporation.
B. As a partnership.
C. As an estate.
D. Both A and B.

81. When can the expenses incurred during a complete liquidation of a corporation be deducted?

A. In the year they are incurred.
B. On the final corporate return.
C. In the year they are accrued.
D. Never. Liquidation expenses of a corporation are not a deductible business expense.

82. Qualset Corporation initiates a section 1031 exchange of an airplane (adjusted basis $30,000) for another airplane (FMV $75,000). Qualset pays an additional $40,000 of cash to complete the exchange. What is Qualset's basis in the new plane?

A. $70,000
B. $75,000
C. $105,000
D. $115,000

83. Robin invests $1,000 in the Dayton Partnership in return for a 20% general partnership interest. The Dayton Partnership takes out a $500,000 loan and incurs $100,000 of losses during the first year. What is Robin's basis in the partnership and how should she treat the loss?

A. $20,000 nondeductible loss; $101,000 basis
B. $20,000 deductible loss; $81,000 basis
C. $20,000 nondeductible loss; $0 basis
D. $20,000 deductible loss; $0 basis

84. For a business expense to be deductible, it must be each of the following except:

A. Ordinary.
B. Reasonable in amount.
C. Necessary.
D. Required.

85. All of the following characterize a complex trust except:

A. It may make discretionary distributions of principal.
B. It reports its accounting income on Form 1041.
C. It may make distributions to charity.
D. It is not allowed to accumulate income.

86. When can a business carry back a net operating loss for longer than the normal two years?

A. When the business has filed for bankruptcy protection.
B. When a corporation has average gross annual receipts totaling less than $5 million.
C. When the NOL is due to a casualty or theft.
D. When the IRS has approved a request for an extension of time for payment of tax because of undue hardship.

87. Which of the following exempt organizations is required to file an annual information return?

A. A church.
B. A governmental unit.
C. A private foundation.
D. All of the above.

88. Amara formed Kubik Corporation in 2015 as a wholly-owned S corporation and contributed $75,000 of capital to the business. During 2015, Kubik had the following results:

Ordinary income	$52,000
Short-term capital loss	4,000
Tax-exempt interest income	5,000
Charitable contributions	5,000
Section 179 deduction	20,000

On June 3, Amara received a $20,000 cash distribution from the corporation. What is the adjusted basis of her stock on December 31, 2015?

A. $83,000
B. $108,000
C. $103,000
D. $118,000

89. Which of the following businesses would not be required to file Form 4626, *Alternative Minimum Tax-Corporations*?

A. A corporation that claimed the credit for prior year minimum tax.
B. A corporation that claimed the qualified electric vehicle passive activity credit from prior years.
C. A corporation with $4 million of average annual gross receipts.
D. A corporation that claims any general business credit.

90. Chris became a limited partner in the Dubishar Partnership by contributing $12,000 of cash upon formation of the partnership. The adjusted basis of his partnership interest at the end of the current year is $21,000, which includes his $15,000 share of partnership liabilities. At the end of the year, Chris sells his partnership interest for $10,000 of cash. How must Chris report this transaction?

A. $4,000 capital gain
B. $2,000 capital loss
C. $19,000 capital gain
D. $6,000 capital gain

91. Anne-Marie died in 2015. At the time of her death, she had not received $5,000 of wages from her employer or $1,000 of rental income from a duplex she owned. A couple of weeks after her death, Anne-Marie's sole heir, her son, Mateo, received checks for the wages and the rent. He deposited the checks into his own bank account. How should Mateo treat this income?

A. Since Mateo received the funds as an inheritance, they are not taxable to Mateo.
B. This income must be reported on Anne-Marie's final tax return (Form 1040), not on Mateo's.
C. This is income in respect of a decedent. Mateo must include $6,000 of IRD in his gross income. IRD is always treated to favorable capital gains rates.
D. This is income in respect of a decedent. Mateo must include $6,000 of IRD in his gross income. The income will retain its character as ordinary income for the wages and as passive activity rental income.

92. A 501(c)(3) corporation has $1,200 in unrelated business income. How should this income be reported?

A. The entity should report the unrelated business income on Form 1120.
B. The IRS will revoke the exempt status of a charitable organization if it has business income.
C. The entity should report the unrelated business income on Form 990-T.
D. The entity should report the income on Form 990, and include a letter of explanation.

93. Which of the following property is not eligible for the section 179 deduction?

A. Inventory.
B. Qualified leasehold, retail, and restaurant improvements.
C. Off-the-shelf computer software.
D. Livestock.

94. Drew operates a farming business as a sole proprietorship and has the following income and expenses:

Sales of grain and produce	$2,000,000
Sales of livestock raised on the farm	200,000
Crop insurance proceeds	150,000
Rental income from excess land	100,000
Proceeds from the sale of used farm machinery	24,000
Car and truck expenses	100,000
Depreciation expense	700,000
Fertilizer and other supplies	500,000
Contribution to SEP-IRA	25,000
Utilities	200,000
Repairs	100,000

Based on the information above, what amount of net farm profit or loss should be reported on Drew's Schedule F?

A. $850,000
B. $750,000
C. $874,000
D. $825,000

95. Best Notary Service has gross receipts of $11,253 and supply expenses of $3,175 in 2015. The owner, Cecelia, uses her own car for business. Her written mileage log shows she drove 1,200 business-related miles. She uses the standard mileage rate to determine her driving expenses. How much can Cecilia deduct for her total business expenses on Schedule C?

A. $3,865
B. $690
C. $8,078
D. $7,388

96. Flooding destroyed a warehouse owned by Telecast Corporation, and the company received $45,000 as an insurance reimbursement. The adjusted basis of the warehouse was $20,000, and the FMV of the building at the time of the flood was $50,000. Telecast spends $41,000 of the insurance proceeds on qualifying replacement property. What is Telecast's taxable gain (or loss) from this involuntary conversion?

A. $4,000 gain
B. $5,000 loss
C. $9,000 gain
D. No gain or loss is recognized in this involuntary conversion.

97. Which of the following occurs when a corporation cannot deduct the full amount of its alternative net operating loss (ATNOL)?

A. The ATNOL cannot be carried back or forward.
B. The ATNOL can be carried back two years or forward up to 20 years.
C. The ATNOL can be carried back two years, but it cannot be carried forward.
D. The ATNOL can be carried forward up to five years.

98. Which of the following would make a corporation ineligible to elect S corporation status?

A. A shareholder is a partnership.
B. A shareholder is a bankruptcy estate.
C. The corporation has both voting and nonvoting stock.
D. The corporation has 100 shareholders.

99. Bethany and Allen are long-time business partners. Allen dies suddenly on September 18, 2015, and Bethany takes over Allen's former ownership in the business following his death. When is the final partnership tax return due?

A. December 31, 2015
B. January 15, 2016
C. January 18, 2016
D. April 15, 2016

100. Naylor Corporation is going through a complete liquidation. Jackson, a shareholder, receives a liquidating distribution of property (a truck). Naylor Corporation's basis in the truck is $12,000 and its fair market value is $52,000. However, the truck is encumbered by a liability of $60,000 (an unpaid loan), which Jackson assumes. How much gain would the corporation recognize, and what is the amount of Jackson's liquidating distribution?

A. $40,000 taxable gain to corporation; $60,000 liquidating distribution to Jackson.
B. $48,000 taxable gain to corporation; $48,000 liquidating distribution to Jackson.
C. $48,000 taxable gain to corporation; $0 liquidating distribution to Jackson.
D. $40,000 taxable gain to corporation; $0 liquidating distribution to Jackson.

Please review your answer choices with the correct answers in the back.

Part 3: Representation Sample Exams

Sample Exam #5
Sample Exam #6

#5 Sample Exam: Representation

1. The Department of the U.S. Treasury now has the power to revoke or suspend U.S. Passports for taxpayers who owe more than _____ to the IRS.

A. $10,000
B. $15,000
C. $25,000
D. $50,000

2. What is a federal tax lien?

A. A preliminary assessment of tax.
B. A legal seizure of the taxpayer's property to satisfy a tax debt.
C. A legal claim to the property of the taxpayer as security for a tax debt.
D. A collection action by the courts.

3. Alexander is an enrolled agent. A client asks him the odds of being audited if he claims certain deductions. Alexander replies that the risk is very low, with only 1% of similar tax returns being audited. Is Alexander in violation of Circular 230?

A. Yes. He cannot take into consideration whether a tax return may or may not be audited on a certain issue.
B. No. He is providing good service in helping his client pay the lowest amount of tax.
C. No, but only if the advice he provides is oral and not in writing.
D. Circular 230 does not address this issue.

4. Marion is an enrolled agent. She has a client named Leo who has several unpaid invoices. Marion prepared Leo's tax return, and called him to pick it up. Later that week, Leo comes to Marion's office and demands return of his records. He refuses to pay for any outstanding invoices. What is Marion required to do in this case?

A. Marion must promptly return any and all records belonging to the client that are necessary for him to comply with his federal tax obligations. She is not required to give Leo the tax return that she prepared.
B. Marion must promptly return any and all records, including the tax return that she prepared, regardless of any fee dispute.
C. Marion is not required to return the client's records while there is an ongoing fee dispute.
D. Marion is required to return the client's records only when the client pays in full.

5. When the IRS considers an offer in compromise and is evaluating a taxpayer's ability to pay, it will take into account all of the following assets and liabilities except:

A. Equity in real property.
B. Alimony owed.
C. Child support owed.
D. All of the items listed would be considered.

6. Max argued his case before the U.S. Tax Court, but took a patently frivolous position. What penalty could Max face?

A. Doubling of his tax liability.
B. Up to $5,000 penalty.
C. Up to $10,000 penalty.
D. Up to $25,000 penalty.

7. Which of the following is illegal under the Internal Revenue Code?

A. Tax avoidance.
B. Tax evasion.
C. Offshore bank accounts.
D. Foreign trusts.

8. What action must an enrolled agent take with the IRS if he chooses to end his representation of a particular client?

A. Nothing. It is the taxpayer's responsibility to notify the IRS.
B. He must send a statement to the IRS via mail or e-mail.
C. He must write "WITHDRAW" across the top of Form 2848 and send it to the IRS via mail or fax.
D. Either B or C.

9. When does a durable power of attorney expire?

A. When a taxpayer either marries or divorces.
B. When a taxpayer becomes mentally or physically incapacitated.
C. When a taxpayer dies.
D. Both B and C are correct.

10. The IRS Office of Appeals:

A. Provides an independent forum for taxpayers to resolve their disagreements with the IRS.
B. Acts as a mediator between the IRS and the U.S. Tax Court.
C. Acts as an advocate for the taxpayer against the examination and collection divisions of the IRS.
D. All of the above statements are correct.

11. On a jointly filed return (MFJ) both spouses are _____ for all the tax due even if only one spouse earns any income.

A. Independently liable.
B. Jointly and severally liable.
C. Partially liable.
D. Not responsible.

12. Which of the following practitioners has the most limited area of practice before the IRS?

A. Enrolled agent.
B. Certified public accountant.
C. Attorney.
D. Enrolled actuary.

13. If an enrolled agent is disbarred from practice, the IRS:

A. Will still allow the practitioner to represent clients before the IRS examination division.
B. Will not recognize a power of attorney that names the individual as a representative.
C. Will retain limited practice rights for representation of past clients.
D. None of the above.

14. Enrolled agents are allowed to assert a limited practitioner confidentiality privilege relating to:

A. Noncriminal tax matters brought before the IRS, or noncriminal tax proceedings brought in federal court.
B. Noncriminal tax matters, including communications regarding tax shelters.
C. Communications in furtherance of a crime or fraud.
D. Criminal tax matters brought before the IRS.

15. Tax practitioners should use "best practices" when representing a client before the IRS. All of the following are cited as examples of best practices in Circular 230 except:

A. Advising the client regarding any potential accuracy-related penalties.
B. Acting fairly and with integrity in dealings with the IRS.
C. Establishing the facts and evaluating the reasonableness of assumptions or representations, relating the applicable law to the relevant facts, and arriving at a conclusion supported by the client's information.
D. Clearly communicating with clients and the IRS.

16. The statute of limitations for the criminal offense of willfully attempting to evade or defeat any tax is:

A. Three years.
B. Six years.
C. Ten years.
D. Indefinite.

17. Which of the following may be grounds for denial of enrollment?

A. Failure to have a valid Social Security number.
B. Failure to have valid U.S. citizenship.
C. Failure to timely pay personal income taxes.
D. When the EA candidate is insolvent or going through bankruptcy proceedings.

18. Alma filed for bankruptcy during the year. She has an existing federal tax debt. What are the consequences in this scenario?

A. The 10-year collection statute will be suspended by the length of time Alma is in bankruptcy, plus 6 months.
B. A levy will be filed automatically against the taxpayer.
C. Delinquent returns will be filed on the taxpayer's behalf (SFR; substitute for return).
D. The filing of a Tax Court petition will be delayed.

19. Delfina owes a tax debt of $60,000. She files an installment agreement request. Which of the following statements regarding installment agreements is TRUE?

A. The IRS is restricted from issuing a levy while an installment agreement request is pending.
B. The taxpayer must wait to file any delinquent returns until after the installment agreement is accepted.
C. Delfina must file a hardship application before she files an installment agreement request.
D. Since the amount Delfina owes exceeds $50,000, her installment agreement will be denied.

20. The more commonly-used name of a Statutory Notice of Deficiency is the:

A. 30-day letter.
B. 90-day letter.
C. A federal tax levy.
D. A federal tax lien.

21. Reginald was disbarred from practice by the IRS. How many years must he wait before he can petition the IRS for reinstatement?

A. One year.
B. Five years.
C. Ten years.
D. Disbarment is permanent.

22. Which of the following statements regarding the Earned Income Tax Credit is correct?

A. U.S. citizens and resident aliens with a valid SSN can claim EITC.
B. Only U.S. citizens with a valid SSN can claim EITC.
C. Only U.S. citizens with a valid SSN who are physically present in the U.S. for at least six months can claim EITC.
D. Resident aliens can claim the EITC using a valid ITIN.

23. Which of the following tax professionals is allowed to practice before the U.S. Tax Court without first passing the tax court exam?

A. Enrolled agent.
B. CPA.
C. Attorney.
D. Enrolled Actuary.

24. Esther is an enrolled agent. She has a former client named Kent. During the year, Esther receives an IRS summons relating to Kent, with an order for her to appear before the IRS. What must Esther do about the summons?

A. Esther must respond to the summons.
B. Esther is not required to respond to the summons, but she must attempt to notify the IRS by mail that Kent is no longer her client.
C. Esther is required to forward the summons to Kent, but she is not required to respond to it since Kent is no longer her client.
D. Esther is not required to respond to the summons, nor is she required to notify her former client of the summons.

25. Who is responsible for paying the trust fund recovery penalty?

A. Any person with authority and control over funds to direct their disbursement.
B. Any employee within an organization who has the duty to perform and the power to direct the collecting, accounting, and paying of employment (trust fund) taxes.
C. A member of the board of trustees for a nonprofit charity.
D. All of the above may be responsible for paying the trust fund recovery penalty.

26. If the IRS discovers an understatement of a taxpayer's liability due to an unreasonable position taken by tax return preparer, what is the applicable penalty?

A. There is no preparer penalty in this case. The penalty would be assessed against the taxpayer.
B. The greater of $1,000 or 50% of the income derived by the tax return preparer related to the return or claim for refund.
C. The lesser of $1,000 or 50% of the income derived by the tax return preparer related to the return or claim for refund.
D. The greater of $5,000 or 100% of the income derived by the tax return preparer related to the return or claim for refund.

27. Under Circular 230, a tax preparer is required to keep which of the following?

A. Copies of all tax returns prepared. They may be stored electronically or kept as hard copies.
B. A list of clients and tax returns prepared that includes information about the taxpayer, tax year, and type of return prepared. The list may be stored electronically or kept as a hard copy.
C. Either A or B.
D. Either a copy of all tax returns prepared, or a list of clients and tax returns prepared. However, hard copies are required in both cases. Electronic storage is acceptable, but is not by itself adequate and must be supplemented with hard copies of all required documents.

28. Once a tax liability is _____, the statute of limitations for collections begins to run.

A. Determined.
B. Levied.
C. Estimated.
D. Assessed.

29. Under the June 2014 revision to Circular 230, practitioners are expected to demonstrate _____ when representing their clients.

A. "Intelligence."
B. "Proficiency."
C. "Competence."
D. "High personal morals."

30. Taxpayers may enter into a voluntary agreement with the IRS to extend the statute of limitations on their return. Which of the following forms is used to formally extend the statute of limitations?

A. Form 872-A
B. Form 2848
C. Form 8821
D. Form 9465

31. A tax return preparer relies on the language of an IRS publication in taking a risky position on a client's return. The return is audited, and the client is assessed an accuracy-related penalty for substantially understating income under section 6662. Could the tax preparer also face an accuracy-related penalty?

A. No. Section 6662 applies to taxpayers only and not to tax return preparers.
B. No, because an IRS publication is official guidance and can be relied upon to avoid accuracy-related penalties.
C. Yes, because an IRS publication is not substantial authority under federal tax law.
D. Yes, even though an IRS publication is considered substantial authority under federal tax law.

32. Which of the following types of IRS guidance generally has the highest authority in establishing precedence for all taxpayers?

A. Revenue ruling.
B. Private letter ruling.
C. Technical advice memorandum.
D. Information letter.

33. Lacey wants to designate her tax preparer as the third party designee on her individual tax return. Based solely on the third party authorization, which of the following actions will her preparer not be able to take on Lacey's behalf?

A. Call the IRS for information about the processing of her return.
B. Receive copies of notices or transcripts related to her return.
C. Respond to IRS notices about math errors on her return.
D. Receive (but not cash) her tax refund check on her behalf.

34. Martha is a taxpayer who is unable to pay her tax liability. She applied for an offer in compromise to settle her debt, but the IRS rejected her offer. Martha has _____ to appeal the rejected offer in compromise.

A. 30 days.
B. 60 days.
C. 90 days.
D. No specific time limit.

35. In which situation may the IRS contact the taxpayer directly, even if a recognized representative is in place?

A. When the taxpayer is outside the United States.
B. When the taxpayer is an estate.
C. When a recognized representative has unreasonably delayed or hindered an examination.
D. When the recognized representative is not a tax practitioner.

36. Zena is an enrolled agent. She represents Thiago, whose tax return is under examination by the IRS. Thiago's tax return was filed jointly with his wife, but they have since divorced. Thiago does not know the whereabouts of his ex-wife. Thiago still wants Zena to represent him before the IRS. What is the proper course of action in this case?

A. Zena cannot represent Thiago during the examination of his previously filed joint return, because she does not have authorization from his ex-wife (who was listed on the return).
B. Zena is allowed to represent Thiago during the examination of his joint return, but only if he agrees to amend his filing status to married filing separately.
C. Zena is allowed to represent Thiago during the examination of his joint return, provided Thiago signs a valid power of attorney (Form 2848).
D. Thiago must represent himself during the examination of his joint return.

37. Which of the following immediately stops all IRS assessment and collection actions for a taxpayer, regardless of the year and type of assessment?

A. When a taxpayer files in Tax Court.
B. When a taxpayer files in bankruptcy court.
C. When a taxpayer's authorized representative signs a Form 2848 and contacts the IRS on his behalf.
D. When a taxpayer files Form 1127, *Extension of Time for Payment Due to Hardship.*

38. Benjamin Lopez is an enrolled agent. He wants to print new business cards for his office. Which of the following descriptions would be prohibited by Circular 230?

A. Benjamin Lopez, enrolled agent, certified to practice before the Internal Revenue Service.
B. Benjamin Lopez, enrolled agent, enrolled to practice before the Internal Revenue Service.
C. Benjamin Lopez, enrolled agent, authorized to practice before the Internal Revenue Service.
D. Benjamin Lopez, EA, enrolled to practice before the IRS.

39. All of the following are true about installment agreements except:

A. Penalties and interest continue to accrue during the term of the agreement.
B. A taxpayer who owes $25,000 or less may request to have his Notice of Federal Tax Lien withdrawn after entering into a direct debit installment agreement.
C. A taxpayer may use an installment agreement to negotiate a lower tax liability.
D. The IRS charges a one-time user fee to set up an installment agreement.

40. Which of the following disclosures of taxpayer information is not allowed without a taxpayer's written consent?

A. When there is a disclosure of taxpayer information for preparation of state or local tax returns.
B. When a tax preparation firm discloses return information to others in the firm for purposes of assisting in the preparation of the tax return.
C. When a disclosure is made to a taxpayer's fiduciary.
D. When a disclosure solicits business from an existing client and the business is not related to the IRS.

41. Which of the following is not required as a part of a tax preparer's due diligence related to the Earned Income Credit?

A. Filing Form 8867 along with the taxpayer's EITC claim.
B. Conducting a thorough interview with the taxpayer every year.
C. Authenticating the taxpayer's Social Security number with the federal government.
D. Completing the EITC worksheet.

42. Yasmin is an enrolled agent. She has just learned that one of her clients is being investigated for criminal tax fraud. What should Yasmin do?

A. Contact a criminal defense attorney and arrange a deal to jointly represent the client in the criminal proceedings.
B. Contact the authorities who are investigating her client and offer to turn over all of her client's records.
C. End representation immediately.
D. Enter into discussions with the client in order to prepare a case to defend him against possible criminal charges.

43. Nellie is an enrolled agent who received a complaint from the Office of Professional Responsibility. The formal complaint from the OPR is not required to disclose:

A. The nature of the complaint.
B. The deadline for response to the complaint.
C. The identity of the employee who drafted the complaint.
D. The specific sanctions recommended against the practitioner.

44. All of the following are examples of disreputable conduct that can lead to suspension or disbarment for an enrolled agent except:

A. Failing to include a valid PTIN on tax returns.
B. Willfully failing to e-file returns electronically if the preparer falls under the e-filing mandate.
C. Solicitation of former clients using direct mail.
D. Maintaining an active partnership with a practitioner who has been disbarred (but does not sign returns).

45. Cora is an enrolled agent who is cleaning up her office. When is the earliest she may shred the records related to her continuing professional education?

A. Four years following the date of the EA renewal for which the CPE is credited.
B. Six years following the date of the EA renewal for which the CPE is credited.
C. Immediately after the date of the EA renewal for which the CPE is credited.
D. Cora should not destroy her CPE records as long as she is in active status.

46. IRS Form 2848 now provides space for the information and signatures of up to _____.

A. Two spouses.
B. One tax year.
C. Four authorized representatives.
D. Three taxpayers.

47. An enrolled agent is able to represent tax clients before all of the following except:

A. The IRS Appeals division.
B. Revenue agents.
C. A U.S. district court.
D. IRS Collections division.

48. What is the minimum number of CPE hours that an enrolled agent must take each year of his renewal cycle?

A. A minimum of 16 hours, two of which must be ethics hours.
B. A minimum of 18 hours, two of which must be ethics hours.
C. A minimum of 72 hours, two of which must be ethics hours.
D. A minimum of 16 hours.

49. If an e-filed return is rejected, what is the preparer required to do?

A. The preparer must take reasonable steps to inform the taxpayer within 72 hours of the rejection.
B. The preparer must take reasonable steps to inform the taxpayer within 48 hours of the rejection.
C. The preparer must take reasonable steps to inform the taxpayer within 24 hours of the rejection.
D. It is the taxpayer's responsibility to ensure that his e-filed return is correctly submitted.

50. Etta is an enrolled agent, and she employs several tax return preparers in her firm. One of Etta's employees prepares a return for a client. The return is later selected for examination, and one of the larger deductions is disallowed. Etta will not be subject to a preparer penalty if:

A. She does not sign the return, and instead directs her employee to sign it.
B. There was a reasonable basis and substantial authority for the position, and the preparer acted in good faith.
C. She warned the preparer that the deduction was an aggressive position to take.
D. The preparer based the return on the information provided by the client.

51. When does the taxpayer need to be present during an examination, assuming a power of attorney is filed?

A. When the taxpayer is represented by his brother.
B. When the taxpayer is represented by an unenrolled tax preparer who prepared the tax return under audit.
C. When the taxpayer is represented by an enrolled agent.
D. When the taxpayer is represented by a licensed attorney.

52. Jana is an enrolled agent with a new client who has several rental properties. In reviewing his prior year tax returns, she discovers that he has failed to claim depreciation for any of the rental properties. What should Jana do in this case to be in compliance with Circular 230 requirements?

A. Insist on amending the client's prior year tax returns.
B. Promptly advise the client of the error and the consequences of not correcting the error.
C. Contact the IRS, in confidence, to notify revenue agents about the error.
D. Nothing. Claiming depreciation deductions is a choice a taxpayer is free to make, but it is not required.

53. In 2015, Janus does not have qualifying health coverage and he does not qualify for an exemption. As a result, Janus owes $325 in tax because of an individual shared responsibility penalty. He does not owe any other taxes. Regarding this tax, which of the following is true?

A. The amount owed is not subject to penalties, levies or the filing of a Notice of Federal Tax Lien. However, interest will continue to accrue and the IRS may offset federal tax refunds until the balance is paid in full.
B. The amount owed is subject to penalties, levies, and the filing of a Notice of Federal Tax Lien.
C. The amount owed is subject to penalties and interest will accrue and the IRS may offset federal tax refunds until the balance is paid in full.
D. The taxpayer does not have to pay the shared responsibility payment if he files a formal appeal.

54. Disbarred individuals are still allowed to:

A. File powers of attorney with the IRS.
B. State that they are eligible to practice before the IRS.
C. Prepare or file documents (including tax returns) or other correspondence with the IRS.
D. Appear before the IRS as a trustee, receiver, guardian, administrator, executor, or other fiduciary if duly authorized under the law of the relevant jurisdiction.

55. Andrea is a tax return preparer. When preparing a return for her client, Darius, Andrea learns that he does not have a bank account to receive a direct deposit of his tax refund. Andrea offers to use her account to receive the direct deposit, and says she will turn the money over to Darius once the refund is deposited. Is this an acceptable action?

A. Yes.
B. No.
C. Only if Darius signs Form 2848, *Power of Attorney and Declaration of Representative*, giving Andrea the right to receive his refund.
D. Only if Andrea receives prior written consent from Darius.

56. In which of the following cases is a power of attorney (Form 2848) not required?

A. When an enrolled agent represents a taxpayer before the IRS appeals division.
B. When a taxpayer wishes to be represented during an IRS examination.
C. By an attorney of record in a case that is docketed in the Tax Court.
D. When a general partner wishes to represent his partnership before the IRS.

57. The IRS will release an existing tax lien in all of the following cases except:

A. When the tax debt is fully paid.
B. When the taxpayer requests an offer in compromise.
C. When payment of the debt is guaranteed by a bond.
D. When the statute of limitations for collection has ended.

58. All of the following persons may practice before the IRS except:

A. Certified public accountants.
B. Certified financial planners.
C. Enrolled actuaries.
D. Enrolled retirement plan agents.

59. The IRS requires tax preparers to take appropriate steps to safeguard taxpayers' private information. Which of the following is not an IRS recommendation to help keep information secure?

A. Assess the security risks in his own office with regard to taxpayer information.
B. Write a plan of how the business will safeguard taxpayer information and put appropriate safeguards in place.
C. Use only service providers who have policies in place to maintain an adequate level of information protection.
D. Store all client information electronically rather than retain hard copies of information

60. Starting in 2015, the IRS created a new online directory of tax return preparers. This listing includes:

A. All tax practitioners with a current EFIN.
B. All current PTIN holders.
C. Enrolled agents, attorneys, and CPAs with a current PTIN.
D. All enrolled practitioners with a current PTIN as well as AFSP Record of Completion holders.

61. Manuel is an enrolled agent. He sends out a targeted direct mail advertisement during the year. How long must he retain a copy of the advertisement?

A. 36 months from the date of the first mailing or use.
B. 24 months from the date of the last mailing or use.
C. 36 months from the date of the last transmission or use.
D. Four years from the date of the last transmission or use.

62. An S corporation filing 250 returns or more a year is generally required to file Form 1120S in the following manner:

A. On paper.
B. On magnetic media.
C. By using IRS e-file only.
D. Any of the above methods is acceptable.

63. Eva is an enrolled agent with a client that wishes to take an aggressive tax position regarding a particular tax credit. Eva does some research and discovers that this issue is currently being litigated in the courts, and the IRS is appealing the issue in several pending cases. It is possible that the issue will continue to be litigated for years. Based on the individual circumstances of her client's case, Eva determines that her client has a good argument for his position. What is Eva's responsibility in this case?

A. Eva cannot file the return or recommend a position that is contrary to a current IRS position.
B. Eva should request a private letter ruling for her client. Otherwise, she may not take the position on the return.
C. Eva can claim the credit on her client's tax return as long as the position is not incorrect, inconsistent, or incomplete; is not frivolous; and is adequately disclosed.
D. Eva can claim the credit on her client's tax return as long as the position is not incorrect, inconsistent, or incomplete, and is not frivolous. Additional disclosure is not required.

64. If a taxpayer fails to file a return and the failure is due to fraud, the penalty is:

A. 15% for each month or part of a month that the return is late, up to a maximum of 50%.
B. 15% for each month or part of a month that the return is late, up to a maximum of 25%.
C. 5% for each month or part of a month that the return is late, up to a maximum of 50%.
D. 15% for each month or part of a month that the return is late, up to a maximum of 75%.

65. Webster just became an enrolled agent. He now wants to apply to become an authorized e-file provider. Which of the following is not a requirement to become an IRS e-file provider?

A. To be a United States citizen or a legal U.S. alien lawfully admitted for permanent residence (a green card holder).
B. To be at least 18 years old as of the date of application.
C. To have a permanent business location outside his home, in order to ensure the safety of client confidentiality and client records.
D. To meet applicable state and local licensing or bonding requirements for the preparation and collection of tax returns.

66. In 2015, Diego plans to submit Form W-7 for his client, Anne, who needs to request an ITIN in order to file her return. What type of identifying documents must accompany the ITIN application?

A. Form W-7 must include photocopies of supporting documentation, such as a passport or birth certificate.
B. Form W-7 must include original or certified copies of supporting documentation, such as a passport or birth certificate. Photocopies are no longer sufficient.
C. Form W-7 must include original or notarized copies of supporting documentation, such as a passport or birth certificate. Photocopies are not sufficient.
D. Form W-7 does not require any additional documentation as long as it is filed with an original return.

67. Fraud is distinguished from negligence, because fraud is always:

A. More complex.
B. Intentional.
C. Harder to detect.
D. More difficult to prosecute.

68. When multiple tax preparers are involved in preparation of a single return, who is required to sign the return?

A. Any preparer who has the proper licensing to sign the return.
B. Any of the preparers involved in the task of preparation may sign.
C. The signing tax preparer should be the individual preparer who has the primary responsibility for the overall accuracy of the return.
D. Multiple preparers may sign in the preparer section of the return, because all the preparers have joint and several liability for the return's accuracy.

69. What is a practitioner's duty to a client if he advised the client regarding a position on a tax return for which penalties may be incurred?

A. A practitioner cannot advise a client about the possibility of penalties resulting from a tax return that he prepared.
B. A practitioner must advise the client of the penalties that are reasonably likely to apply regarding a position on a tax return, if he advised the client regarding the position or if he prepared the tax return.
C. A practitioner must advise the client of the possibility of the tax return being audited and estimate the risk of that occurring.
D. Both B and C are correct.

70. IRC section 6695 deals with which of the following issues?

A. Disclosure requirements for tax preparers.
B. Civil and criminal penalties for tax preparers who wrongfully disclose or use a taxpayer's private information.
C. E-filing requirements for tax preparers.
D. Penalties for tax preparers for violations in connection with preparing tax returns for other persons.

71. An official IRS censure:

A. Prohibits a practitioner from practicing before the IRS.
B. Prohibits a practitioner from filing tax returns.
C. Prohibits a practitioner from practicing before the IRS and from filing tax returns.
D. Does not prevent a practitioner from filing tax returns or representing taxpayers before the IRS.

72. Sarina is an enrolled agent. Her client tells her that he used his automobile 100% for business purposes. The client does not own any other vehicles. Can Sarina rely on his statement without further information?

A. Yes.
B. No. She needs to verify the information with third parties.
C. No. She must make reasonable inquiries of her client.
D. No. She must review a mileage log and other documents provided by her client before she can claim any deductions.

73. A practitioner is required to be in compliance with all his existing tax obligations in order to maintain his licensing. Under Circular 230, what is the definition of "tax compliance"?

A. When all returns that are due have been filed.
B. When all returns that are due have been filed and all taxes that are due have been paid (or acceptable payment arrangements have been established).
C. When all returns that are due have been filed and all taxes that are due have been paid. A payment arrangement is not sufficient; the taxes must be paid in order to be in compliance.
D. When all taxes that are due have been paid (or acceptable payment arrangements have been established), even if there are unfiled returns.

74. Bruno owes $10,000 of tax. He does not dispute the amount, but does not have the ability to pay the full amount because he is disabled and cannot work. Bruno agrees to pay $5,000 of his liability as part of an offer in compromise with the IRS based on grounds of:

A. Doubt as to liability.
B. Undue hardship.
C. Doubt as to collectability.
D. Effective tax administration (exceptional circumstances).

75. A taxpayer's return fraudulently contains the Earned Income Tax Credit (EITC). The taxpayer already received and spent his $3,000 refund when an audit notice is issued. During the examination, the taxpayer cannot provide documentation to support his EITC claim. What is likely to happen in this case?

A. The EITC will be disallowed, and the taxpayer will have a balance due, including penalties.
B. The EITC will be disallowed, and the taxpayer will have a balance due, including penalties and interest. In addition, the taxpayer may be disallowed from claiming EITC in future years.
C. The EITC will be disallowed, but the taxpayer will not owe any additional penalties.
D. The EITC will not be disallowed for the current year return, but it may be disallowed in future years.

76. Shelby is a sole proprietor who owns a small manufacturing business. She claims a product's cost of production as $50 when its actual cost is $20. Her factory makes 10,000 of the products, and Shelby's tax return reports a loss of $300,000 on their sales. Shelby would be subject to which of the following penalties?

A. Substantial understatement penalty.
B. Substantial valuation misstatement penalty.
C. Manufacturer fraud penalty.
D. Frivolous return penalty.

77. Kira is a tax preparer who plans to retire this year. She sells her practice to Agnes, who is a CPA. What must occur when a tax business is sold?

A. Agnes is required to submit a new e-file application and request her own EFIN.
B. Kira may transfer her EFIN to Agnes, as long as the physical location of the practice does not change.
C. Agnes is not required to submit a new e-file application as long as Kira gives her written permission to use the existing one. A formal transfer is not required.
D. The IRS will issue a new EFIN automatically when the preparer's PTIN information changes on the submitted returns.

78. How long must a paid preparer retain a copy of a client's tax return?

A. Three years after the close of the return period.
B. Four years after the close of the return period.
C. Six years after the close of the return period.
D. Indefinitely.

79. All of the following may cause a practitioner to face disciplinary action by the Office of Professional Responsibility except:

A. A misdemeanor conviction for public drunkenness.
B. Misconduct while representing a taxpayer.
C. A felony drug possession conviction.
D. Giving a false opinion through gross incompetence.

80. A tax preparer who is convicted of criminal fraud and false statements relating to a client's individual tax return can face a maximum penalty of:

A. A $25,000 fine.
B. A $50,000 fine and/or up to one year in prison, along with the costs of prosecution.
C. A $100,000 fine and/or up to one year in prison, along with the costs of prosecution.
D. A $100,000 fine and/or up to three years in prison, along with the costs of prosecution.

81. Which of the following returns can be e-filed?

A. Prior year returns.
B. Amended tax returns.
C. Tax returns with adoption taxpayer identification numbers (ATIN).
D. Both A and C are correct.

82. During the IRS examination process, a taxpayer has the right to:

A. Request that an enrolled practitioner represent him.
B. Appeal any determination made by the IRS examination division.
C. Decline an IRS summons.
D. Both A and B are correct.

83. At the end of 2015, the following enrolled agents totaled their CPE hours for the year. Which of them has not met the minimum yearly educational requirements for license renewal?

Preparer	Regular CPE	Ethics CPE
Sebastian	24 hours	1 hour
Gloria	16 hours	2 hours
Mona	14 hours	4 hours

A. Sebastian.
B. Gloria.
C. Mona.
D. None of these enrolled agents have met their minimum yearly CPE requirement.

84. Which of the following statements regarding the IRS Collection Appeals Program (CAP) is incorrect?

A. A taxpayer cannot appeal a CAP hearing decision to the U.S. Tax Court.
B. The CAP process is generally quicker and is available for a broader range of collection actions than a collection due process hearing.
C. A Low Income Tax Clinic may represent taxpayers who qualify.
D. A taxpayer may go to court if he disagrees with the CAP decision.

85. Which of the following documents is a practitioner not required to return to a client upon the client's request?

A. Documents obtained from the client's attorney that were used to render advice on a position taken on the client's tax return.
B. A tax return prepared by the practitioner that is being withheld pending payment of fees associated with the client's tax return.
C. The taxpayer's original mileage log, Form W-2, and brokerage statements.
D. All of the above must be returned to the client.

86. Russell is an enrolled agent. In 2015, he was found to have knowingly disclosed confidential taxpayer information to a third party for profit. This was biographical information that Russell had collected from his clients when he was preparing their tax returns. What is the preparer penalty for unauthorized disclosure of taxpayer information?

A. $250 for each unauthorized disclosure.
B. $1,000 for each unauthorized disclosure.
C. Either A or B may apply.
D. 30 days incarceration and a $10,000 fine.

87. Beatrice is a full-time accountant for Ortega Brothers Partnership. As part of her job duties, she prepares the partnership return for Ortega Brothers, including Schedules K-1 for each of the individual partners. She does not prepare any other returns for compensation. Is Beatrice required to obtain a PTIN?

A. Yes, she is a preparer and must obtain a PTIN.
B. No, she is not a preparer and she is not required to obtain a PTIN.
C. Beatrice is allowed to forgo obtaining a PTIN only if the IRS provides her a written waiver.
D. She is not required to obtain a PTIN in 2015, but she will be required to do so in 2016.

88. Which provides a higher degree of rights to a practitioner, Form 2848 or Form 8821?

A. Form 2848.
B. Form 8821.
C. Neither form is used by a preparer; they are used by taxpayers to receive tax transcripts.
D. Both forms confer an equal degree of rights to a practitioner.

89. Under expedited suspension procedures, the Office of Professional Responsibility can take quicker disciplinary action against a practitioner who:

A. Has been convicted of a crime involving dishonesty.
B. Has been convicted of a crime involving a breach of trust.
C. Has failed to file his federal income tax returns in four of the five previous tax years.
D. All of the above.

90. What is a 30-day letter?

A. A revenue agent report.
B. A summons to appear before an IRS examiner.
C. A notice explaining a taxpayer's right to appeal and statement of proposed tax owed after an IRS examination.
D. A notice of collection action that will be taken within 30 days if the taxpayer fails to pay tax owed.

91. Circular 230 is found in _____ of the Code of Federal Regulations, which governs practice before the Internal Revenue Service.

A. Title 31.
B. Title 26.
C. The Uniform Commercial Code (UCR).
D. Title 53.

92. What documentation is sufficient for a taxpayer to claim a charitable deduction for a cash donation of $250 or more?

A. No documentation is needed for cash donations of under $500.
B. A receipt or written acknowledgment from the organization listing the date of the donation and the amount contributed.
C. A receipt or written acknowledgment with the items listed in answer B, plus a statement from the organization regarding whether the qualified organization gave any goods or services as a result of the contribution.
D. No receipt is required, but the organization must write a good faith estimate of the value of goods and services provided by the organization as a result of the contribution.

93. Which of the following situations may represent a conflict of interest for a practitioner?

A. When the representation of a taxpayer would be in conflict with the practitioner's personal interests.
B. When the practitioner provides tax planning services for one spouse and the other spouse may have opposing interests.
C. When the practitioner provides tax planning services for a married couple who are in the midst of a divorce proceeding.
D. All of the above.

94. What is Direct Pay?

A. A third-party payment service that charges a fee to withdraw an IRS payment.
B. Direct Pay is a secure IRS service that may be used to pay an individual tax bill or estimated tax payment. The IRS charges a nominal fee for Direct Pay.
C. Direct Pay is a free IRS service that may be used to pay an individual tax bill or estimated tax payment.
D. Direct Pay is an IRS service that processes individual tax returns for free.

95. Which of the following practitioners would be allowed to use the term "enrolled agent" to describe their status?

A. A person who has passed all three parts of the EA exam, but who has not received his confirmation of enrollment yet.
B. An enrolled agent who has been placed on inactive status.
C. An enrolled agent who is currently appealing an official OPR censure.
D. An enrolled agent who has let his license lapse.

96. In both criminal and civil fraud cases, the burden of proof rests with the:

A. Taxpayer.
B. Tax preparer.
C. Government.
D. Tax Court.

97. Katherine and Michael are married. Michael is currently serving in a combat zone, and Katherine has no way to contact her husband for several months. When one spouse is serving in a combat zone, what is required in order to file a joint return?

A. Both spouses must sign, so Katherine must appeal to the IRS for a special exemption.
B. Katherine may sign the joint return on her husband's behalf, but only if she secured a power of attorney in advance.
C. Katherine may sign on behalf of her husband, whether or not she has a signed power of attorney.
D. Katherine may delay filing the tax return until Michael has returned to the United States and can sign the return.

98. What happens when a taxpayer has a late payment on an installment agreement?

A. The late payment will generate an automatic 30-day notice.
B. The late payment will extend the statute of limitations for collecting the tax.
C. The late payment will cause the installment agreement to default.
D. The IRS will file a Notice of Deficiency.

99. Kimberly is a bookkeeper who prepares a number of tax returns and is subject to the e-file mandate. She has a client who refuses to e-file his tax return. What is the proper action for Kimberly to take?

A. She must decline the engagement.
B. She must refer the client to a different tax return preparer.
C. She can prepare the client's return on paper and attach Form 8948.
D. She should encourage the taxpayer to file electronically. If the client refuses, Kimberly does not need to sign the return as a paid preparer.

100. A practitioner would like to rely on the advice of another practitioner's work product. Can he do so without question?

A. Yes, if the practitioner is another member of the first practitioner's firm.
B. Yes, in all circumstances.
C. No, reliance on another preparer's work product is prohibited.
D. Generally, yes, but only if the advice is reasonable and in good faith.

Please review your answer choices with the correct answers in the back.

#6 Sample Exam: Representation

1. How often must enrolled agents renew their enrollment?

A. Every three years.
B. Every five years.
C. Every year.
D. None of the above.

2. Under Circular 230, an employer of other tax preparers must:

A. Furnish the IRS a record of all tax return preparers employed.
B. Keep a record of all tax return preparers employed and make it available for IRS inspection upon request.
C. Document each tax preparer's performance and keep a record that must be made available for IRS inspection upon request.
D. All of the above.

3. In which of the following situations must a tax return preparer obtain client consent to disclose or receive sensitive tax return information?

A. The preparer receives a grand jury subpoena requesting client records.
B. The preparer reports a possible crime to authorities involving one of his clients.
C. For purposes of peer reviews.
D. None of the above requires permission from a client.

4. A single financial account is limited to _____ electronically-deposited tax refunds per tax year.

A. One.
B. Two.
C. Three.
D. No limit.

5. Which of the following is not a reason for the IRS to abate interest on a taxpayer's tax liability?

A. Managerial act.
B. Ministerial act.
C. Reasonable cause.
D. When the interest was incurred while the taxpayer was in a combat zone or declared disaster area.

6. Stacy is an enrolled agent with two clients who are both parties in the potential sale of a business. The sale is not prohibited by law. Stacy believes she can provide competent and diligent representation to each client. Which statement best describes the action Stacy must take to fulfill the requirements of Circular 230 before representing both clients?

A. Since she has already researched the situation and determined she is competent to handle the matter, Stacy is not required to take further action.
B. Stacy must obtain either oral or written permission from both clients, stating they have been made aware of the potential for conflict of interest.
C. Stacy must meet with both clients at the same time to inform them of the potential for conflict of interest.
D. Stacy must inform each client of the potential for conflict of interest and then obtain written waivers of the conflict from both clients.

7. In evaluating a taxpayer's ability to pay his tax liability, which of the following expenses is the IRS least likely to challenge (because it is not indicative of a lifestyle choice)?

A. $10,000 a year for court-ordered child support.
B. $10,000 a year for restaurant meals.
C. $10,000 a year for tuition.
D. $10,000 a year for rent.

8. During the examination of a taxpayer's Form 1040, the IRS examiner found numerous errors resulting in additional tax. One of the adjustments was a large amount of unreported income discovered in a concealed bank account. Some deductions were supported with altered or defaced documents. The taxpayer gave false information and misrepresented the facts throughout the examination. All of the acts of the taxpayer, when seen as a whole, indicate:

A. Negligence.
B. Fraud.
C. Noncompliance.
D. A tax protester argument.

9. Which IRS insignia may a practitioner use in his advertising?

A. The official IRS e-file logo.
B. The U.S. Treasury seal.
C. The IRS eagle insignia.
D. The FMS insignia.

10. Which of the following accurately describes an IRS levy?

A. A levy is not a legal seizure of property.
B. A levy on salary or wages will end when the time expires for legally collecting the tax.
C. A levy can only be released by the filing of a lien.
D. A levy does not apply to the taxpayer's clothing and undelivered mail.

11. Trent decided to represent himself in an IRS audit. When he arrived at the IRS office, he became agitated during the initial examination interview and requested to speak to a representative. Which of the following statements is correct?

A. The taxpayer may leave the examination and finish the audit through correspondence.
B. An IRS interview must be suspended when the taxpayer clearly requests the right to consult with a representative.
C. If the taxpayer chooses to suspend the interview, he must return in person with his representative.
D. The IRS is not required to cease an examination when the taxpayer requests a representative.

12. A practitioner who has been disciplined by the IRS can do which of the following?

A. Represent a taxpayer before the IRS.
B. Accompany a taxpayer to a conference or meeting with the IRS and argue the merits of any issue raised in the taxpayer's case.
C. Accompany a taxpayer to a conference or meeting with the IRS and respond to questions and provide facts and/or documents.
D. None of the above.

13. Which of the following taxpayer numbers is valid for claiming the Earned Income Tax Credit?

A. Social Security number.
B. Adoption taxpayer identification number.
C. Individual tax identification number.
D. All of the above.

14. The IRS has the authority to issue a summons in all of the following instances except:

A. To prepare a substitute return when a taxpayer has not filed one.
B. To determine the liability of a taxpayer.
C. To collect any internal revenue tax liability.
D. To require a taxpayer to create a tax return when he has not filed one.

15. Louie is a tax preparer. His new client, Minerva, wants to claim the Earned Income Tax Credit. Which of the following issues would automatically disqualify Minerva from claiming the Earned Income Tax Credit for the 2015 tax year?

A. Investment income of $3,450.
B. Minerva files as Married Filing Separately.
C. Minerva files her tax return using a valid ITIN.
D. All of the above would disqualify her from claiming the credit.

16. Clarence is an enrolled agent. His client wants to know if their discussions during normal tax preparation are privileged. Which statement is correct?

A. Under Circular 230, discussions surrounding the preparation of a tax return are considered privileged communications if the preparer is a practitioner.
B. Discussions surrounding the preparation of a tax return are not privileged, regardless of whether the preparer is a practitioner.
C. Discussions surrounding the preparation of a tax return are always privileged, even if the practitioner is an unenrolled tax return preparer.
D. None of the above is correct.

17. In which of the following situations is an IRS power of attorney required?

A. Allowing the IRS to discuss return information with a third party designee.
B. Allowing a tax matters partner to perform acts for the partnership.
C. Allowing the IRS to discuss return information with a fiduciary.
D. Allowing the tax practitioner to receive, but not cash, taxpayer refund checks.

18. Asher is a tax return preparer who accepts electronic signatures. He has a client who lives in a different state. How is Asher required to authenticate the identity of the taxpayer?

A. The taxpayer must mail or fax a copy of his Social Security card to Asher for review.
B. The taxpayer must mail or fax a copy of his driver's license, with a picture ID, to Asher for review.
C. Asher must verify that the name, Social Security number, address, date of birth, and other personal information provided by the taxpayer are consistent with information obtained through record checks with applicable agencies or institutions, or through credit bureaus or similar databases.
D. No special verification procedures are required.

19. The IRS may accept an offer in compromise based on three grounds. Which of the following is not a valid basis for submitting an offer in compromise to the IRS?

A. Doubt as to collectability.
B. Effective tax administration.
C. Doubt as to liability.
D. Legitimate hardship argument.

20. In 2015, the IRS instituted stricter procedures for ITINs. ITINs will now automatically expire after _____ years of non-use.

A. One.
B. Two.
C. Three.
D. Five.

21. Lloyd is an enrolled agent. He has a new client, Kelly, who has self-prepared her own returns in the past. Lloyd notices that Kelly has been claiming head of household status on her tax returns. However, she does not qualify for this status, because she does not have a qualifying person. What is Lloyd required to do?

A. Amend the incorrect returns.
B. Refuse any future engagement with Kelly unless she corrects the prior year returns.
C. Notify Kelly of the error and tell her the consequences of not correcting the error.
D. Notify Kelly of the error and correct the error by amending her prior year returns.

22. What practice rights do all enrolled agents have?

A. Unlimited practice rights before the IRS.
B. Unlimited practice rights before the IRS and the U.S. Tax Court.
C. Limited practice rights.
D. All of the above.

23. Erin files jointly with her husband, who has delinquent student loans. Their tax refund check is applied against his past due student loans. Erin would like to claim her portion of their tax refund, so she files for _____ relief.

A. Innocent spouse.
B. Equitable.
C. Injured spouse.
D. Separation of liability.

24. Which type of practitioner fee is prohibited by Circular 230?

A. Charging a fee for direct deposit.
B. Fixed fees for bookkeeping services.
C. Hourly fee rates for tax consulting.
D. Charging a fee for e-filing a return.

25. Which would have the highest degree of substantial authority for all taxpayers, assuming each was addressing the same tax issue?

A. A revenue ruling issued in the year 2015.
B. A private letter ruling issued in the year 2000.
C. A revenue ruling issued in the year 2000.
D. All have the same degree weight of substantial authority.

26. A tax preparer must complete the paid preparer section of the tax return in which of the following scenarios?

A. An employee preparer who completes employment tax returns for his employer.
B. An enrolled agent who prepares her own tax return.
C. A CPA who prepares a return for her brother and charges him only $30.
D. An enrolled agent who prepares his neighbor's return for free.

27. What is a reportable transaction?

A. A transaction of a type that the IRS has determined as having the potential for abusive tax avoidance or evasion.
B. A court decision to which the IRS has officially nonacquiesced.
C. Another name for a private letter ruling.
D. A transaction of a type that the IRS has determined will benefit the public interest.

28. Under Circular 230, in which of the following cases may the IRS suspend a certified public accountant from practice before the IRS?

A. If a CPA moves outside the U.S. and attempts to represent overseas taxpayers.
B. If a CPA is suspended from practice by a state board of accountancy for a matter unrelated to taxation.
C. If a CPA takes an aggressive position on a tax return.
D. If a CPA hires unenrolled preparers to work in his office.

29. As part of the application to become an authorized IRS e-services provider, which of the following categories of tax professionals is required to be fingerprinted?

A. Enrolled agents and unenrolled tax return preparers.
B. All e-services applicants must be fingerprinted by the IRS.
C. Unenrolled tax return preparers.
D. Only CPAs and tax attorneys must be fingerprinted, because they are licensed by the state, not the federal government.

30. Which of the following is not a requirement when a taxpayer requests innocent spouse relief?

A. The taxpayer filed a joint return that has an understatement of tax (deficiency) that is solely attributable to a spouse's erroneous item.
B. When the taxpayer signed the joint return, he or she did not know, and had no reason to know, that there was an understatement of tax on the return.
C. Taking into account all the facts and circumstances, it would be unfair to hold the taxpayer liable for the understatement of tax.
D. The taxpayer must have already filed for divorce or legal separation when innocent spouse relief is requested.

31. In serving a complaint against a practitioner, the Office of Professional Responsibility may use all of the methods listed below except:

A. Private delivery service.
B. E-mail.
C. First class mail.
D. In person.

32. When it comes to possible preparer penalties, the reasonable cause and good faith exceptions do not apply to an understatement of income that is a result of:

A. A taxpayer who misrepresents information to the preparer.
B. An unreasonable position.
C. A preparer's mathematical error.
D. None of the above.

33. Under Internal Revenue Code §6695, a tax preparer who violates EITC due diligence requirements faces what penalty for tax year 2015?

A. A $505 fine for each violation.
B. A $1,000 fine for each violation.
C. A $50 fine for each violation.
D. A $1,000 fine for each violation and imprisonment up to one year.

34. Which of the following statements is correct?

A. The IRS is not required to notify the taxpayer of an audit.
B. In certain circumstances, the IRS may audit tax returns for up to six years after the filing date.
C. Tax returns can only be audited for up to two years after they are filed.
D. An original tax return that is filed late does not extend the statute of limitations for an audit on the return.

35. How long is an IRS power of attorney authorization valid?

A. Until the taxpayer's retirement.
B. For three years.
C. Until the close of the taxable year for which it was filed.
D. Until revoked.

36. Which of the following is an example of an individual filing a frivolous tax return?

A. A taxpayer who incorrectly claims the Earned Income Credit when he is not eligible for it because he did not read the instructions.
B. A taxpayer who files a tax return and strikes out the jurat.
C. A preparer who files a delinquent tax return because the taxpayer refused to file.
D. A fiduciary who files an incorrect tax return and later amends it.

37. Which of the following statements is not correct regarding a practitioner's fees for his services?

A. He is allowed to publish a written schedule of fees.
B. He is allowed to charge a fee for an initial consultation with a client.
C. He is allowed to charge an unconscionable fee for services in connection with any matter before the IRS.
D. He is allowed to charge a contingent fee based on an IRS examination of an original tax return.

38. Taxpayers must sign their returns:

A. Under penalty of perjury.
B. With a physical signature.
C. Before the return has been prepared.
D. Before paying their tax preparer.

39. Suzanne is an enrolled agent who is interviewing a new client who wants to claim the Earned Income Credit. The information the client offers seems incorrect to Suzanne. Under her due diligence requirements, what should she do?

A. Refuse to accept the engagement.
B. Report the client to the IRS fraud hotline.
C. Take note of the woman's inconsistent answers and go ahead and submit the EITC claim anyway.
D. Ask additional questions if the information furnished seems incorrect or incomplete.

40. An enrolled agent becomes official on the date:

A. He passes the final Special Enrollment Exam.
B. He receives his enrollment card in the mail.
C. He completes Form 23.
D. The IRS's Return Preparer Office issues his enrollment card.

41. Which one of the following tax preparers is required to e-file his clients' returns?

A. A paid preparer who anticipates filing 11 or more Forms 1120.
B. A paid preparer who anticipates filing 11 or more Forms 1040.
C. A paid preparer who anticipates filing 11 or more Forms 1065.
D. All of the preparers listed above are subject to the e-file mandate.

42. Which of the following actions is not considered "disreputable conduct" by the IRS?

A. Willfully failing to e-file returns electronically if they fall under the e-filing mandate.
B. Failing to include a valid PTIN on tax returns.
C. Performance as a notary by a practitioner.
D. Willfully failing to file a tax return.

43. Rachel is a CPA. She is taking an aggressive position on a tax return, which requires disclosure. Which form is used to disclose a position on a tax return?

A. Form 8275.
B. Form 8823.
C. Form 656.
D. Form 1040X.

44. Judith, an enrolled agent, prepares William's income tax return. William gives Judith power of attorney, including the authorization to receive his federal income tax refund check. Accordingly, the IRS sends William's $1,000 refund check to Judith's office. William is very slow in paying his bills and owes Judith $500 for tax services. Judith should:

A. Use William's check as collateral for a loan to tide her over until William pays her.
B. Refuse to give William the check until he pays her the $500.
C. Get William's written authorization to endorse the check, cash the check, and reduce the amount William owes her.
D. Turn the check directly over to William.

45. Which of the following actions is not considered practice before the IRS?

A. Appearing as a taxpayer's witness before the IRS.
B. Corresponding with the IRS on behalf of a taxpayer.
C. Communicating with the IRS for a taxpayer regarding the taxpayer's rights.
D. Representing the taxpayer at an examination.

46. A preparer is required to provide a copy of the tax return to a client. Which of the following statements is not correct?

A. The preparer must provide a complete copy of the tax return to the taxpayer.
B. A scanned copy of the tax return is sufficient to meet this requirement.
C. The IRS requires the client receive a paper copy of the tax return.
D. The client copy does not need to contain the Social Security number of the paid preparer.

47. What is a private letter ruling?

A. A private letter that a taxpayer writes to the IRS and that becomes public once Tax Court litigation begins.
B. A private letter issued by the U.S. Tax Court.
C. A communication from the Internal Revenue Service in response to a taxpayer's written request for guidance on a particular tax issue.
D. A response from Congress to the IRS to clarify Congressional action on a specific tax issue.

48. Circular 230 states a practitioner may not willfully, recklessly, or through gross incompetence sign a tax return or claim for refund that the practitioner knows, or reasonably should have known, contains a position that:

A. Understates the liability for tax.
B. Is reckless or has intentional disregard of rules or regulations.
C. Lacks a reasonable basis.
D. All of the above.

49. What is the dollar limit for the U.S. Tax Court small case division?

A. $50,000 or less
B. $50,000 or more
C. $15,000 or less
D. $100,000 or less

50. Which of the following is not a type of Treasury regulation?

A. Legislative regulation.
B. Interpretative regulation.
C. Congressional regulation.
D. Procedural regulation.

51. Amanda is an enrolled agent, and she prepares approximately 300 returns for compensation during the year. Which of the following numbers is required in order for her to prepare tax returns for compensation?

A. Electronic filing identification number (EFIN).
B. Preparer tax identification number (PTIN).
C. Both A and B.
D. Employer identification number (EIN).

52. Under Circular 230, employers of other tax practitioners are prohibited from taking certain actions. These include all of the following except:

A. To not employ or accept assistance from a practitioner who has been disbarred.
B. To not employ or accept assistance from a practitioner who has been suspended from practice.
C. To not employ or accept assistance from a practitioner who has received a reprimand from the IRS.
D. To not accept assistance from a former government employee, such as an individual who worked for the IRS, when that employee personally and substantially participated in the matter while employed by the government.

53. The IRS will waive or abate penalties assessed to a taxpayer under certain circumstances. Which of the following is not an instance in which that will happen?

A. When the penalty is incurred due to a major disaster affecting a large number of taxpayers in a given geographical area.
B. When the penalty is incurred as a result of tax preparer advice provided on a Form 1040 tax issue.
C. When there is "reasonable cause" due to circumstances beyond the taxpayer's control.
D. When the penalty is due to an IRS computation error.

54. If a disbarred practitioner seeks reinstatement, he may still practice before the IRS:

A. While the reinstatement proceedings are pending.
B. While the appeals process takes place.
C. After an appeals petition is filed with the Office of Professional Responsibility.
D. None of the above. A disbarred practitioner may not practice before the IRS, except to represent himself. He may not represent a client.

55. A third party designee has the right to do which of the following tasks?

A. Sign a binding agreement for the taxpayer.
B. Respond to IRS notices about math errors, offsets, and return preparation.
C. Represent the taxpayer before the IRS.
D. Receive refund checks.

56. Isabel is an enrolled agent, and Javier is her client. Isabel did a review of Javier's past tax returns, and noticed that Javier missed a big deduction on his 2012 tax return, was filed on time on March 10, 2013. Javier wants to amend his 2012 return, because the amendment will result in a refund. What is the deadline for Javier to amend his return and obtain a refund?

A. It is too late for him to amend his 2012 return and obtain a refund.
B. April 18, 2016
C. March 10, 2016
D. April 15, 2017

57. Circular 230 explicitly defines all of the following except _____ as practice before the IRS:

A. Filing documents with the IRS.
B. Representing a client at a hearing before the IRS.
C. Rendering legal advice on a tax issue.
D. Rendering written advice concerning a plan with the potential for tax evasion.

58. What is the purpose of a Centralized Authorization File (CAF) number?

A. It is an IRS file designed to prevent the theft of taxpayer identification numbers.
B. It is an IRS file containing the PTINs of all paid tax preparers.
C. It is an IRS file containing information from Forms 2848 only.
D. It is an IRS file containing authorization information from both Forms 2848 and Forms 8821.

59. Who is allowed to determine the time and place for an audit of a taxpayer?

A. The IRS.
B. The taxpayer.
C. The taxpayer's representative and the IRS have an equal say in the determination of the time and location of an audit.
D. The IRS, the taxpayer, and the taxpayer's representative have an equal say in determining the time and location of an audit.

60. A taxpayer would like assistance from the Taxpayer Advocate Service. All of the following are considerations in determining whether a request will be granted, except situations in which:

A. The taxpayer will suffer irreparable injury or a long-term adverse impact if relief is not granted.
B. The taxpayer is facing a significant and unexpected tax liability.
C. The taxpayer is experiencing economic harm or is about to suffer economic harm.
D. The taxpayer is facing an immediate threat of adverse action.

61. Preparers are required to exercise greater due diligence in preparing Earned Income Credit claims for their clients. Which of the following is not a due diligence requirement?

A. Submitting Form 8867 to the IRS with every EITC claim.
B. Personally answering the due diligence questions on Form 8867.
C. Submitting the EITC worksheet to the IRS with every EITC claim.
D. Retaining documentation of the questions asked a client during an EITC interview.

62. Renata is an enrolled agent. A client wants to use direct deposit. Which of the following statements is incorrect?

A. Renata must accept any direct deposit election to any eligible financial institution designated by the client.
B. The client may designate refunds for direct deposit to up to three qualified accounts.
C. A taxpayer should not request a deposit of his refund to an account that is not in his own name.
D. The taxpayer may designate refunds for direct deposit to credit card accounts.

63. Which of the following is considered an authoritative source material for federal tax law?

A. IRS publications.
B. IRS tax forms and instructions.
C. Congressional committee reports.
D. Internal Revenue Manual.

64. A rejected electronic individual income tax return can be corrected and retransmitted without new signatures if changes do not differ from the amounts on the original electronic return by more than:

A. $50 of total income or AGI
B. $100 of tax due
C. $50 of tax due
D. A rejected e-file return cannot be retransmitted without new signatures.

65. Cherie has a 21-year-old daughter named Abby. Abby's tax return was chosen for examination by the IRS. Cherie is not an enrolled agent, attorney, or CPA. Which of the following statements is correct?

A. Cherie may represent her daughter before all levels of the IRS if Abby signs a Form 2848.
B. Cherie may not represent her daughter before the IRS because Abby is no longer a minor and Cherie is not enrolled to practice before the IRS.
C. Cherie may not represent her daughter because she is not a trained tax accountant.
D. A parent may not represent a child because of privacy regulations.

66. Natalie became a new enrolled agent two years ago. For renewal purposes, which of the following statements is incorrect?

A. She is required to take a minimum of 16 hours of CPE each year.
B. She is required to take a minimum of two hours of ethics CPE per year.
C. She must still fulfill the overall CPE requirement of 72 hours, even though she has only been an EA for two years of the enrollment cycle.
D. For renewal purposes, the annual CPE requirements only apply for the years in which she was an enrolled agent.

67. Before a tax preparer is formally assessed a penalty under IRC section 6694, how many days does he have to file an appeal before the penalty is assessed?

A. 10 days.
B. 30 days.
C. 45 days.
D. The penalty is assessed immediately, and must be appealed retroactively.

68. All of the following are options for how a taxpayer may direct his tax refund except to:

A. Receive the refund as a paper check.
B. Split the refund, with a portion applied to next year's estimated tax and the remainder received as direct deposit or a paper check.
C. Use the refund to purchase municipal bonds.
D. Use the refund (or part of it) to purchase U.S. Series I Savings Bonds.

69. Which of the following disputes may not be resolved by a proceeding in the U.S. Tax Court?

A. Gift tax.
B. Income tax.
C. Employment taxes.
D. Innocent spouse relief.

70. An IRS power of attorney must contain all of the following information except:

A. The type of tax involved.
B. The name and address of the representative.
C. The name and taxpayer identification number of the taxpayer.
D. The specific date the tax return was filed, if delinquent.

71. If there is substantial unreported gross income (over 25%), the IRS may audit tax returns for up to _____ after the filing date.

A. Three years.
B. Five years.
C. Six years.
D. Ten years.

72. The IRS must give a taxpayer reasonable notice before contacting third parties in connection with examinations or collecting tax liability. However, the IRS is not required to give notice in which of the following instances?

A. Any pending criminal matter.
B. When providing notice would jeopardize collection of any tax liability.
C. When providing notice may result in reprisal against any person.
D. All of the above.

73. If a practitioner uses radio, television, Internet, signage, or other advertising methods, which of the following statements is correct?

A. The practitioner must keep a copy of the advertising for a minimum of 30 days after the last transmission or use.
B. The practitioner must keep a copy of the advertising until the end of the calendar year following the last transmission or use.
C. The practitioner must keep a copy of the advertising for at least three years following the last transmission or use.
D. The practitioner is not required to keep a copy of the advertising.

74. Which of the following sanctions will the Office of Professional Responsibility not impose on a practitioner?

A. Disbarment.
B. Censure.
C. Formal reprimand.
D. Criminal penalties.

75. What penalty does a taxpayer who files a "frivolous" return face?

A. $1,000
B. $5,000
C. $10,000
D. $100,000

76. Penny has an installment agreement in place with the IRS. In March 2015, she gets into a bad car accident and misses a payment. The IRS sends her a notice 30 days later and terminates her installment agreement. Which of the following statements is incorrect?

A. Penny has no appeal rights once the installment agreement is in default.
B. The IRS cannot levy until 30 days after the termination of an installment agreement.
C. If Penny appeals within a 30-day period after the termination, the IRS will be prohibited from levying until her appeal is completed.
D. Penny may call the telephone number shown on the notice and explain that she wants to appeal the termination.

77. Under IRS regulations, which of the following does not constitute an "understatement of liability"?

A. Taking a tax protester position on a return.
B. Overstating the net amount creditable or refundable.
C. Taking a position with no realistic possibility of success.
D. Answers choices A and C are correct

78. Which of the following statements is incorrect?

A. A taxpayer is prohibited from recording his meeting with an IRS auditor unless the taxpayer is represented by an enrolled agent, CPA, or tax attorney.
B. A taxpayer may record the examination interview with the IRS.
C. The request to record the examination meeting must be made in writing.
D. A taxpayer must notify the IRS ten days in advance in order to record an examination.

79. Which of the following individuals is not under the jurisdiction of Circular 230?

A. An unlicensed tax return preparer who files Form 2848 for a client he is representing in an examination.
B. A state licensed attorney who prepares tax returns for clients.
C. An enrolled agent who does representation work for clients before the IRS, but does not prepare tax returns.
D. An employee of a tax preparation firm who collects receipts, organizes records, and gathers information for a practitioner.

80. Which of the following statements is correct regarding practitioners?

A. A practitioner is prohibited from charging contingent fees in all cases.
B. A practitioner may not notarize documents for the clients that he represents before the IRS.
C. A practitioner may not represent two clients when there is a conflict of interest.
D. A practitioner is forbidden from discussing tax shelters with a client.

81. A paid preparer is required by law to:

A. Charge a fee for e-filing.
B. Sign a tax return and fill in the preparer areas of the form.
C. Include his Social Security number on the tax return.
D. Charge a contingency fee.

82. Luther is an enrolled agent who was subject to a disbarment proceeding. The administrative law judge upheld the OPR's decision to disbar him from practice. Does Luther have any appeal rights at this point?

A. Within 60 days after the administrative law judge makes a decision on a disciplinary action, the practitioner may appeal the decision to the Return Preparer Office.
B. Within 60 days after the administrative law judge makes a decision on a disciplinary action, the practitioner may appeal the decision to the Treasury Appellate Authority.
C. Within 30 days after the administrative law judge makes a decision on a disciplinary action, the practitioner may appeal the decision to the Treasury Appellate Authority.
D. No, Luther does not have any appeal rights after the administrative law judge makes his decision.

83. Sophie is a taxpayer who receives a notice of deficiency in the mail. She fails to respond to the letter within 90 days. What is Sophie's option if she wants to contest her tax deficiency?

A. She can request an extension to the period of time for petitioning the Tax Court.
B. She cannot contest her tax deficiency in the Tax Court. She must pay the amount owed and sue the IRS for a refund in a U.S. district court or Court of Federal Claims.
C. She cannot contest her tax in the Tax Court. She must sue the IRS for a refund in a U.S. district court or Court of Federal Claims. She does not have to pay the amount owed first.
D. She has no more appeals rights and must pay her tax deficiency.

84. Sterling is an enrolled agent. A long-time client starts a new business in an industry with numerous specialized tax regulations and incentives. Sterling begins working on the client's tax return, but finds he does not understand most of the elections and credits. Can Sterling prepare and sign this tax return?

A. Yes. It is not unusual for a tax preparer to lack understanding in certain complex areas of tax law.
B. Yes, but only if Sterling has another member of his firm review the return before Sterling signs it.
C. Yes, but only if Sterling accepts a reduced fee for the work from his client.
D. No. Sterling cannot prepare or sign a tax return if he lacks sufficient competence.

85. Which of the following statements regarding revenue rulings is incorrect?

A. Revenue rulings can be used to avoid IRS penalties.
B. Revenue rulings cannot be used to avoid IRS penalties.
C. A revenue ruling is an official interpretation by the IRS of the Internal Revenue Code.
D. A revenue ruling can be challenged in court.

86. What is the penalty a taxpayer faces if he fails to pay his taxes on time?

A. 5% of the unpaid taxes for each month or part of a month after the due date that the taxes are not paid.
B. ½ of 1% (0.5%) of unpaid taxes for each month or part of a month after the due date that the taxes are not paid, up to a maximum amount of 25% of the unpaid taxes.
C. A minimum of $500.
D. A minimum of $1,000.

87. Under Circular 230, the definition of a "tax return" includes:

A. A claim for a refund, an original return, and an amended return.
B. Only an original return or an amended return.
C. A Tax Court petition.
D. A request for a Private Letter Ruling.

88. Can multiple preparers in one office share a single PTIN?

A. Yes.
B. Yes, but only at the same office location.
C. Yes, but only if the principal preparer continues to sign the tax returns.
D. No, each preparer must obtain his own PTIN.

89. Enrolled agents are allowed a limited confidentiality privilege with their clients. Confidential communications do not extend to:

A. Noncriminal tax matters before the IRS.
B. Noncriminal tax proceedings brought in court.
C. Correspondence audits.
D. Tax shelter opinions.

90. The Freedom of Information Act (FOIA) does not require the IRS to release all documents that are subject to FOIA requests. The IRS may withhold information:

A. Due to budget cuts.
B. Due to the statute of limitations for FOIA requests.
C. If the requester fails to provide notarized identification along with the request.
D. For an IRS record that falls under one of the FOIA's nine statutory exemptions, or by one of three exclusions under the Act.

91. Rajeev is a tax preparer. He would like to become an electronic return originator (ERO)so he can e-file his clients' returns. What is the first step he should take in this application process?

A. Create an IRS e-Services account by supplying certain required personal information to the IRS.
B. Undergo a thorough background check of his tax compliance history.
C. Apply for a PTIN.
D. Apply for an electronic filing identification number.

92. Which of the following statements is incorrect regarding an IRS power of attorney?

A. A newly-filed power of attorney concerning the same matter will revoke a previously-filed power of attorney.
B. The filing of Form 2848 will not revoke any Form 8821, *Taxpayer Information Authorization*, which is in already in effect.
C. A signed Form 8821 is sufficient for a practitioner to represent a taxpayer before the IRS.
D. A power of attorney held by a student volunteering at a Low Income Tax Clinic is valid for only 130 days from the received date and will automatically be revoked.

93. Don is an enrolled agent. He mailed an advertisement announcing a flat rate of $100 for preparation of a single tax return. Don later changes his mind and wants to increase the price. Don is bound by this advertised rate for a minimum of _____ days after the last date on which the fee schedule was published:

A. 20 days.
B. 30 days.
C. 45 days.
D. 60 days.

94. If the IRS declares a taxpayer to be in currently not collectible status (known as status 53), which of the following will happen?

A. All collection actions, including levies, will be stopped for two years.
B. Penalties and interest will be suspended and will not be added to the tax debt while the taxpayer remains in this status.
C. The IRS will issue a criminal warrant.
D. The taxpayer will be guaranteed this status for at least one year.

95. Omar is an enrolled agent. His client, Fatima, has a large tax deficiency. Fatima tells Omar she has no intention of paying her tax liability, no matter what. Knowing that his client is not compliant, Omar advises Fatima to submit a request for a collections due process hearing in order to stop collection activity. Is Omar in violation of Circular 230?

A. Yes, he is in violation of Circular 230 standards.
B. No. This gives Omar's client additional time to pay her tax liability.
C. No. Omar cannot control his client's actions and is simply advising his client to contest her tax liability.
D. Insufficient information to determine the answer.

96. Conner is in charge of his firm's tax practice. He does not directly supervise all of the members of his firm. Can he be subject to discipline if one of the members of his firm violates Circular 230?

A. Yes.
B. No. He would not be subject to discipline for any other members of his firm, whether he supervised them or not.
C. No. He would be subject to discipline only for members of his firm whom he supervised.
D. Circular 230 does not address this issue.

97. Which of the following persons may represent a taxpayer at an IRS appeals conference?

A. An unenrolled tax preparer who prepared the tax return in question.
B. An enrolled agent.
C. A friend of the taxpayer.
D. A disbarred practitioner with a current PTIN.

98. Which of the following professional designations is not always required to obtain a PTIN?

A. CPAs.
B. Attorneys.
C. Enrolled agents.
D. Both A and B.

99. In the licensing of enrolled agents, an enrollment cycle refers to:

A. The enrollment year preceding the effective date of renewal.
B. The three successive enrollment years preceding the effective date of renewal.
C. The year in which the enrolled agent receives his initial enrollment.
D. The amount of continuing professional education required each year of enrollment.

100. Alexa is an enrolled agent, and she files approximately 300 individual tax returns every year. This year, she has a new client named Iker. Iker is distrustful of modern technology and he does not wish to e-file his tax return. What must Alexa do in this case?

A. Iker may file his tax return on paper, and no additional forms are necessary.
B. Form 8948 must be mailed along with Iker's paper return.
C. Form 2848 must be submitted with Iker's paper return, along with a reason for each return that is not e-filed. There is no penalty.
D. If her client refuses to e-file, Alexa must decline the engagement.

Please review your answer choices with the correct answers in the back.

Test Answers

Answers to Exam #1: Individuals

1. The answer is C. Failing to withdraw an RMD by the applicable deadline may result in the taxpayer owing the IRS an excise tax equal to 50% of the amount not withdrawn. A taxpayer is required to start taking withdrawals from a traditional IRA account when she reaches age 70½. Unlike traditional IRAs, Roth IRAs do not require withdrawals until after the death of the owner.

2. The answer is C. Neither is eligible for the American Opportunity Credit, because they both had previously completed four years of postsecondary studies and the AOC applies only to the first four years of postsecondary studies. The Lifetime Learning Credit is easy to calculate because it is based on 20% credit for up to $10,000 in allowable expenses ($10,000 × 20% = $2,000 maximum credit). Since Benedict and Emma have $11,700 ($4,800 + $6,900) in qualified education expenses (which is more than the maximum allowed of $10,000), their deduction is $2,000.

3. The answer is A. Although Royce is not required to take his employer's offer of coverage, if anyone in Royce's tax family is without coverage and without an exemption, then the taxpayer would be responsible for a Shared Responsibility Payment. In 2015, health coverage is considered "unaffordable" if the cost exceeds 8.05% of the modified adjusted gross income of the taxpayer's household (which includes the taxpayer, the taxpayer's spouse (if a joint return is filed), and any dependents claimed by the taxpayer). Since the coverage that was offered to Royce did not exceed this threshold, he would be responsible for paying the additional tax (unless he qualified for another exemption).

4. The answer is A. Herb has a $1,000 short-term capital loss and a $7,000 ($5,000 + $2,000) long-term capital gain. The loss on the sale of the ABC Co. stock is short-term, because he owned the stock for less than a year. The gain on the sale of the empty lot is long-term gain, because inherited property is always treated as long-term property, regardless of how long the beneficiary holds the property. The gain on the sale of the XYZ Co. stock is also long-term gain, because Herb held the stock for over a year.

5. The answer is B. Life insurance proceeds are not taxable. However, interest or investment gains earned on a life insurance installment contract are taxable. The face amount of the policy is $270,000. Therefore, the excluded part of each installment is $1,500 ($270,000 ÷ 180 months), or $18,000 for an entire year. The rest of each payment, $300 a month (or $3,600 for an entire year), is interest income to Sheila.

6. The answer is A. All the gain is excludable under section 121, because Cristina meets the ownership and use tests. Cristina meets the use test because she lived in the home for five years with Joe. She also meets the ownership test because, if ownership of a home is transferred to a former spouse in a divorce, the transferee is considered to have owned it during any period of time when the other spouse owned it. In other words, since Joe was required to transfer the property due to their divorce settlement, the period that Joe owned the home is also considered time that Cristina owned the home. Therefore, all of Cristina's gain is excludable.

7. The answer is D. Hailey must file as MFS, and she will be forced to itemize deductions. On an MFS return, if one spouse itemizes deductions, the other spouse must also itemize and cannot claim the standard deduction. Hailey also cannot claim the dependency exemption for Vincent, because she is not the custodial parent. If the parents separated during the year and the child lived with both parents before the separation, the custodial parent is the one with whom the child lived for the greater number of nights during the rest of the year. Neither spouse qualifies for head of household filing status, because they did not separate until September 2015.

8. The answer is B. Lucille's main home is her rental apartment in Denver because she lives there most of the time. If she were to sell the ski home in Lake Tahoe, she would not qualify for the section 121 exclusion on the sale because it is a vacation home and not her primary residence.

9. The answer is B. The kiddie tax is based only on a child's unearned income, not on her wages or other earned income. Since Anya's unearned income totaled more than $2,100 in 2015, a portion of her income will be taxed at her parents' tax rate instead of her own. The kiddie tax applies to children under age 18, those under age 19 whose earned income was not more than half of their own support for the year, or full-time students under age 24 whose earned income was not more than half of their own support for the year.

10. The answer is B. Qualified foreign income taxes may be deducted on Schedule A as an itemized deduction. Taxpayers have the option to choose the Foreign Tax Credit or to deduct foreign income taxes as an itemized deduction.

11. The answer is B. The adjusted basis of the house at the time of the change in its use was $182,000, of which $20,000 was attributable to land and $162,000 to the house. The basis for depreciation on the house is the fair market value on the date of the change ($147,000), because it is less than the allocable portion of Carlos's adjusted basis ($162,000). When a primary residence is changed to rental use, the basis of the property for depreciation will be the lesser of its fair market value or its adjusted basis on the date of conversion. Land is not subject to depreciation.

12. The answer is B. Lester cannot claim the Earned Income Tax Credit. As a noncustodial parent, he does not meet the residency test because the child did not live with him for more than half of the year. Only a custodial parent can claim the Earned Income Tax Credit based on a dependent child. If the noncustodial parent qualifies to claim the dependency exemption for a child, he can claim the Child Tax Credit if the other requirements for claiming the credit are met. The Child Tax Credit can only be claimed by the parent claiming the dependency exemption.

13. The answer is A. The basis of property received from a decedent's estate is generally the fair market value of the property on the date of the decedent's death. However, when an executor elects the alternate valuation date, the basis to the heirs is normally the fair market value of the assets six months after the date of death. However, for assets distributed prior to six months after death, the basis to the heir in these particular assets is the fair market value as of the date of distribution (IRC Sect. 2032). Since the alternate valuation date was elected, the stock's basis is the fair market value as of February 26, 2015 (the date of distribution), so Immanuel's basis in the inherited stock is $26,000. His holding period is long-term, because inherited property is always treated as long-term property, regardless of how long the beneficiary holds the property.

14. The answer is D. Since Peter filed a joint return but is not responsible for the debt, he is entitled to a portion of the refund. He may request his share of the $5,000 by filing Form 8379, *Injured Spouse Allocation*.

15. The answer is D. Generally, the value of a gift is its fair market value on the date of the gift. In this case, the value of $40,000 exceeds the annual exclusion amount of $14,000 for gifts in 2015. Even if Bianca and her husband took advantage of the gift-splitting option for purposes of the gift to her brother, the value would exceed their combined exclusion amount of $28,000, and would need to be reported on Form 709.

16. The answer is D. To be eligible for the Premium Tax Credit, a taxpayer, his spouse (if filing a joint return), or his dependents must have been enrolled at some point during the year in one or more qualified health plans offered through the Health Insurance Marketplace (both federal and state exchanges). One or more of the individuals listed on the return generally cannot have been eligible for minimum essential coverage through another source, such as through an employer, unless the eligible employer plan was not "affordable." Affordability is generally defined as a plan with an annual premium for self-only coverage that exceeds 9.5% of the taxpayer's household income. The Premium Tax Credit is refundable and is based on a taxpayer's household income, which must be at least 100%, but not more than 400%, of the federal poverty line for its family size.

17. The answer is D. Only the expenses of hosting a foreign exchange student are deductible, assuming the student has been sponsored by a qualified organization. The other expenses are not valid as charitable contributions.

18. The answer is B. The aggregate portion of his estate distributed to his grandchildren ($10 million) would be reduced by his exclusion amount for GST ($5.43 million) and the remainder of $4.57 million would be subject to GST.

19. The answer is A. Alejandro's loss must be reduced by his insurance reimbursement ($5,000 loss - $3,500 insurance reimbursement = $1,500). He does not have a theft loss deduction because his loss after applying the $100 reduction ($1,500 - $100 = $1,400) is less than 10% of his adjusted gross income ($2,050). The problem is figured as follows:

Loss after insurance	$1,500
Loss after $100 reduction	1,400
Subtract 10% × $20,500 = $2,050	2,050
Theft loss deduction	**$0**

20. The answer is B. Mai Lin can deduct only $15,000 ($25,000 - [50% × $20,000]) of the rental losses in the current year. Taxpayers (other than real estate professionals) who actively participate in a rental real estate activity can deduct up to $25,000 of loss from the activity from nonpassive income. However, the $25,000 allowance is phased out if modified adjusted gross income (MAGI) is between $100,000 and $150,000. The $25,000 limit gets phased out by $1 for every $2 that the taxpayer's MAGI is over $100,000. If the taxpayer's MAGI is $150,000 or more ($75,000 or more if married filing separately), there is no special allowance. This special allowance is an exception to the general rule disallowing losses in excess of income from passive activities.

21. The answer is C. Only Enoch qualifies for the Child Tax Credit. A qualifying child must:
- Be a son, daughter, stepchild, foster child, brother, sister, stepbrother, stepsister, or a descendant of any of them (for example, a grandchild, niece, or nephew);
- Be under age 17 at the end of 2015;
- Have not provided over half of his own support for 2015;
- Have lived with the taxpayer for more than half of 2015;
- And be a U.S. citizen, a U.S. national, or a U.S. resident alien.

22. The answer is C. Because Linda is over 65 and she and Mitchell are filing jointly, they can deduct the portion of their medical expenses that exceeds 7.5% of their AGI. However, Linda's facelift is a cosmetic procedure and not deductible. Over the counter medications (the aspirin) are not deductible unless a doctor prescribes them. Allowable medical expenses are therefore $4,380 ($3,000 + $500 + $480 + $400). This amount exceeds 7.5% of their AGI of $2,100 ($28,000 × 7.5%) by $2,280 ($4,380 - $2,100), so this is their allowable medical expense deduction.

23. The answer is C. Mavis does have minimum essential coverage (MEC). She is required to report this on page 2 of her Form 1040. The fact that she files separately from her husband is irrelevant, as long as she has qualifying health coverage. Employer-sponsored coverage is generally considered "minimum essential coverage." If an employee has employer-sponsored coverage that covers other family members, such as a spouse, those family members are also considered to have qualifying coverage.

24. The answer is D. A taxpayer can make a tax-free rollover of funds from a traditional IRA or a Roth IRA into a high deductible health savings account (HSA), subject to certain restrictions. In 2015, the distribution cannot be more than:
- $3,350 for an individual health plan, or
- $6,650 for a family health plan.

An additional $1,000 contribution is allowed for taxpayers age 55 and over. This type of rollover can be done only once in a taxpayer's lifetime. The distribution must be made directly by the trustee of the IRA to the trustee of the HSA. If a taxpayer has already contributed to her HSA for the year, she can roll over an amount equal to or less than her HSA maximum contribution limit.

25. The answer is C. Since the trip was mainly for business, Valentina can deduct the round-trip airfare, parking, hotel costs, and the meals (subject to the 50% limit) connected with her professional continuing education. The meal costs incurred while sightseeing are not deductible. The answer is calculated as follows:

Roundtrip airfare to New Orleans	$360	$360
Parking at the airport	24	24
Meals while at the conference	220	220 × 50% = 110
Meals while sightseeing	72	NOT ALLOWABLE
Hotel costs during the conference	450	450
Allowable costs before application of the 2%-of-AGI limit		**$944**

26. The answer is C. For 2015, the maximum exclusion for the foreign earned income exclusion is $100,800.

27. The answer is B. On Quinn's tax return, he can deduct $3,000 of the capital loss. The unused part of the loss, $4,000 ($7,000 − $3,000), can be carried over to the following year. Quinn's adjusted gross income is $29,000 ($32,000 − $3,000 capital loss). Capital losses can be deducted on a taxpayer's return and used to reduce other income, such as wages, up to an annual limit of $3,000 (or $1,500 if married filing separately).

28. The answer is C. Josiah's basis in the 10 shares of stock received from his father would presumably be his father's adjusted basis, or $100. (This is normally the case, although his basis could possibly also include any gift tax paid by his father related to the appreciation of the stock's value while he held it.) Josiah's basis in the stock he purchased would be $620. When shares of stock are sold from lots acquired at different times and the identity of the shares sold cannot be determined, the sale is charged first against the earliest acquisitions (first-in, first-out). The 20 shares sold in 2015 would be presumed to be the 10 shares acquired by gift from Josiah's father and half of the shares purchased in 2012. Therefore, the basis of Josiah's Rust Valley Corporation shares he still owns would be half the basis of the purchased shares, or $310.

29. The answer is C. Under the optional method of calculating the home office deduction, a taxpayer can deduct $5 per square foot for the space in the home that is used for business, with a maximum allowable square footage of 300 square feet. Therefore, the maximum deduction is $1,500. The criteria for who qualifies for the deduction remain the same, but the calculation and recordkeeping requirements have been simplified. There is no depreciation expense and no recapture of depreciation upon sale of the home. Home-related itemized deductions, such as for mortgage interest and real estate taxes, may be claimed in full on Schedule A, without allocation of portions to the home office space.

30. The answer is A. The additional Medicare tax of .9% is applied only to earned income ($188,000 + $10,000 + $56,000 = $254,000 earned income) above the threshold for a taxpayer's filing status. Therefore, Katrina owes $486 ($254,000 - $200,000 = $54,000 × .009 = $486). The interest income and the inheritance do not figure into the calculation.

31. The answer is D. Line 21 of Form 1040 is used for all other types of miscellaneous taxable income that is not otherwise listed elsewhere on the return or on other schedules. Examples of the types of income reported on line 21 include the following:
- Gambling winnings
- Prizes and awards
- Jury duty pay
- Alaska Permanent Fund dividends
- Taxable distributions from a Coverdell education savings account (ESA)
- Hobby income

32. The answer is D. For income tax purposes, Pastor Green excludes $31,000 from gross income ($24,000 fair rental value of the parsonage plus $7,000 from the allowance for utility costs). He will report $60,000 as regular income ($59,500 salary plus $500 of unused utility allowance). His income for SE tax purposes, however, is $91,000 ($67,000 salary + $24,000 fair rental value of the parsonage). Services that a duly ordained, commissioned, or licensed minister performs in the exercise of his ministry are generally covered under the Self-Employment Contributions Act. That means the minister is exempt from Social Security and Medicare withholding, but he is then responsible for paying self-employment tax on his net earnings from self-employment. The fair rental value of a minister's parsonage is excludable from income only for income tax purposes. No exclusion applies for self-employment tax purposes.

33. The answer is B. It is determined as follows:

Required textbooks	$450
Required lab equipment	1,260
Tuition ($6,800 - $4,750)	2,050
Qualifying costs for the AOC	**$3,760**

The GI Bill is a benefit that is not taxable or reportable. However, to figure the amount of qualifying educational expenses for purposes of the AOC credit, Reggie must first subtract the $4,750 GI Bill payment from his tuition expenses ($6,800 - $4,750). The books and lab equipment are allowable expenses, but the student health fees are specifically disallowed (even if they are mandatory). Parking fees, transportation costs, and commuting costs are not allowable for the tuition and fees deduction, American Opportunity Credit, or the Lifetime Learning Credit.

34. The answer is D. Because she was covered by a retirement plan at work and her modified AGI was over $71,000 in 2015, Brittany cannot deduct the IRA contribution. The deductibility of traditional IRAs is phased out above certain thresholds. However, she is still allowed to contribute to a traditional IRA. Brittany must designate this contribution as a "nondeductible contribution" by reporting it on Form 8606, *Nondeductible IRAs*.

35. The answer is B. Brock's gross profit percentage is 12.5% ($15,000 ÷ $120,000). Brock would report 12.5% of each payment (12.5% × $30,000) = $3,750) as installment sale income from the sale for the tax year he receives the payment (after subtracting interest, if any). The balance of each payment, exclusive of interest, is the tax-free return of his adjusted basis.

36. The answer is A. Early withdrawal penalties from certificates of deposit (CDs) or other time deposit accounts are deductible as an adjustment to income. Answers B and C are incorrect because penalties for early withdrawal from retirement accounts are never deductible.

37. The answer is B. Dianne can file as head of household because her husband did not live with her for the last six months of the year. There is a special exception that applies to married persons who live apart from their spouses for at least the last six months of the year. In this case, the taxpayer will be "considered unmarried" for head of household filing purposes.

38. The answer is C. Income derived from a business carried on by an estate (or trust) generally is not included in determining the self-employment earnings of the estate. Even if a taxpayer was self-employed while he was alive and the business continues to generate income after his death, that income is not subject to self-employment tax. However, it will be subject to income tax.

39. The answer is C. The answer is calculated as follows: ($35,000 + $80,000 + $2,300 = $117,300). If a taxpayer buys property and assumes an existing mortgage on the property, the basis includes the amount of the assumed mortgage. The basis also includes the settlement fees and closing costs for buying a property. The following items are examples of settlement fees or closing costs that are included in a property's basis.
- Abstract fees (abstract of title fees)
- Charges for installing utility services
- Legal fees and recording fees
- Transfer taxes
- Owner's title insurance
- Any amounts the seller owes that the buyer agrees to pay, such as delinquent property taxes or interest, recording or mortgage fees, charges for improvements or repairs, and sales commissions

40. The answer is B. Lupe's dividends should be reported on Form 1040. Lupe meets the requirements for reporting the capital gain distribution directly on Form 1040. If the total amount of dividends received is over $1,500, Schedule B must also be filed with the tax return. Since Lupe's dividends did not exceed $1,500, Schedule B is not required. The capital gain from the sale of stock should be reported on Schedule D. In some circumstances, the sale of stock may also have to be reported on Form 8949.

41. The answer is A. Life insurance proceeds payable to Amelia's beneficiaries would be included in the calculation of her gross estate. The gross estate includes the value of property that the taxpayer owns at the time of death. In addition to the value of life insurance proceeds, the gross estate includes the following:
- The value of certain annuities payable to the estate or to the taxpayer's heirs, and
- The value of certain property transferred within three years before the taxpayer's death.

42. The answer is B. Chelsea has a taxable gain of $30,000. Her basis in the new home is $80,000. The part of her gain that is taxable is $30,000 ($130,000 − $100,000), the unspent part of the payment from the insurance company. The rest of the gain ($20,000) is not taxable, because it was reinvested into the replacement home. This follows the rules for involuntary conversions (IRC section 1033). The basis of the new home is calculated as follows:

Cost of replacement home	$100,000
Subtract gain not recognized	(20,000)
Basis of the replacement home	**$80,000**

43. The answer is C. If a taxpayer claims a deduction for a charitable contribution of noncash property worth more than $5,000, the taxpayer is required to obtain a qualified appraisal and must fill out Form 8283, *Noncash Charitable Contributions*.

44. The answer is B. If a taxpayer is entitled to deduct depreciation on the part of a home used exclusively for business, she cannot exclude the part of the gain equal to any depreciation she deducted (or could have deducted) for periods after May 6, 1997. Of the gain Araceli realizes, $26,000 qualifies for section 121 exclusion, while $14,000 must be reported as ordinary income.

45. The answer is B. Leslie does not need to pay estimated tax because she expects her current year income tax withholding ($10,250) to be more than her prior year tax of $9,224. Therefore, Leslie qualifies for the safe harbor rule and is not required to make estimated tax payments. Her expected income tax withholding is also more than 90% of the expected tax liability on her current year return ($11,270 × 90% = $10,143). A taxpayer is not required to pay estimated tax for the current year if:
- The taxpayer had no tax liability in the prior year
- The taxpayer was a U.S. citizen or resident alien
- The current tax year covered a 12-month period.

The taxpayer also does not have to pay estimated tax if she pays enough through withholding so that the tax due on the return (minus the amounts of tax credits or paid through withholding) is less than $1,000. For a taxpayer with AGI of $150,000 or less, estimated tax payments must be made if she expects the amount owed after withholding and credits to be less than the smaller of:
- 90% of the tax liability on the current year tax return, or
- 100% of the tax liability on the prior year tax return.

Note: For high-income taxpayers with adjusted gross income of *over* $150,000 ($75,000 if married filing separately), the estimated tax safe harbor threshold for the amount owed would be 110% of the previous year's tax liability rather than 100%.

46. The answer is A. Charlene would report $1,200 in business income. Generally, the FMV of property exchanged for services is includable in income. However, if services are performed for a price agreed on beforehand, the price will be accepted as the FMV if there is no evidence to the contrary.

47. The answer is B. The donor is generally responsible for paying gift tax. A gift is not taxable to the recipient, but may need to be reported on Form 709. The annual exclusion amount for gifts made to a donee during 2015 is $14,000. The general rule is that any gift over $14,000 is a taxable gift. However, there are many exceptions to this rule. Generally, the following gifts are not taxable gifts:
- Gifts that are not more than the annual exclusion amount
- Tuition or medical expenses paid for someone directly to a college or a medical provider (the educational and medical exclusions)
- Gifts to a spouse who is a U.S. citizen
- Gifts to a political organization for its own use

48. The answer is B. The $30,000 in debt cancellation is treated as a reduction in basis in the property and should be reported on line 10b of Form 982, *Reduction of Tax Attributes Due to Discharge of Indebtedness*. In addition, the box on line 1e of Part I of Form 982 must be checked as well. The debt cancellation is covered by the qualified principal residence indebtedness exclusion and is not counted as taxable income on the return. Form 8949, *Sales* *and Other Dispositions of Capital Assets*, and Schedule D are not required because Paloma did not dispose of the home.

49. The answer is B. In 2015, the individual shared payment responsibility provision of the Affordable Care Act took effect. All taxpayers are expected to have health coverage that meets certain requirements (called minimum essential coverage), unless they have an exemption. There are more than 30 exemptions that excuse a taxpayer from the requirement to obtain minimum essential coverage. Having a short coverage gap is a legitimate exemption reason. However, a short coverage cap is defined as having "less than three consecutive months," not four consecutive months as stated in the question. If a taxpayer does not have minimum essential coverage in 2015 and does not have an approved exemption from coverage, he will face a penalty called the *shared responsibility payment* (SRP) when he files his tax return. A taxpayer owes one-twelfth of the annual SRP for each month he or his dependents do not have coverage and do not qualify for an exemption. While a foreclosure, by itself, does not automatically result in an exemption from the Shared Responsibility Payment for 2015, it may be considered in the determination of a potential hardship exemption allowed for under the Affordable Care Act.

50. The answer is A. Gains from the sale of personal-use assets, such as Mandy's painting, are taxable and must be reported. The auction house's commission is $1,800 ($6,000 × 30%). Mandy's gain is $4,180 ($6,000 - $20 basis - $1,800 commission).

51. The answer is B. The estate tax return is generally due nine months after the date of death.

52. The answer is D. Gregory has a wash sale, and he cannot deduct the capital loss. A wash sale occurs when a taxpayer sells stock or other securities at a loss and, within 30 days before or after the sale or disposition, the taxpayer buys or acquires substantially identical stock or securities. The wash sale rules also apply if a taxpayer sells stock and then the taxpayer's spouse immediately buys identical stock. Since Gregory's wife purchased identical securities within 30 days after Gregory sold his stock, he has a wash sale. The wash sale rules apply regardless of whether a husband and wife file separate tax returns. Gregory's $4,000 loss is instead added to the cost basis of the new stock. The result is an increased basis in the new stock. This adjustment postpones the loss deduction until the disposition of the new stock or securities. The holding period for the new stock includes the holding period of the stock or securities sold.

53. The answer is B. Even though a taxpayer files Form 4868, *Application of Automatic Extension of Time to File U.S. Individual Income Tax Return*, he will owe interest and a late payment penalty on the amount owed if he does not pay the tax owed by the regular due date.

54. The answer is C. Because he is a transportation worker covered under special DOT rules, Howard can deduct 80% of his business meal expenses, instead of the normal 50%. The answer is calculated as follows: $3,080 × .80 = $2,464. Other employees covered under the DOT rules include interstate truck and bus drivers; airline pilots, mechanics, flight crew, and control tower operators; certain railway employees; and certain merchant mariners.

55. The answer is A. If a taxpayer's spouse dies during the year, the surviving spouse is considered married for the entire year and can choose either married filing jointly or married filing separately as his or her filing status (assuming the taxpayer did not remarry during the year).

56. The answer is B. Under the section 121 exclusion, Hugh and Nicole may exclude $500,000 of the gain on their primary residence, so they must recognize $32,000 of capital gain ($805,000 - $273,000 = $532,000) in 2015. The exclusion may be claimed only on a main home and not on a second home, and is subject to both ownership and occupancy tests. A loss on a personal residence, regardless of whether it is a main home or a second/vacation home, is not deductible.

57. The answer is A. Ted can claim $250 (the maximum amount allowed for 2015) for the educator expense deduction. Maya is not eligible because the deduction is available only to kindergarten through grade 12 teachers, instructors, counselors, principals, and aides who worked at least 900 hours during the year. If Maya had been an eligible educator, the couple could have claimed a maximum deduction of $500.

58. The answer is B. The calculation of Theresa's gross estate includes all of the assets she owned outright at the date of her death, including the life insurance proceeds payable to her beneficiaries. However, only half of the amounts of the assets she owned jointly with her husband would be included in the calculation. Therefore, the answer is figured as follows: $150,000 IRA + $15,000 automobile + $750,000 life insurance + $30,000 checking account + $50,000 ($100,000/2) brokerage account + $250,000 ($500,000/2) other jointly-held property = $1,245,000. Debts not paid before the decedent's death, including medical expenses subsequently paid on her behalf, are liabilities that can be deducted from the gross estate on the estate tax return.

59. The answer is C. Ryan has a long-term capital gain of $370 ($1,320 sale price - $950 transferred basis). The basis of a gift generally remains the same for the gift recipient/donee as it was for the donor. Therefore, Ryan's basis in the stock, for purposes of determining gain, is $950 (transferred basis). The holding period is also transferred, so the three years that Dante held the stock is added to Ryan's holding period, which makes the disposition a long-term capital gain.

60. The answer is D. Gambling income does not qualify as earned income for purposes of the Earned Income Tax Credit. For purposes of the EITC, earned income includes:
- Wages, salaries, and tips
- Union strike benefits
- Long-term disability benefits received prior to minimum retirement age
- Net earnings from self-employment
- Nontaxable combat pay

The taxpayer can elect to have nontaxable combat pay included in earned income for the Earned Income Tax Credit.

61. The answer is D. The cleaning deposits are refundable to the tenants, so they are not considered rental income. The advance rent must be included in Kelsey's 2015 rental income. This is because Kelsey had constructive receipt of the rent, and advance rent is always taxable when it is received, regardless of the taxpayer's accounting method. A taxpayer is deemed to have constructive receipt of income when the amount is made available without restriction. A taxpayer cannot hold checks or postpone taking possession of income from one tax year to another in order to avoid paying tax. The fact that Kelsey waited to cash the check is irrelevant, because she had rights to the funds. Kelsey must calculate her rental income as follows:

$$\begin{array}{l}\$11,700\ (\$1,300 \times 9\text{ months in 2015}) \\ \$1,800\ (\$600 \times 3\text{ months in 2015}) \\ \underline{\$600\ (\text{rent paid in advance})} \\ \textbf{\$14,100 rental income for 2015}\end{array}$$

62. The answer is B. Traditional IRA distributions are taxable to the receiver. In the case of a deceased IRA holder, the distribution to the beneficiary is subject to income tax, but is not subject to the 10% early withdrawal penalty, regardless of the age of the beneficiary.

63. The answer is A. The basis of the new property is $37,000 (equal to the adjusted basis of the old property, $17,000, plus the amount of cash she paid, $20,000). If a taxpayer trades property in a like-kind exchange and also pays money, the basis of the property received is the adjusted basis of the property given up increased by the money paid.

64. The answer is D. The wages, interest, alimony, and unemployment compensation are taxable income and will be shown on Donna's tax return ($26,200 + $5,400 + $7,400 + $5,300 = $44,300). Child support, inheritance, and worker's compensation are nontaxable income and will not be shown on Donna's tax return. Unlike unemployment compensation, worker's compensation is not taxable, because it is a form of insurance providing wage replacement and medical benefits to employees injured in the course of employment. Compensation for injuries is generally not taxable.

65. The answer is D. Because Zeke does not meet the age test, Inez's son is not her qualifying child. Because he does not meet the gross income test, Zeke is not her qualifying relative. As a result, he is not Inez's qualifying person for head of household purposes and she cannot claim her son as a dependent. However, if Zeke was permanently disabled, he would be considered a qualifying child, regardless of his age.

66. The answer is B. Judy must report $300 of the recovery in her taxable income. A taxpayer must include a recovery in income for the year it is received, but only up to the amount by which a deduction reduced her taxable income in an earlier year. Thus, the only portion of the $900 reimbursement that must be included in Judy's income for 2015 is the amount that was actually deducted in the prior year ($300).

67. The answer is C. Larry may choose to report the bond interest in one of two ways. He can:
- Report $250 of interest income when the bond matures (this is the difference between the $500 value at maturity and the amount he paid for the bond); or
- Report $7 of interest income at the end of the first year. This is the increase in value at the end of the year ($257 - $250 = $7). Larry would then be required to report interest income each year until maturity.

68. The answer is C. Victoria can claim $26,400 in alimony paid as an adjustment to income on her individual Form 1040, the total of the medical expenses and the regular alimony paid ($15,000 + $11,400). Alimony paid is an adjustment to income and is claimed on page 1 of Form 1040. A taxpayer does not need to itemize deductions in order to claim an adjustment for alimony paid. The payer can deduct the full amount if it is required by the divorce agreement. Alimony is a payment to or for a spouse or former spouse under a divorce or separation agreement. Alimony does not include voluntary payments that are not made under a divorce or separation decree. Payments to a third party (such as the payment directly to the hospital) on behalf of an ex-spouse under the terms of a divorce or separation agreement can qualify as alimony. These include payments for an ex-spouse's medical expenses, housing costs (rent, utilities, etc.), taxes, and tuition. The payments are treated as received by the spouse and then paid to the third party.

69. The answer is B. Melanie turned 13 on May 1 and is no longer a qualifying person for purposes of this credit. For the Child and Dependent Care Credit, the child must be under the age of 13 (or be disabled, of any age). Rayna can use the $2,000 of expenses for Melanie's care January through April before she turned 13 to figure her credit, because it is less than the $3,000 yearly limit for qualifying expenses for a taxpayer with one qualifying child. If there is more than one qualifying child, the total amount of qualifying expenses is limited to $6,000 in 2015.

70. The answer is D. Mason must report $12,000 of gambling winnings. He should also report the $1,300 withholding on his return. Mason can deduct his gambling losses as an itemized deduction on Schedule A, but the losses are limited to the amount of his gambling winnings. Therefore, Mason cannot deduct more than $12,000 of gambling losses. If a taxpayer does not itemize deductions, he is not allowed to deduct gambling losses. Gambling winnings over certain amounts are reported to a taxpayer on Form W-2G, *Certain Gambling Winnings*.

71. The answer is B. Reiko can contribute to a Roth IRA, but her contribution is subject to a phase-out because of her MAGI. Taxpayers can contribute to a Roth IRA if they have qualifying compensation and their modified AGI in 2015 is less than:
- $131,000 (phase-out begins at $116,000) for single, head of household, or married filing separately (if the taxpayer did not live with his or her spouse at any time during the year)
- $193,000 (phase-out begins at $183,000) for married filing jointly or qualifying widower
- $10,000 (phase-out begins at $0) for married filing separately (and living with spouse)

72. The answer is D. A statutory nonemployee is the most likely to be subject to estimated taxes. There are three categories of statutory nonemployees: direct sellers, licensed real estate agents, and certain companion sitters. These taxpayers are treated as self-employed for FICA purposes and are usually required to pay estimated taxes. Answers A and C are incorrect because household employees and statutory employees would have Medicare and Social Security taxes withheld by their employers. Answer B is incorrect because taxes are withheld from the earnings of a taxpayer subject to backup withholding and investment income is not subject to SE tax.

73. The answer is C. Gary can claim the American Opportunity Credit for Devon and Brianna, but cannot for Keisha, because she is a graduate student who had already completed four years of college as an undergraduate. A taxpayer can claim the American Opportunity Credit for qualified education expenses paid for a dependent child, the taxpayer, or a spouse listed on the return. If a taxpayer has multiple qualifying students, the taxpayer can claim multiple credits on the same return. In Gary's case, since he has two qualifying students, he can claim a maximum of $5,000 ($2,500 × 2) in American Opportunity Credits. Gary may be able to take the Lifetime Learning Credit for Keisha's education expenses, if she otherwise qualifies.

74. The answer is D. The passive losses from the real estate activity may be used only to the extent of the $4,000 of passive income from the investment partnership. Since the taxpayers' MAGI of $169,000 exceeds the phase-out threshold of $150,000, the remaining $500 of rental losses are not allowed against non-passive income. However, the disallowed rental loss of $500 may be carried forward to the next year. The answer is calculated as follows:

Wages for Ellie	$60,000
Wages for Timothy	105,000
Income from a passive investment partnership	4,000
Rental loss	(4,500)
Adjusted gross income	164,500
Add back rental loss	4,500
Modified adjusted gross income	**$169,000**

75. The answer is A. The term "points" is used to describe certain interest charges paid by a borrower to obtain a home mortgage. Points may also be called loan origination fees, maximum loan charges, loan discount points, or discount points. A taxpayer generally cannot deduct the full amount of points paid for a refinance in the year paid. Taxpayers must calculate and amortize points on a monthly basis, calculated over the life of the loan. In this case, the taxpayer had a 30-year loan that began on November 1, 2015. The answer is calculated as follows:
- $1,800 ÷ 30 years = $60 in deductible interest per year
- $60 ÷ 12 months = $5 of interest per month
- $5 × two months (November and December) = $10 of deductible interest in 2015

Whitney can claim a deduction of $10 in 2015.

76. The answer is B. Martina will report $30,850 on Form 1040, line 7. This is the total of her W-2 income and her unreported tip income ($25,600 + $4,950 + $300). The unemployment compensation must be reported as income and the state income tax refund may have to be reported if Martina had itemized her deductions in the prior year, but neither would be reported on the return as wages.

77. The answer is A. The expenses paid for an unsuccessful adoption attempt in the United States may still be deductible. Qualified adoption expenses include court costs, attorney fees, traveling expenses (including meals and lodging while away from home), and other expenses directly related to the legal adoption of an eligible child. Qualified adoption expenses do not include expenses for adopting a spouse's child, expenses for a surrogate arrangement, or any expenses that were reimbursed by an employer or another organization. Expenses connected with a foreign adoption (in which the child was not a U.S. citizen or resident at the time the adoption process began) qualify only if the adoption is successful.

78. The answer is D. Nonresident aliens are limited in the deductions they are allowed to claim on their tax returns. Jae Hwa cannot claim the mortgage deduction for a home he owns in the United States. Nonresident aliens can claim deductions only to the extent they are connected with income related to their U.S. trade or business. Nonresidents are allowed to claim the following deductions:
- State and local income taxes
- Qualifying charitable contributions to U.S. nonprofit organizations
- Casualty and theft losses
- Miscellaneous itemized deductions

79. The answer is A. The allowable casualty loss is calculated as follows:

Basis of property	$4,000
Minus (the $100 rule)	(100)
Allowable loss	3,900
Minus 10% of $24,000 AGI (the 10% rule)	(2,400)
Audrey's allowable casualty loss deduction	$1,500

An individual can claim a personal casualty loss as an itemized deduction on Form 1040, Schedule A. For property held for personal use (not business use), the taxpayer must subtract $100 from each casualty that occurred during the year. Those amounts are then added before 10% of adjusted gross income is subtracted from the total to calculate the allowable casualty and theft losses for the year. Casualty losses of business and investment property are not subject to the same $100 and 10%-of-AGI limitations.

80. The answer is A. A tax preparer should advise Braden to amend his tax return using Form 1040X, removing his personal exemption from the return. Once the amended return is processed, Larissa may file her tax return normally, claiming her son as a dependent. If necessary, an extension may be filed for Larissa if Braden's amended return has not been processed by the original due date. A taxpayer should file an amended return when a return that has already been filed needs to be corrected. For example, a taxpayer should file an amended return if he:
- Received another Form W-2, a corrected Form W-2, or another income statement that was not reported on the original return
- Received an additional Form 1099 that was not reported on the original return
- Claimed a personal or dependency exemption on the return when someone else was entitled to claim it
- Claimed deductions or credits that should not have been claimed
- Did not claim deductions or credits they could have claimed
- Should have used a different filing status

81. The answer is D. The full amount is subject to self-employment tax and income tax. Theo must report the $12,400, as well as the $2,500 of other cash payments, as self-employment income on his Schedule C. It does not matter whether he receives a 1099-MISC or not. All of the income is taxable as self-employment income. Therefore, it is subject to income tax, as well as to SE tax.

82. The answer is B. If a taxpayer claimed the First-Time Homebuyer Credit for 2008, it is repaid as an additional tax on subsequent years' tax returns. Veronica is required to repay the credit in equal payments over 15 years. Each payment is reported on Line 60b of Form 1040.

83. The answer is D. Allie has a loss on the sale of the rental property, calculated as follows:

($230,000 FMV on the date of conversion - $18,000 depreciation) = $212,000 tax basis
($212,000 tax basis - $205,000 sale price) = **$7,000 loss**

A loss from the sale of a primary residence is not deductible. However, if a primary residence is converted to a rental, the loss is generally deductible. The loss is calculated on the adjusted tax basis of the rental property. The basis of the converted property is the lesser of:

- The cost basis when the property is placed in service as a rental; or
- The fair market value when it is placed in service.

The adjusted basis is the basis at the date of conversion plus any improvements that were made while the property was a rental, minus any depreciation.

84. The answer is A. Capital gain distributions, such as those from mutual funds and real estate investment trusts (REITs), are taxable income. These distributions are treated as long-term capital gains, regardless of how long the taxpayer holds the shares. The other types of distributions listed are not taxable. A return of capital reduces a taxpayer's stock basis. Stock dividends reduce the basis of the individual shares held prior to the distribution. Dividends paid to cash-value life insurance policyholders are also considered nontaxable distributions.

Note: Do not confuse *"capital gains"* with *"capital gain distributions."* A capital gain occurs when a taxpayer sells stock, shares of a mutual fund, or other capital asset. A capital gain distribution occurs when the mutual fund sells assets for more than their cost and distributes the realized gain to its investors.

85. The answer is A. Harvey is over the age limit of 70½ for making a traditional IRA contribution. There is no age limit for Roth IRA contributions. Cindy can contribute $5,500 to her Roth IRA, but Harvey cannot contribute anything to his traditional IRA, because of his age.

86. The answer is C. James has $1,100 of net long-term capital gains ($1,600 gain - $500 loss). The gain on the Harris stock is short-term because the shares were not held for more than a year.

Activity	Bought	Sold	Gain/Loss	Character
1400 shares for $3,000 (basis: $1,400)	1/3/2013	12/1/2015	$1,600	LT gain
200 shares for $500 (basis: $1,000)	1/3/2012	12/25/2015	($500)	LT loss
50 shares for $1,700 (basis: $1,500)	2/1/2015	9/12/2015	$200	ST gain

87. The answer is C. The gift is not taxable, but it must be reported on Form 709. The gift limit in 2015 is $14,000. If both spouses consent to splitting the gift, a married couple can give up to $28,000 to a person without making a taxable gift. When a married couple splits a gift, each spouse must generally file his or her own individual gift tax return. However, certain exceptions may apply that allow for only one spouse to file a return if the other spouse signifies consent on the donor spouse's Form 709.

88. The answer is B. To qualify for a deduction, job search expenses must be related to the taxpayer's *current* occupation. A taxpayer cannot deduct expenses incurred while looking for a job in a new occupation or while looking for a job for the first time. Job search expenses are claimed as a miscellaneous itemized deduction on Schedule A and are subject to the 2%-of-AGI threshold.

89. The answer is D. Neither Harold nor Trish has taxable income from this exchange. Although canceled debt is usually included in income, since Trish filed for bankruptcy, the canceled debt is excludable.

90. The answer is B. Individuals who have been physically present for at least 183 days over a three-year period, including the current year, meet the requirements of the substantial presence test and will be taxed as a resident of the U.S. The substantial presence test requirements include 183 days of physical presence over a three-year period comprising the current year (must be at least 31 days); the first year before the current year (where each day present in the U.S. is counted as one-third of a day); and the second year before the current year (where each day present in the U.S. is counted as one-sixth of a day).

91. The answer is C. Marcel and Anna have two reporting requirements. They are required to file the FBAR as well as Form 8938. They must file an FBAR by June 30, 2016, directly with the Treasury Department using their online FBAR submission website. Form 8938 must be filed with the IRS by the due date (including extensions) of their tax return. In general, Form 8938, *Statement of Specified Foreign Financial Assets*, must be filed by:

- MFJ taxpayers who hold foreign financial assets with an aggregate value that exceeds $100,000 on the last day of the year ($50,000 for other filing statuses), or
- MFJ taxpayers who hold foreign financial assets that exceed $150,000 at any time during the tax year ($75,000 for other filing statuses).

FinCEN Form 114, *Report of Foreign Bank and Financial Accounts (FBAR)*, must be filed by U.S. taxpayers with foreign accounts of more than $10,000. The report must be filed electronically with the Treasury Department's Financial Crimes Enforcement Network (FinCEN) by June 30, 2016.

92. The answer is A. Health insurance for a sole proprietor is deductible, but not on Schedule C. Instead, it is claimed as an adjustment to income on page one of Form 1040. For self-employed individuals filing Schedule C or Schedule F, the insurance policy can be either in the name of the business or in the name of the individual.

93. The answer is B. The medical expenses are subject to a 10%-of-AGI limit for taxpayers under 65 years of age. The unreimbursed work expenses are subject to a 2% of AGI limit. The gambling losses are deductible to the extent of the gambling winnings ($3,000).

Type of Expense	Actual	Allowable	Reason
Medical expenses	$10,400	$7,080	Subject to 10% of AGI floor
Mortgage interest on main home	6,700	6,700	Allowable in full
Property tax on main home	2,300	2,300	Allowable in full
Misc. unreimbursed work expenses	1,200	536	Subject to 2% of AGI floor
Charitable donation to his church	1,600	1,600	Allowable in full
Gambling losses	4,600	3,000	Limited to gambling winnings
Allowable deductions on Schedule A		**$21,216**	

To calculate the allowable amount of medical expenses:
- $33,200 AGI × 10% = $3,320
- $10,400 medical expenses - $3,320 = $7,080 allowable expense
- To calculate the allowable miscellaneous unreimbursed work expenses:
- $33,200 AGI × 2% = $664
- $1,200 employee expenses - $664 = $536 allowable expense

94. The answer is A. Each will be treated as having received $900 of rents ($1,800 × 50%) and $600 of taxable interest ($1,200 × 50%). An amount distributed to a beneficiary retains the same character for the beneficiary that it had for the estate.

95. The answer is B. Monique may qualify for relief as an innocent spouse even when she is responsible for all or part of the tax liability. A spouse requesting innocent spouse relief must not have known that income was underreported or that the tax shown on the return was otherwise incorrect. The taxpayer must complete and attach Form 8857, *Request for Innocent Spouse Relief,* to apply for innocent spouse relief.

96. The answer is D. The entire gain can be excluded from income. Aiden meets the ownership and use tests in order to exclude the gain, because he owned and lived in the home for more than two years during the five-year period ending on the date of sale. The required two years of ownership and use do not have to be continuous, nor do they have to occur at the same time. A taxpayer will meet the tests if he can show that he owned and lived in the property as a main home for either 24 full months or 730 days (365 × 2) during the five-year period ending on the date of sale.

97. The answer is B. To qualify for the Child Tax Credit, the dependent must be under the age of 17 and claimed on the taxpayer's return. The Child Tax Credit is worth as much as $1,000 per qualifying child. A qualifying child is someone who meets the qualifying criteria of seven tests: age, relationship, support, dependent, citizenship, residence and the joint return test.
- Age test: A child must have been under age 17 at the end of the year.

- Relationship test: The child must be a son, daughter, stepchild, foster child, brother, sister, stepbrother, stepsister, or a descendant of any of these individuals.
- Support test: The child must not have provided more than half of his own support.
- Dependent test: The taxpayer must claim the child as a dependent on his federal tax return.
- Citizenship test: The child must be a U.S. citizen, U.S. national, or U.S. resident alien.
- Residence test: The child must have lived with the taxpayer for more than half the year. Temporary absences (for school or hospitalization, etc.) are allowable.
- Joint return test: The child must not file a joint tax return with another taxpayer for the year (unless it is only to claim a refund of withheld income tax or estimated tax paid).

The Additional Child Tax Credit is the refundable component of this credit. If the amount of the Child Tax Credit is greater than the amount of tax liability on the return, the taxpayer may qualify for the Additional Child Tax Credit.

98. The answer is B. Claudia can use her minimum tax credit carryforward to reduce her regular tax, but not below the tentative minimum tax of $4,000. Thus, the amount she can use is the difference of $750 between her regular tax of $4,750 and the tentative minimum tax of $4,000. The balance of $850 ($1,600 - $750) can be carried forward. The minimum tax credit is a nonrefundable credit that may be available to individuals, estates, and trusts for alternative minimum tax paid in prior years to the extent that a taxpayer's regular tax in the current year is greater than his tentative minimum tax. If applicable, the credit is calculated on Form 8801, *Credit for Prior Year Minimum Tax – Individuals, Estates, and Trusts*.

99. The answer is B. Using an IRA as security for a loan is a prohibited transaction. A prohibited transaction is the improper use of a traditional IRA by a taxpayer, a beneficiary, or any other disqualified person (disqualified persons include a fiduciary and family members). Prohibited transactions include:
- Borrowing money from an IRA
- Selling property to an IRA
- Receiving unreasonable compensation for managing an IRA
- Using the IRA as security for a loan
- Buying property for personal use with IRA funds

If a prohibited transaction occurs, the IRA ceases to be an IRA, and the full amount of the account becomes taxable as of the first day of that year. The other actions listed in the question (early withdrawal of IRA funds, making excess contributions, and failing to take required minimum distributions) are not prohibited transactions, but they will result in additional taxes and penalties for the taxpayer.

100. The answer is B. Stephanie may file as single, claiming her daughter as a dependent, and claim the Earned Income Credit. Hannah is a qualifying child of both Stephanie and Fred, because she meets the relationship, age, residency, support, and joint return tests for both of them. However, only one taxpayer can claim the child as a dependent. Since Stephanie did not pay the costs of keeping up the home, she does not qualify for head of household filing status.

Answers to Exam #2: Individuals

1. The answer is B. Angelo will not owe an underpayment penalty. Even though he will owe tax at the end of 2015, Angelo will not incur the underpayment penalty for 2015 because he had no tax liability in 2014.

2. The answer is A. There is a special rule for homes that are rented for fewer than 15 days a year. In this case, the rental income is not reported. A taxpayer's home can be rented out for less than 15 days each year without the need to report the rental income. This is the "de minimis rental" rule. In this scenario, the house is still considered the taxpayer's personal residence, so the owner can deduct mortgage interest and property taxes on Schedule A as they normally would. The rental expenses would not be deductible.

3. The answer is B. Starting in 2015, a taxpayer can make only one rollover from one IRA to another IRA in any 1-year period. However, the taxpayer can continue to make unlimited trustee-to-trustee transfers between IRAs because this type of transfer is not considered a rollover. There is no limit to the number of IRA conversions (a conversion from a traditional IRA to a Roth IRA).

4. The answer is D. To qualify for the Premium Tax Credit, married taxpayers generally must file jointly (with limited exceptions for situations such as spousal abuse or abandonment). They meet the income eligibility requirements, since household income must be from 100-400% of the federal poverty line for their family size. It is not necessary for each taxpayer to have been enrolled for all 12 months of the year. A taxpayer, his spouse (if filing a joint return), or his dependents must have been enrolled at some point during the year in one or more qualified health plans offered through the Health Insurance Marketplace (both federal and state exchanges).

5. The answer is A. The nanny is a household employee. Household employees include housekeepers, maids, babysitters, gardeners, and others who work in or around a taxpayer's private residence as employees. If an employer pays a household employee wages of less than $1,900 in 2015, the employer does not have to report and pay Social Security and Medicare taxes on that employee's wages. However, the wages are still taxable to the nanny and must be reported on her own tax return. This threshold goes up from $1,900 to $2,000 in 2016.

6. The answer is D. There are two separate reporting requirements that may apply for taxpayers who hold certain types of foreign assets or who have certain amounts of funds in foreign bank accounts. An FBAR generally must be filed with the Treasury Department if a taxpayer has more than $10,000 in offshore bank accounts. Taxpayers also must file a statement with the IRS if they hold foreign financial assets with an aggregate value that exceeds $50,000 ($100,000 MFJ) on the last day of the tax year, or that exceeds $75,000 ($150,000 MFJ) at any time during the tax year. In Collette's case, since her funds in her foreign accounts totaled $52,000 on the last day of the tax year, she is required to file both Form 8938, *Statement of Specified Foreign Financial Assets,* and an FBAR. The FBAR must be filed electronically by June 30, 2016.

7. The answer is B. The sales price was $4,400, which was $1,900 more than the original basis of $2,500 ($2,400 cost + $100 commission) of the shares. The broker's commission would be deducted when figuring the amount of gain. The gain is the difference between the sales price and the adjusted basis.

8. The answer is C. The additional Medicare tax of .9% is applied to their earned income ($155,000 + $18,000 + $176,000 = $349,000) above the threshold for a taxpayer's filing status. Tracy's court settlement is not taxable because it is for an injury or illness. Therefore, Tracy and Kevin owe $891 ($349,000 - $250,000 = $99,000 × .009 = $891). Employers are required to withhold the additional Medicare tax if the individual is paid more than $200,000, regardless of the individual's filing status. Tracy and Kevin may request additional withholding by their employers (or make estimated tax payments) since their compensation is over the $250,000 earned income threshold for this tax for couples filing jointly.

9. The answer is C. The maximum amount of investment income he can have and still claim the Earned Income Credit is $3,400 for tax year 2015.

10. The answer is B. Only one of the children, Patricia, received a gift in excess of the 2015 exemption amount of $14,000. The excess portion of $2,500 ($16,500 - $14,000 yearly gift limit) would be considered a taxable gift for purposes of filing a gift tax return. However, Shane can use a portion of his basic exclusion amount to avoid payment of gift tax in 2015. A gift tax return would need to be filed to report the gift.

11. The answer is B. Jenni is allowed to take a portion of the rental losses, but her deduction is limited. The special allowance is limited to $12,500 for married individuals who file MFS, if they lived apart from their spouses during the tax year. For married taxpayers who live together and file separately, the rental losses are completely disallowed in the current year and must be carried forward.

12. The answer is D. Only the amount that exceeds the value of the benefit received (the dinner) would be deductible as a charitable gift. Therefore, Pearl must deduct the value of the dinners ($20 × 6 tickets = $120) from the amount she paid. The answer is $160 ($280 - $120 = $160).

13. The answer is A. It is calculated as follows:

Wages #1 job	$5,000
Wages #2 job	18,500
Gross wages	23,500
Subtract allowable capital loss	(3,000)
Gross income	20,500
Early withdrawal penalty	(130)
Adjusted gross income	**$20,370**

The allowable capital loss is $3,000. Individuals can deduct up to $3,000 of net capital losses against non-capital gain income. This allowable capital loss is subtracted from total gross wages to determine gross income. The early withdrawal penalty is allowed as an adjustment to income to arrive at adjusted gross income (AGI).

14. The answer is C. Amounts contributed to an FSA are not subject to employment or federal income taxes. Health flexible spending arrangements (FSAs) allow employees to be reimbursed for medical expenses. FSAs are usually funded through voluntary salary reduction agreements with an employer. Employers may also contribute. Unlike HSAs and Archer MSAs, for which contributions must be reported on Form 1040, there are no reporting requirements for FSAs on a taxpayer's individual return.

15. The answer is B. Bernhard can claim only one personal exemption on his Form 1040NR. Nonresident aliens are generally not allowed to claim dependency exemptions. They are also not allowed to claim the standard deduction.

16. The answer is C. For 2015 IRA contributions, a taxpayer may contribute at any time during 2015 and up until April 18, 2016 (the filing deadline for 2015 individual returns). Filing an extension does not extend the IRA contribution deadline. However, if the taxpayer makes a contribution after January 1, but before the April 18 deadline, he will still need to designate the contribution year.

17. The answer is B. The gift is subject to both the gift tax and the generation-skipping transfer tax. The generation-skipping transfer tax is imposed separately and *in addition to* estate and gift taxes.

18. The answer is C. The taxpayer can undo the conversion through a recharacterization. A taxpayer may undo or reverse a rollover or conversion from one type of IRA to a different type of IRA through a *recharacterization*. Essentially, by recharacterizing an IRA, it is as if the conversion or rollover never occurred. A recharacterization can only be done through a trustee, and it must be completed by October 15 of the year after the taxpayer made the initial conversion. The deadline applies even if the taxpayer did not request an extension to file her return, and filed her return on or before the April 15 deadline.

19. The answer is B. For individuals, a 3.8% tax is imposed on the lesser of:

- The individual's net investment income for the year, or
- Any excess of the individual's modified adjusted gross income for the tax year over certain thresholds.

Net investment income does not include earned income, such as wages or self-employment earnings. Retirement income is also not included in net investment income, so Phil's net investment income is $36,000, the total of his capital gains, rental income, and dividend income. Phil's MAGI exceeds the threshold for single filers by $71,000 ($271,000 - $200,000). Since $36,000 is less than $71,000, that is the amount on which the net investment income tax would be calculated ($36,000 × 3.8% = $1,368).

20. The answer is C. Because Kaia provides over one-half of her own support, she will claim her own exemption. Therefore, she is also responsible for her own health coverage.

21. The answer is D. Individuals, estates, and trusts may receive a tax credit for alternative minimum tax paid in a prior year, if they are not liable for AMT in the current year. The credit is figured on Form 8801, *Credit for Prior Year Minimum Tax-Individuals, Estates, and Trusts*. A taxpayer must calculate how much of the AMT paid in prior years was related to deferral items, which generate credit for future years, as opposed to exclusion items, which are not deductible for the AMT. Any applicable credit from prior years is then carried forward to the current year. The amount of the minimum tax credit that is carried forward then reduces a taxpayer's regular tax for the current year, but the amount cannot be reduced below the tentative minimum tax. Any additional amount of the credit not used would be carried forward to the subsequent year.

22. The answer is C. Leonard's gross estate totals $6,750,000 ($50,000 of income in respect of a decedent + $700,000 of cash and investments + $1 million of life insurance proceeds + $5 million of other property). Allowable deductions of $90,000 are made from the gross estate ($40,000 burial expenses + $30,000 administration expenses + $20,000 state death tax) to arrive at the taxable estate of $6,660,000. The basic exclusion amount is $5.43 million in 2015, but Leonard had used $2 million of that amount during his lifetime, so only $3.43 million of his estate can be shielded from estate tax. Therefore, the amount of Leonard's estate that is subject to estate tax in 2015 is $3.23 million ($6.66 million minus $3.43 million). The self-employment earnings he had earned, but had not been paid at the time of his death, is income in respect of a decedent (IRD). IRD is included in the decedent's estate and may be subject to estate tax.

23. The answer is B. Since both Ling and Bao are under the age of 65, they can deduct only the portion of their medical expenses that exceeds 10% of their AGI ($68,000 × .10 = $6,800). Their deduction is calculated as follows: ($19,500 in medical expenses - $6,800 10% of AGI) = $12,700 in allowable deductions.

24. The answer is D. Taxpayers can deduct the cost and upkeep of uniforms if the uniforms are not suitable for everyday use. Taxpayers cannot deduct the cost of regular clothing used for work. The clothing must be specifically required by the employer. Eddie can only claim the amount of expenses that exceeds 2% of his adjusted gross income. The expense is deductible on Schedule A (Form 1040) as a miscellaneous itemized deduction, subject to the 2% floor.

25. The answer is A. A taxpayer's gross estate will be valued either on the date of death or six months after the date of death, which is the alternate valuation date and is determined by the executor of an estate. If a taxpayer dies on March 18, the alternate valuation date is September 18.

26. The answer is C. Because she signed a joint return knowing that it was false, Kaitlyn would not qualify for innocent spouse relief or relief from separation of liability. However, given her personal circumstances, Kaitlyn may be eligible for equitable spouse relief. The IRS will review equitable spouse relief requests to determine the fairness of a tax assessment in light of an individual taxpayer's circumstances. In some cases, the spouse requesting relief may have known about the understated or underpaid tax on a return, but did not challenge the treatment for fear of her spouse's retaliation. Under revised rules, the taxpayer has up to ten years to request equitable relief. Form 8857, *Request for Innocent Spouse Relief*, is used to request all three types of relief: innocent spouse, separation of liability, and equitable spouse.

27. The answer is C. Wilson's office is 20% (240 ÷ 1,200) of the total area of his home. Therefore, his business percentage is 20%. His expenses for the year were $12,000 ($1,000 per month × 12 months) and $600 ($50 × 12 months). The answer is calculated as follows:

$12,000 total rent
$600 total utilities
$12,600 total expenses for the year × 20% (business-use percentage) = **$2,520.**

28. The answer is A. Debt cancellation that occurs prior to filing for bankruptcy does not qualify for the exclusion. However, canceled debts may be excluded from taxable income if the debts are forgiven as part of a Title 11 bankruptcy proceeding. The debt must be discharged through bankruptcy and not before the filing.

29. The answer is A. Kayla meets the support test because she did not provide half of her own support. The support test determines the level of support by the child, not the person who wants to claim the child as a dependent. A person's own funds are not counted as support unless they are *actually spent* for support. Children generally do not provide more than half of their own support during the tax year. Since Kayla's income was deposited into a trust fund for college, it is not figured in the support calculation. Therefore, Kayla's parents can claim their daughter as a dependent on their return.

30. The answer is A. Keith and Tiffany can deduct the interest on their loans because the total amount of the home equity loan throughout 2015 ($72,000) does not exceed $100,000, and it is not more than the home's fair market value minus any outstanding acquisition debt ($230,000 - $30,000 = $200,000).

31. The answer is A. A foster child may be treated just like a biological child for purposes of the Earned Income Credit. A child is an eligible foster child if the child is placed with the taxpayer by an authorized placement agency or by judgment, decree, or other order of any court.

32. The answer is B. Josh and Heather can each make a maximum contribution of $5,500 to a traditional IRA. This is because Josh, who has no compensation, can add Heather's compensation, reduced by the amount of her IRA contribution ($50,000 - $5,500 = $44,500) to his own compensation ($0) to figure his maximum contribution to a traditional IRA. Only those age 50 and above can contribute $6,500 to an IRA in 2015.

33. The answer is D. The stock is restricted, so Faith does not have constructive receipt of it. She should not report any income until she receives the stock without restrictions. Constructive receipt does not require physical possession of the item of income. However, there are substantial restrictions on the stock's disposition, because Faith must complete another four years of service before she can sell or otherwise dispose of the stock.

34. The answer is C. Dylan's deductible expense would be calculated as follows: $300 + $245 + $150 + $30 ($60 × 50%) = $725. All of the expenses are qualifying work-related educational expenses, but the meal expense must be reduced by 50%. Employees can deduct work-related educational expenses as a miscellaneous itemized deduction on Form 1040, Schedule A. The deduction is subject to the 2% of adjusted gross income limitation.

35. The answer is C. Chuck can exclude up to $250,000 of gain on a separate or joint return for 2015. The $500,000 maximum exclusion for joint returns does not apply because Julie does not meet the use test.

36. The answer is B. In 2015, the Adoption Credit is nonrefundable. Therefore, Vanessa will receive a carryover of $1,500 that she can use in the following year (or, if needed, up to five years following the year the credit was generated). To claim the credit, the taxpayer must complete Form 8839, *Qualified Adoption Expenses*, and attach it to her Form 1040.

37. The answer is D. Income in respect of a decedent (IRD) is any taxable income that was earned but not received by the decedent by the time of death. IRD is not taxed on the final return of the deceased taxpayer. IRD is reported on the tax return of the person (or entity) that receives the income. This could be the estate, in which case it would be reported on Form 1041. Otherwise, it could be the surviving spouse or another beneficiary, such as a child. IRD is included in the decedent's estate and may be subject to estate tax. If it is received by a beneficiary and subject to income tax on the beneficiary's return, the beneficiary can claim a deduction for estate tax paid on the IRD. This deduction is taken as a miscellaneous itemized deduction on Schedule A and is not subject to the 2% floor.

38. The answer is A. Long-term care expenses are an itemized medical deduction, only deductible to the extent they exceed 10% of AGI (or 7.5% if the taxpayer is 65 or older). The other answers are all deductions that are allowed as adjustments to income on Form 1040.

39. The answer is C. Sarah's venture is most likely a hobby. It is presumed that an activity is not a hobby if it generated a profit in three of the last five years, including the current year. Income from a hobby is taxable and is reported on Form 1040, Line 21 as "other income". Sarah can deduct her expenses, but only up to the amount of her hobby income. She would report $950 as a miscellaneous expense, subject to the 2%-of-AGI threshold.

40. The answer is C. Jennifer's total itemized deduction for taxes is $4,000 ($2,000 + $1,900 + $100 = $4,000). The $250 homeowners' association fee is not deductible. All the other costs are deductible as taxes.

41. The answer is A. Contributions are not deductible for federal tax purposes. Section 529 plans are also known as qualified tuition programs. They are generally maintained by states or by educational institutions.

42. The answer is A. The value of the free use of a taxpayer's property is not allowed as a charitable deduction. Qualified contributions must be made in cash or property.

43. The answer is B. The Lifetime Learning Credit is limited to $2,000 per tax return. The credit is calculated as 20% of the first $10,000 of qualifying costs, regardless of the number of qualifying students, with a maximum credit of $2,000 ($10,000 × .20). The Lifetime Learning Credit can be used for a student who is not eligible for the American Opportunity Credit. However, a taxpayer cannot claim both the American Opportunity Credit and the Lifetime Learning Credit for the same student on the same return.

44. The answer is A. The distribution from the estate would be reported to Madison on Schedule K-1 (Form 1041). Nonpassive distributions would be reported on Schedule E (Form 1040). How a taxpayer reports distributions from an estate depends on the character of the income in the hands of the estate. Each item of income retains the same character. For example, if the income distributed includes dividends, tax-exempt interest, or capital gains, it would retain the same character in the hands of the beneficiary. Business income and other nonpassive income that is distributed from an estate would be reported on Part III of the taxpayer's Schedule E (Form 1040). The estate's personal representative (executor) should provide a Schedule K-1 (Form 1041) to each beneficiary who receives a distribution from the estate. The personal representative handling the estate must furnish Schedule K-1 to each beneficiary by the date on which Form 1041 is filed.

45. The answer is D. A recovery is a refund or return of an amount for which a taxpayer deducted or took a credit in an earlier year. A taxpayer must include a recovery in income in the year he receives it, to the extent the deduction or credit reduced his tax in the earlier year. Refunds of federal income taxes are never included in a taxpayer's income because they are not allowed as a deduction.

46. The answer is A. Although Lenny owned the ten shares he received as a nontaxable stock dividend for only three months, all the stock has a long-term holding period. Stock acquired as a stock dividend has the same holding period as the original stock owned. Because he bought the stock for $1,500 three years ago, his holding period is long-term. Lenny has a long-term capital gain of $530 on the sale of the 510 shares.

47. The answer is C. Raymond is allowed to roll over his traditional IRA into a government deferred-compensation plan (section 457 plan). Taxpayers are allowed to roll over their traditional IRA to any of the following plans without incurring tax or penalty:
- A rollover into another traditional IRA
- A qualified plan
- A tax-sheltered annuity plan (section 403(b) plan)
- A government deferred-compensation plan (section 457 plan)

IRAs cannot be held jointly, so spouses are not allowed to roll over funds into each other's retirement plans. However, a taxpayer is allowed to roll over an IRA from a deceased spouse. After death, the surviving spouse may elect to treat the IRA as his own and roll it over into another traditional IRA.

48. The answer is B. Any amount that is reduced due to a contingency related to the child (such as the child dying, getting married, or going to school) is considered by the IRS to be child support, rather than alimony. Child support payments are neither deductible by the payer nor taxable to the payee.

49. The answer is C. A taxpayer generally cannot deduct charitable contributions that exceed 50% of her adjusted gross income. The 50% limit applies to contributions made to churches; hospitals; most schools; state or federal government units; and corporations, trusts, or foundations organized solely for charitable, religious, educational, scientific, or literary purposes or for the prevention of cruelty to children or animals. Certain other organizations, including veterans groups, fraternal societies, and nonprofit cemeteries, are subject to a 30%-of-AGI limitation. The Veterans of Foreign Wars is a 30% organization, so the deductible portion of this contribution could be limited to $18,000 ($60,000 × 30%). Roxanne's total deduction is limited to $30,000 ($60,000 AGI × 50%).

50. The answer is A. The basis of property received as a gift is figured differently than property that is purchased. Generally, the basis of gifted property is the same in the hands of the donee as it was in the hands of the donor, but it may also include the amount of gift tax paid by a donor, if any. If the fair market value of the property on the date of the gift is less than the transferred basis, the donee's basis for gain is the transferred basis. However, if the donee reports a loss on the sale of gifted property when the property's FMV was less than the donor's basis at the time of the gift, his basis is the FMV of gifted property at the time of the gift. The sale of gifted property can also result in no gain or loss. This happens when the sale proceeds are greater than the gift's FMV, but less than the transferred basis when the property's FMV was less than the donor's basis at the time of the gift. Lawrence has a $1,500 gain because he uses the donor's adjusted basis at the time of the gift ($50,000) plus the amount that he spent to clear the property ($1,500) as the basis to figure gain. Therefore, since he sold the property for $53,000, he has a $1,500 gain, calculated as follows:

$$(\$50,000 + \$1,500) = \$51,500 \text{ basis}$$
$$(\$53,000 - \$51,500) = \mathbf{\$1,500 \text{ gain on sale}}$$

51. The answer is A. Unlike a traditional IRA, Roth IRAs do not require minimum distributions at age 70½.

52. The answer is C. Walter must repay the excess advance premium tax credit payments that were paid to his insurance company. When enrolling in a Health Insurance Marketplace plan, a taxpayer must choose whether to have some or all of the expected Premium Tax Credit paid to his insurance company or wait to claim the benefit on his tax return. A taxpayer who chooses advance credit payments must file a tax return, regardless of whether he meets any other filing requirements, in order to reconcile the advance credit payments with the actual Premium Tax Credit earned. This reconciliation is calculated on Form 8962. If the credit allowed is less than the advance credit payments received, normally the difference will be subtracted from the taxpayer's refund or added to his balance due.

53. The answer is D. The full amount of $5,000 is taxable to Clark, because if a student is not a degree candidate, all scholarships are subject to federal income tax, even if they are spent on educational expenses. The student must also attend an eligible educational institution.

54. The answer is C. For an involuntary conversion in a federally-declared disaster area, the taxpayer has up to four years after the end of the tax year in which any gain is realized to replace her principal residence (rather than the normal two-year replacement period) or to pay tax on any gain. Real property that is held for investment or used in a trade or business is allowed a three-year replacement period. The replacement period is generally for four years for livestock involuntarily converted because of weather-related conditions.

55. The answer is D. Rebecca is a statutory nonemployee. Veranda would issue Rebecca a Form 1099-MISC for commissions, and Rebecca would file Schedule C to report her income and expenses. There are generally two categories of statutory nonemployees: direct sellers and licensed real estate agents. They are treated as self-employed for all federal tax purposes, including income and employment taxes, if:
- Substantially all payments for their services as direct sellers or real estate agents are directly related to sales or other output, rather than to the number of hours worked, and
- Their services are performed under a written contract providing that they will not be treated as employees for federal tax purposes.

56. The answer is C. Janice must file a Schedule C for the restaurant showing her net profit of $25,000, and Marty must file his own Schedule C for the carpentry business showing his net loss of $1,500. Janice's Schedule SE will show total earnings subject to SE tax of $25,000. Even if taxpayers file a joint return, they cannot file a joint Schedule SE. This is true whether one spouse or both spouses have earnings subject to self-employment tax. Married taxpayers cannot use losses from each other's businesses to offset self-employment tax. However, if an individual taxpayer operates multiple businesses, he must combine the net profit (or loss) from each to determine total earnings subject to SE tax. A loss from one business offsets the profit from another business. For example, if

Janice had been running two businesses, the loss from the second business would have reduced her overall profit and also her self-employment tax.

57. The answer is B. The maximum amount taxpayers can claim for the nonrefundable Child Tax Credit is $1,000 for each qualifying child. The amount actually claimed on Form 1040 depends on the taxpayer's tax liability, modified adjusted gross income (MAGI), and filing status. This credit is phased out once MAGI reaches the following income levels:
- Married filing jointly: $110,000
- Single, head of household, or qualifying widow(er): $75,000
- Married filing separately: $55,000

In the phaseout range, the Child Tax Credit is reduced by $50 for each $1,000 of income above these threshold amounts.

58. The answer is B. Nora does not need to itemize deductions in order to claim the adjustment for the penalty on early withdrawal of savings. The deduction can be claimed on Form 1040 or Form 1040A.

59. The answer is A. If a taxpayer has more than one employer and her total compensation is over the $118,500 Social Security base limit for 2015, too much Social Security tax may have been withheld. In this case, Zoe can claim the excess as a credit against her income tax. If she files Form 1040, she would enter the excess amount on line 71.

60. The answer is D. All of the charges are deductible as mortgage interest, so their deduction is $14,370 ($12,200 + $50 + $120 + $2,000). Taxpayers can deduct a late payment charge on a mortgage loan as mortgage interest. Sometimes, if a person pays off his home mortgage early, he must pay a penalty. The taxpayer can deduct a prepayment penalty as home mortgage interest, provided the penalty is not for a specific service performed or cost incurred in connection with the mortgage loan. When taxpayers sell their home, they can deduct home mortgage interest paid up to, but not including, the date of the sale.

61. The answer is D. Unlike divorce, an annulment legally invalidates a marriage and is effective on a retroactive basis. A court decree of annulment deems that no valid marriage ever existed. Therefore, the taxpayer is considered unmarried even if he filed joint returns for earlier years. A taxpayer whose marriage is annulled must file Form 1040X claiming single or head of household status for all tax years affected by the annulment that are not closed by the statute of limitations for filing an amended tax return. Taxpayers may choose to file MFJ if they are:
- Married and living together as husband and wife.
- Living together in a common law marriage recognized by their state.
- Married and living apart but not legally separated under a decree of divorce or separate maintenance.
- Separated under an interlocutory (not final) decree of divorce.
- Married to a nonresident alien and elect to file jointly. The nonresident spouse must request an ITIN in order to file jointly.

62. The answer is C. When the owner of a traditional IRA reaches 70½ years old, the funds must be distributed in annual required minimum distributions (RMDs). The first RMD payment can be delayed until April 1 of the year following the year the taxpayer turns 70½. The distribution for each subsequent year must be made by December

31. The amount of each RMD is based on IRS tables. Since Sharon reaches age 70½ on August 8, 2015, she must take her first RMD by April 1, 2016.

63. The answer is C. A legitimate nonbusiness bad debt is reported as a short-term capital loss on Form 8949, *Sales and Other Dispositions of Capital Assets,* and Schedule D. It is subject to the capital loss limit of $3,000 per year, or $1,500 if the taxpayer files MFS. The taxpayer must include a detailed bad debt statement with a description of the debt, the amount, and the date it became due; the name of the debtor; the efforts made to collect the debt; and the reason the debt is worthless.

64. The answer is D. It is calculated as follows:

Wages reported on Form W-2	$42,000
Gambling winnings	2,000
Gambling losses	NO DEDUCTION
Dependent care benefits (spent $3,200 on childcare)	n/a
Capital loss carryover from prior year	(3,000)
Gross income shown on return	**$41,000**

The dependent care benefits are not taxable because Luke's dependent care expenses exceeded the benefit payments. The gross gambling winnings must be included in income. The gambling losses are only deductible as an itemized deduction and only to the extent of gambling winnings. If Luke does not itemize, he cannot deduct his gambling losses. The capital loss carryover is deductible, but only up to $3,000, the annual capital loss deduction limit.

65. The answer is D. If a taxpayer must file a U.S. tax return, or is listed on a tax return as a spouse or dependent and does not have and cannot obtain a valid SSN, he must apply for an ITIN.

66. The answer is C. Abigail must include $4,000 in her gross income. The distributable net income is less than the amounts authorized for distribution by Gerald's will, so Abigail must include $4,000 in her gross income ([$5,000 ÷ $7,500] × $6,000), and the daughter must include $2,000 in her gross income ([$2,500 ÷ $7,500] × $6,000).

67. The answer is D. In the case of personal-use property (such as a personal home or vehicle), any casualty losses are subject to reductions of $100 and 10%-of-AGI. This means that once Penelope has subtracted any insurance reimbursement, she must subtract $100 from each casualty. Then she must further reduce the aggregate loss amount by 10% of adjusted gross income. The answer is calculated as follows:

$58,000 casualty loss - $50,000 insurance reimbursement = $8,000 realized loss $8,000 loss - $100 reduction = $7,900 $22,000 AGI × 10% = $2,200 $7,900 - $2,200 (10% of the taxpayer's AGI) = **$5,700 allowable casualty loss deduction**
Note: Remember that casualty losses of business property are not subject to the reductions of $100 and 10%-of-AGI; they are deductible in full.

68. The answer is D. Employee business expenses are a miscellaneous itemized deduction, not an adjustment to income. Some of the most common adjustments to income include:
- Individual retirement arrangements (IRAs)
- Alimony paid
- Bad debt deduction
- Moving expenses
- Student loan interest deduction
- Tuition and fees deduction
- Educator expense deduction
- Self-employed health insurance
- Jury duty pay given to the taxpayer's employer

69. The answer is B. Royalties from copyrights, patents, and oil, gas, and mineral properties are taxable as ordinary income. In most cases, royalties are reported as passive income on Schedule E. The amounts are generally subject to income tax, but not to self-employment tax. However, taxpayers who are in business as self-employed writers, inventors, artists, etc. must report this income on Schedule C, in which case the amounts would be subject to SE tax as well as income tax.

70. The answer is A. These expenses are deductible on Schedule A as a miscellaneous itemized deduction, subject to the 2% floor. They are deductible because they relate to Matt's investment activity. The tax code allows for a deduction for the production or collection of income, such as the management of investments. Since investing is not a self-employment activity (unless a person is a bona fide securities dealer), the costs related to this activity, such as the safe deposit box and the subscriptions to the investing magazines, would not go on Schedule C.

71. The answer is C. Jeremiah's gross profit is $25,000 ($125,000 selling price − $100,000 adjusted basis), and his gross profit percentage is 20% ($25,000 ÷ $125,000). He must report 20% of each payment received (excluding the portion representing interest income) as gain from the sale. Thus, $5,000 (20% of the $25,000 down payment) is taxable in 2015.

72. The answer is B. The Saver's Credit, formally known as the Retirement Savings Contribution Credit, is a maximum of $2,000 for couples filing jointly ($1,000 for other filing statuses). The actual credit amount depends on the amount of a taxpayer's eligible contributions to a retirement plan during the year and his AGI. The credit is a percentage of the qualifying contribution amount, with the highest rate for taxpayers at the lowest income levels. The Saver's Credit can be claimed in addition to other tax benefits that may result from retirement contributions, such as deducting part or all of the contributions to a traditional IRA.

73. The answer is B. Because David's new job location is 57 miles farther from his former home than the distance from his former home was to his old job location, he meets the distance test. A move will meet the distance test if the new main job location is at least 50 miles farther from the former home than the old job location was from the former home. For example, if the old job location was three miles from the former home, the new main job location must be at least 53 miles from that former home. Deductible moving expenses include moving household goods and personal effects (including in-transit or foreign-move storage expenses) and traveling (including lodging, but not meals) to a new home. A taxpayer can include the cost of storage and insuring household goods within any period of 30 consecutive days before or after the moving day.

74. The answer is A. The gross estate tax is reduced by the *applicable credit*, also referred to as the *unified credit*, which is a tax credit amount that corresponds with the basic exclusion amount and, if applicable, the DSUE available to a surviving spouse. An applicable credit amount of $2,117,800 in 2015 corresponds with the basic exclusion amount of $5.43 million. Just as with the basic exclusion amount, any portion of the applicable credit amount used to avoid payment of gift taxes reduces the amount of credit available in later years that can be used to offset gift or estate taxes. Since Bonnie had used the full $2,117,800 applicable credit to avoid payment of gift taxes during her lifetime, she exhausted her entire $5.43 million basic exclusion and her estate is liable for tax on the taxable estate without further offset.

75. The answer is A. A taxpayer must recognize income in the year when she has constructive receipt of the funds. Constructive receipt occurred on December 26, 2015, when the check arrived at Janet's home and was available for Janet to deposit. It is not necessary for a taxpayer to have actual physical possession of the income. However, for constructive receipt to have taken place, funds must be available without substantial limitations. If there are significant restrictions on the income or if the income is not accessible to the taxpayer, it is not considered to have been constructively received.

76. The answer is A. VA disability compensation is generally exempt from federal and state income tax, and from Social Security and Medicare taxes. The veteran must have been terminated through separation or discharge under honorable conditions. The VA does not issue Form W-2, Form 1099-R, or any other document for veterans' disability benefits.

77. The answer is C. It is calculated as follows: (7 × $25= $175 + $59 = $234). A taxpayer's deduction for business gifts is limited to $25 per customer or client during the each year. Fees for shipping and packaging do not count toward the $25 limit.

78. The answer is B. All of the income is taxable except the inheritance. Amounts received in the form of gifts or inheritances are not included in taxable income.

79. The answer is A. The depreciable basis for the building is limited to the value of the building ($150,000). Land is never depreciated. Since residential rental property is depreciated over 27.5 years, a basis of $150,000 would generate depreciation of $5,455 per year ($150,000/27.5 years). Rental activity is reported on Schedule E, *Supplemental Income and Loss*. The depreciation of rentals is reported on Form 4562, *Depreciation and Amortization*.

80. The answer is A. The unemployment compensation is not qualifying income for purposes of an IRA contribution. Since his wages were only $5,000 for the year, Kenneth has made a $1,500 excess contribution to his IRA. He must correct the excess contribution, or he will have to pay an excise tax on any excess amount that remains in the account at the end of the year. The tax on excess contributions is 6%.

81. The answer is C. The life insurance premiums and vitamins are not qualified medical expenses. Because George and Kristin are self-employed, they can deduct the health insurance premiums as an adjustment to income on line 29 of Form 1040. The other medical expenses are deductible only to the extent they exceed the 10%-of-AGI limit. The answer is calculated as follows:

Copayments for prescription drugs	$750
Dental fees	1,200
Health insurance premiums (for self-employed taxpayers, these are an adjustment to income and not included in calculation of medical expenses on Schedule A)	8,500
Life insurance premiums	None
Orthodontia fees	1,500
Vitamins	None
Emergency room bill	7,000
Prescription eyeglasses	350
Total qualified medical expenses on Schedule A before application of the AGI limit (not including health insurance premiums)	**$10,800**

$10,800 qualified expenses - $5,800 ($58,000 × 10% = $5,800) = $5,000 allowable deduction on Schedule A.

82. The answer is B. Laverne can deduct $4,500, subject to the 2% limit, as a miscellaneous itemized deduction. Legal fees for a divorce are not a deductible expense. However, because a taxpayer must include alimony received in gross income, she can deduct legal fees related to the collection of alimony. A taxpayer can also deduct fees paid to appraisers, actuaries, and accountants for tax advice or for services related to the determination of correct tax. An individual taxpayer can deduct these legal fees only if she itemizes deductions on Schedule A (Form 1040). They are reported as a miscellaneous itemized deduction subject to the 2%-of-adjusted gross income limit.

83. The answer is B. A debt is genuine if it arises from a debtor-creditor relationship based on a valid and enforceable obligation to repay a fixed or determinable sum of money. There must be a profit motive in order for the loan to qualify as a true debtor-creditor relationship. If a taxpayer lends money to a relative or friend with the understanding that it will not be repaid, it is considered a gift and not a loan. Unless a taxpayer has documentation that proves otherwise, the IRS generally considers loans to relatives or friends to be gifts.

84. The answer is B. The maximum taxable amount of a taxpayer's Social Security benefits subject to tax is 85%. Here, Rose has enough additional income, based on her filing status, to have the maximum amount of Social Security benefits subject to tax. Therefore, the maximum amount that is taxable on Rose's net benefits is 85% or $10,540 ($12,400 × .85).

85. The answer is D. Benny and Arabella must report the amount that was credited to their mutual fund account, regardless of the amount that was actually distributed to them. Capital gains distributions from a mutual fund are always reported as long-term, regardless of how long the taxpayer has held the shares. Investors may have to pay taxes on any capital gains distribution they receive, even if the fund performed poorly after they bought shares.

86. The answer is C. An employee can generally exclude $5,000 from an employer-financed flexible spending account. However, if a taxpayer is filing MFS, the maximum she can exclude is $2,500. Benefits that are in excess of those limits ($5,000/$2,500 for MFS) are included in gross income. Terry cannot take the Child and Dependent Care Credit for any of the remaining amounts, because in order to claim this credit, the taxpayer's filing status generally must be single, head of household, qualifying widow(er), or married filing jointly.

87. The answer is D. Sierra's income is subject to the kiddie tax. Part of a child's investment income may be taxed at a parent's marginal rate if:

- The child's investment income is more than $2,000.
- The child is under age 18 or a full-time college student under age 24.
- The child is required to file a tax return for the tax year.
- At least one of the child's parents was alive at the end of the year.
- The child does not file a joint return for the tax year.

Parents can avoid paying the kiddie tax only if the child is age 18 or older and has enough earned income to provide greater than half of her own support. In that case, the tax would be based on the child's tax rate and not the parent's. Sierra's unearned income is $2,200. This is the total of her dividends ($1,200), taxable interest ($900), and capital gains reduced by capital losses ($500 - $400 = $100). Her wages are considered earned income, rather than unearned income, because they are for work performed. Her tax-exempt interest is not considered in determining unearned income for this purpose.

88. The answer is C. The basic exclusion amount for an estate is $5.43 million in 2015. Since Joaquin had used $2 million of his exclusion to offset payments of gift tax during his lifetime, the amount his estate may exclude was reduced to $3.43 million ($5.43 basic exclusion minus $2 million). That amount is subtracted from his taxable estate, and estate tax will be calculated based upon a net amount of $4.57 million ($8 million minus $3.43 million).

89. The answer is B. Compensatory damages resulting from personal physical injuries or physical sickness, including reimbursement of medical bills (that were not previously deducted) and lost wages, are generally not taxable income, whether they are from a settlement or from an actual court award, unless they are punitive damages. However, interest associated with an award or settlement is always taxable.

90. The answer is A. In 2015, anyone can make a qualified rollover contribution to a Roth IRA regardless of the taxpayer's modified AGI. If a taxpayer wants to convert a traditional IRA to a Roth IRA, he is required to pay federal income taxes on any pretax contributions, as well as any growth in the investment's value. Once the funds are converted to a Roth, all of the investment grows tax-free, and funds can be withdrawn on a tax-free basis. Although there are still income limits as to who can participate in a Roth IRA, anyone may convert an existing traditional IRA to a Roth IRA. Unlike other retirement plans, Roth IRA funds do not have to be withdrawn when a taxpayer reaches 70½.

91. The answer is A. Francis's taxable estate is calculated as follows:

Cash and investments	$325,000
Life insurance proceeds	1,000,000
Personal residence	500,000
Subtotal – gross estate	1,825,000
Funeral expenses	(25,000)
Administration expenses	(50,000)
Debts	(200,000)
Taxable estate before marital deduction	1,550,000
Marital deduction	(1,550,000)
Taxable estate	**$0**

Because Francis's spouse is a U.S. citizen, his estate is entitled to an unlimited marital deduction for assets passing to his spouse (up to the amount of his taxable estate).

92. The answer is B. There are special restrictions on EITC claims by taxpayers who have had previous EITC claims denied. A taxpayer who claimed the EITC due to reckless or intentional disregard of the EITC rules cannot claim the EITC for two tax years. If the error was due to fraud, the taxpayer cannot claim the EITC for ten tax years.

93. The answer is D. If a nonstatutory or nonqualified stock option is actively traded on an established market or its FMV is otherwise readily determinable, the employee who receives the option must recognize compensation income, either at the date of grant if there are no restrictions that affect its value to the employee, or at a later date when any restrictions no longer apply. If the option's FMV is not readily determinable at the date of grant, the difference between the exercise price and the market value of the stock on the exercise date must be recognized as ordinary income when the option is exercised. The employee's basis in the stock is the market value of the stock at grant or exercise (depending on which was used to determine his tax liability) plus any amount paid for the option itself. If he later sells the stock at a price higher than his basis, he would realize taxable gain on that sale.

94. The answer is D. Daniel and Maria can claim three exemptions on their tax return: one for Daniel, one for Maria, and one for Daniel's stepmother. If a taxpayer's qualifying person is a dependent parent, the taxpayer may still take a dependency exemption even if the parent does not live with the taxpayer.

95. The answer is D. A taxpayer may need to increase the federal income tax withheld from his pay or pension or make estimated tax payments to avoid an estimated tax penalty resulting from his liability for employment taxes in connection with household employees, as shown on Schedule H. The taxpayer has several options. He can:

- Increase his federal income tax withheld by giving his employer a new Form W-4
- Increase his federal income tax withheld by giving the payor of his pension a new Form W-4P, *Withholding Certificate for Pension or Annuity Payments*
- Make estimated tax payments by filing Form 1040-ES, *Estimated Tax for Individuals*

Estimated taxes must be withheld or paid as the tax liability is incurred, so a taxpayer cannot wait until he files his return (and Schedule H) to pay household taxes owed. The year is divided into four payment periods for estimated taxes, each with a specific payment due date:

First payment due	April 15
Second payment due	June 15
Third payment due	September 15
Fourth payment due	January 15 (of the following year)

96. The answer is B. Ramon can claim head of household status since his spouse is a nonresident alien who will not file a joint return with him, and he meets all the other qualifications for head of household. There is a special exception that allows U.S. citizens and resident alien spouses who live with their nonresident alien spouses to file as head of household. All of the following requirements must be met:

- The taxpayer is a U.S. citizen or resident alien for the entire year and meets all the rules for head of household except for living with the nonresident alien spouse.
- The nonresident alien spouse does not meet the substantial presence test.
- The nonresident alien spouse does not choose to file a joint return.

97. The answer is A. A refundable credit can reduce tax liability to zero, and the IRS will pay back (refund) any remaining credit to the taxpayer. Examples of refundable credits are the Premium Tax Credit, the Earned Income Tax Credit, and the Additional Child Tax Credit. In contrast, a nonrefundable credit can only reduce a taxpayer's tax liability for the year to zero.

98. The answer is C. Both taxpayers must file. Taxpayers who are under 65, use the married filing separately status, and earn at least $4,000 are required to file a return.

99. The answer is B. Passive activity losses are generally deductible only to the extent of passive activity income. Passive activity income can only be generated by a passive activity. There are only two sources of passive activity income:
1. A rental activity, or
2. A business/activity in which the taxpayer does not materially participate.

Nonpassive activities are businesses in which the taxpayer works on a regular, continuous, and substantial basis. In addition, passive activity income does not include salaries or investment income. Income and losses from the following activities generally would be considered passive: rental real estate, and operation of a farm or any other business in which the taxpayer does not actually participate. There are two exceptions to this passive activity loss limitation. First, when a taxpayer materially participates in a business, it is not generally considered a passive activity. Second, although rental real estate income is generally considered passive activity income, there is an exception in the law for real estate professionals.

100. The answer is C. Gael can choose to take distributions from the inherited IRA in full within five years of Leigh's death or take minimum distributions from the retirement account over his life expectancy. These distributions will be subject to income tax, but it will not be subject to the 10% early withdrawal penalty. He cannot roll over the inherited retirement plan into his own plan. The IRS generally imposes a 10% early withdrawal penalty on early distributions (distributions before age 59½). However, there are many exceptions to this rule, and one is when the original owner of the plan dies. Since Gael was Leigh's son, he cannot choose to roll over the amounts into his own plan (as only surviving spouses have this option).

Answers to Exam #3: Businesses

1. The answer is A. Since Structim Company is on the accrual basis, it reports income when it is earned, not when it is received. Structim must include the entire payment of $22,000 in 2015 income because that is when it was earned.

2. The answer is C. Payments made to an employee under an accountable plan would not be included on the employee's Form W-2. These are amounts that are not taxable to the employee and not reportable as wages. An accountable plan is a formal or written arrangement whereby an employer reimburses an employee for business expenses. The employee provides documentation of the expense, and the employer is allowed to deduct the expenses as normal business expenses. The employee does not have to recognize the reimbursements as income.

3. The answer is D. A closely held corporation generally has a small number of shareholders and no public market for its corporate stock. The corporate ownership and management often overlap. A corporation is considered to be closely held if all of the following apply:
- It is not a personal service corporation.
- At any time during the last half of the tax year, more than 50% of the value of its outstanding stock is, directly or indirectly, owned by or for five or fewer individuals. An individual in this case includes certain trusts and private foundations.

Closely held corporations are exempt from certain at-risk and passive activity limits, which can provide substantial tax benefits.

4. The answer is A. The gain and loss for the two portions of the property must be determined separately, as outlined in the following table. Gabby will have a taxable gain on the business portion of the property. The loss on the residential portion is not deductible.

Activity	Residential Part	Business Part
Condemnation award received	$45,000	$45,000
Minus the legal fees	(1,000)	(1,000)
Net condemnation award	44,000	44,000
Adjusted basis calculation		
Original cost, $75,000	37,500	37,500
Improvements, $15,000	7,500	7,500
Total	45,000	45,000
Minus depreciation	N/A	(20,000)
Adjusted basis, business part	0	25,000
Loss/gain on property	**($1,000)**	**$19,000**

5. The answer is C. The miles to the first site and the miles back home (10+8 =18) 18 miles are commuting miles and, therefore, not deductible. Cotto drives a total of 36 miles on this work day, but only 18 miles (13+ 5) are deductible as a business expense.

6. The answer is B. Mariangel's basis in the factory machinery is $12,000. Her partnership basis is reduced to zero. In a nonliquidating distribution, Mariangel's basis in the partnership must first be reduced by the cash distribution ($6,000). Her basis in the machinery then would be the lesser of:
- her remaining basis in the partnership, or
- the partnership's adjusted basis in the machinery.

The answer is calculated as follows:

Mariangel's starting partnership basis	$18,000
Reduced by cash distribution	(6,000)
Lesser of: $12,000 remaining basis or the partnership's basis in the property	**$12,000**

7. The answer is B. The Fun-ta Corporation exceeded the $50,000 threshold for deductible organizational costs by $3,000, so it must reduce its immediate deduction by this amount. Fun-ta can deduct $2,000 of its organizational costs ($5,000 maximum allowable deduction minus the excess of $3,000) immediately. The remaining amount of organizational costs, $51,000 ($53,000 - $2,000 allowable deduction), must be amortized over 180 months starting in the month it commences business. Although business start-up and organizational costs are generally capital expenditures, a business can elect to deduct up to $5,000 of business start-up and $5,000 of organizational costs.

8. The answer is D. An employee generally must have at least one year of service in order to be eligible. Often, this requirement may be defined as having worked 1,000 hours during the prior year. All of the other statements are correct.

9. The answer is C. Golden Touch Partnership is required to use April 30 as its tax year-end. A partnership generally must conform its tax year to its partners' tax years. If one or more partners own a majority interest (an interest in partnership profits and capital of more than 50%), the partnership must use the tax year of those partners. In this case, since Daisy Corporation and Aster Corporation share the same tax year and their combined partnership interest exceeds 50%, Golden Touch Partnership is required to use April 30 as its tax year-end.

10. The answer is A. A trust designed to claim unallowable deductions, such as depreciation on a personal residence, would be considered fraudulent, and the taxpayer would be subject to civil and/or criminal penalties. The other answers describe legitimate types of trusts.

11. The answer is D. Multitasker's taxable income is determined as follows:

Net income per books	$300,000
Plus federal income tax expense per books	4,000
Plus excess of capital losses over capital gains	10,000
Minus the tax-exempt interest income	(5,000)
Taxable income	**$309,000**

12. The answer is C. Jasmine will not be not required to request an EIN if she operates multiple businesses, as long as those businesses are all sole proprietorships without employees. A taxpayer will need an EIN if any of the following is true:
- She files for bankruptcy under Chapter 7 (liquidation) or Chapter 11 (reorganization) of the Bankruptcy Code.
- She incorporates or takes in partners to operate as a partnership.
- She establishes a pension, profit sharing, or retirement plan.
- She files employment or excise tax returns.

She will not need a new EIN if any of the following is true:
- She changes the name of her business.
- She changes the location or adds locations (stores, plants, enterprises, or branches of the same entity).
- She operates multiple businesses (including stores, plants, enterprises, or branches of the same entity).

13. The answer is B. Mabel's total gain on the sale is $94,000 ($180,000 - $86,000). Because the painting is section 1245 property, she must recognize $39,000 of ordinary income from depreciation recapture. The remaining $55,000 is capital gain.

14. The answer is A. Lori's basis in the stock after a tax-free exchange under section 351 is $3,700 ($6,200 basis of the machinery - $2,500 relief of liabilities that was assumed by the corporation). Generally, when liabilities are assumed in an exchange, the party that is relieved of debt is treated as boot and results in recognition of a gain. However, in a section 351 transaction, the liability relief is normally not treated as boot for recognition purposes. Instead, the basis of the transferor's stock is reduced by the liability assumed by the corporation.

15. The answer is C. Distributable net income is income that is currently available for distribution. In this case, it is $15,250, or the sum of the trust's interest income and capital gain minus the fiduciary fee ($13,000 + $3,000 - $750). Depending on how a trust is written, capital gains may be allocated to income or to the trust's corpus. In the latter case, capital gains would not be included in DNI.

16. The answer is B. The corporation's basis in the land and building is $650,000. The contributing shareholder's basis in the property is $450,000 and any gain that is recognized by Ignacio must be added. Ignacio's recognized gain is the lesser of: (1) his realized gain or (2) the boot received in the transaction. Ignacio's realized gain is $250,000 ($700,000 FMV - $450,000 basis). The boot he received was $200,000. Therefore, the gain recognized is $200,000, and the corporation's basis in the property is $650,000 ($450,000 basis + $200,000 boot).

17. The answer is D. The answer is calculated as follows: $14,960 ($14,000 + $960 sales tax). Generally, the FMV of property exchanged for services is includable in income. The basis of property is usually its cost. However, if services are performed for a price agreed on beforehand, the price will be accepted as the FMV if there is no evidence to the contrary. Since Scott charged $14,000 for his services and agreed to the transfer, $14,000 will be accepted as the FMV. The sales tax on purchase is always added to the basis of an asset, capitalized, and depreciated. The basis of an asset also includes the following items:
- Freight in (shipping costs)
- Installation and testing

- Excise taxes
- Legal and accounting fees (when they must be capitalized)
- Real estate taxes (if assumed for the seller)

18. The answer is B. If a cash-basis business pays an insurance premium in advance, it can generally deduct only the portion that applies to the current tax year, regardless of whether it prepaid the entire amount. Therefore, Galveston Seafood may only deduct the part of the policy that applies to the current year, calculated as follows: $1,800 ÷ 36 (months) = $50 per month; $50 × 12 = $600, the current year insurance expense. There is an exception under the "12 month rule", in which the amounts paid do not relate to periods beyond the earlier of:
- 12 months after the first date on which the business receives the benefit; or
- The end of the tax year following the tax year in which payment is made.

19. The answer is B. Michelle's basis is calculated as follows:

Initial Contribution	$100,000
Increases from pass-through of income	
Ordinary income	48,000
Tax-exempt interest	6,000
Distributions	(25,000)
Decreases from pass-through of expenses	
Short-term capital loss	(5,000)
Charitable contributions	(8,000)
Section 179 deduction	(25,000)
Adjusted basis at December 31, 2015	**$91,000**

20. The answer is A. Based on the information provided, Rico may qualify for a credit of up to 50% of the premiums he paid for his employees. The actual percentage credit is determined by the number of full-time equivalent employees and their average annual wages. Small tax-exempt employers can qualify for a credit of up to 35% of the health insurance premiums paid for their employees. The Small Business Health Care Tax Credit is refundable; is designed for small business employers with fewer than 25 low to moderate income workers; and may be claimed for two consecutive years.

21. The answer is A. A corporation can carry over charitable contributions for five years. It loses any unused amounts after that period. Corporate charitable contributions cannot be carried back.

22. The answer is B. The domestic production activities deduction cannot exceed 50% of W-2 wages paid that are allocable to its domestic production gross receipts. The domestic production activities deduction is designed to stimulate domestic manufacturing and farming. In 2015, the DPAD is equal to 9% of the lesser of:
- The business's qualified production activities income, or
- Taxable income determined without regard to the DPAD.

The deduction is limited to 50% of wages paid on Form W-2 by the company for the year that are allocable to its domestic production gross receipts. Therefore, if a company does not have any employees, it is not eligible for this deduction.

23. The answer is D. Ellen's at-risk amount for this activity includes all her costs, investments, and the debt that she personally absorbs for the business. Since Ellen used her own credit cards for the purchase of business materials, this is also considered an investment in her business. If any of the debt had been nonrecourse, she would not be considered at-risk for those amounts.

24. The answer is C. The destruction of the taxpayer's tractor is a section 1033 involuntary conversion. Travis has until December 31, 2017, to reinvest the insurance proceeds in a new tractor or other qualifying replacement property. The replacement period generally ends two years after the close of the first tax year in which the taxpayer realizes gain from the involuntary conversion. Travis is not required to report the insurance proceeds on his tax return unless he fails to reinvest the proceeds in qualifying replacement property (such as a new tractor).

25. The answer is A. A corporate distribution is taxable to a shareholder as a dividend, but only to the extent of earnings and profits (including current and accumulated E&P). Any distribution in excess of E&P is treated as a return of capital and would reduce the shareholder's basis in his stock. In this case, there are two equal shareholders, April and Charles; the gross distribution is $100,000; and the corporation only had $90,000 in E&P. The answer is calculated as follows:
- Distribution to Charles: $50,000 = ($100,000 × 50%)
- Amount treated as a dividend: $45,000 = (90,000 × 50%)
- Amount treated as a reduction in shareholder's stock basis: $5,000 ($50,000 - $45,000)

26. The answer is D. A de minimis fringe benefit is deductible by the employer, but not taxable to the employee. The IRS defines a de minimis benefit in this way: a benefit for which, considering its value and the frequency with which it is provided, is so small as to make accounting for it unreasonable or impractical. De minimis fringe benefits include occasional snacks, coffee, or doughnuts provided in a company's break room, and limited employee use of a business copy machine for personal purposes. Common examples of fringe benefits that do not qualify as de minimis and thus are taxable to the employee include:
- Cash (except for meal money provided infrequently to allow overtime work)
- Cash equivalents (e.g., savings bonds, gift cards, or certificates)
- Certain transportation passes or costs
- Use of an employer's apartment, vacation home, or boat
- Commuting use of an employer's vehicle more than once a month
- Membership in a country club or athletic facility

27. The answer is A. An individual partner's basis is increased by his share of taxable and nontaxable income. Since Christian is a 50% partner, the income items must be allocated based on his partnership percentage. The answer is calculated as follows:

Starting partnership basis		$1,000
Ordinary income x 50%	$40,000	$20,000
Tax-exempt income x 50%	20,000	10,000
Rental income x 50%	4,000	2,000
Christian's year-end basis		**$33,000**

28. The answer is A. The final deadline for self-employed persons or small employers to establish a SIMPLE IRA for the year 2015 is October 1, 2015. A business can set up a SIMPLE IRA plan effective on any date between January 1 and October 1 of a year, provided the business did not previously maintain a SIMPLE IRA plan. If the business previously maintained a SIMPLE IRA plan, the business can set up a SIMPLE IRA plan only on January 1. A SIMPLE IRA plan cannot have an effective date that is before the date the business actually adopts the plan.

29. The answer is D. Section 1245 applies to most depreciable personal property, but generally does not apply to real property (buildings, homes, etc.). Section 1245 property does not include most permanent buildings and structural components. The term "building" also includes a house, barn, warehouse, or garage.

30. The answer is B. Jerry recognizes a taxable gain of $175,000 on the transaction. In order for the transfer to be nontaxable, Jerry would have to own at least 80% of the total stock. Since he only received 70% of the stock, the exchange does not qualify for section 351 nonrecognition treatment.

31. The answer is C. By definition, an S corporation is not a personal service corporation. A C corporation is classified as a personal service corporation if its shareholders are also employee-owners that perform the personal services within the corporation and account for more than 20% of the corporation's compensation costs. If a corporation is classified as a PSC, there are three major drawbacks:
- Personal service corporations pay a flat corporate rate of 35%. The graduated corporate tax rates that apply to other C corporations do not apply to PSCs.
- A personal service corporation cannot elect to have a fiscal year without prior IRS approval.
- Unlike other C corporations, the at-risk rules and passive loss rules apply to personal service corporations.

32. The answer is A. Unlike limited partners, general partners have joint and several liability in a partnership's debt obligations. Limited partners are only liable up to the amount of their investment.

33. The answer is A. An S corporation may have a shareholder that is an estate. S corporations cannot be owned by C corporations, partnerships, or nonresident aliens. Some exempt entities (notably 501(c)(3) charities) may own stock in an S corporation. Answer C is incorrect because an S corporation that was previously a C corporation cannot have passive investment income that exceeds 25% of its gross receipts for three consecutive tax years. If this occurs, the S election will be terminated and the corporation will revert back to C corporate status. Answer D is incorrect because an S corporation cannot have more than 100 shareholders.

34. The answer is C. An individual partner's basis is increased by her share of partnership debt and decreased by the amount of debt relief. Since Holly was a 30% partner, she retains a corresponding share of the debt. The answer is calculated as follows:

Beginning basis (her adjusted basis in the building)	$60,000
Mortgage debt assumed by partnership	(30,000)
Holly's share of the debt ($30,000 × 30%)	9,000
Holly's basis in the partnership interest	**$39,000**

35. The answer is B. The accumulated earnings tax is assessed on the accumulated earnings and profits of a C corporation. If a corporation allows earnings to accumulate beyond the reasonable needs of the business, it may be subject to an accumulated earnings tax of 20% of the excess amount accumulated. The accumulated earnings tax does not apply to partnerships, sole proprietorships, or S corporations, because these businesses are pass-through entities and do not accumulate earnings from year to year as a C corporation does.

36. The answer is B. May 15 is the deadline for calendar-year nonprofit organizations to file their information returns (Form 990). The organization may also request an extension by using Form 8868. Even though a charity is organized as a corporation, it must still file Form 990, not Form 1120. An exempt entity on a fiscal year is required to file by the fifteenth of the fifth month after the end of its taxable year.

37. The answer is A. If a corporation pays an employee who is also a shareholder a salary that is unreasonably high considering the services actually performed, the excessive part of the salary may be treated as a constructive distribution of earnings to the employee-shareholder.

38. The answer is C. Kerry's basis in her partnership interest is calculated by adding the cash contributed ($10,000) to the basis of the property contributed ($18,000). Her partnership interest is $28,000 ($10,000 + $18,000).

39. The answer is B. The distribution is treated as a sale. Helvetica Corporation would recognize income of $138,000 on the distribution ($200,000 - $62,000 basis). A corporation recognizes gain when it makes a liquidating distribution to its shareholders.

40. The answer is D. The built-in gains tax is imposed at the highest rate of tax that is applicable to corporations (currently 35%).

41. The answer is A. Christopher must recognize dividend income of $150,000 and a taxable gain of $20,000. He must also reduce his stock basis to zero. In this case, the shareholder received dividend income of $150,000 (equal to the corporation's accumulated earnings and profits). Christopher's stock basis was $30,000, so, after reducing his stock basis to zero (for the tax-free return of capital for the $30,000 of distributions following the $150,000 of taxable dividends), he must recognize a taxable gain of $20,000, which is the excess of the distribution over the amount of his stock basis. The answer is calculated as follows:

- ($200,000 distribution - $150,000 accumulated E&P) = $50,000
- ($50,000 remaining distribution - $30,000 return of capital (stock basis reduced to zero) = $20,000
- $20,000 is treated as a gain from the sale or exchange of stock.

42. The answer is C. Guaranteed payments are paid in accordance with the partnership agreement, and they are treated as salary payments. Guaranteed payments are deductible in determining the partnership's ordinary income.

43. The answer is D. In 2015, the following SEP contribution limits apply:
- For an employee: Contributions cannot exceed the lesser of 25% of the employee's compensation or $53,000.
- For a self-employed individual: Contributions cannot exceed the lesser of 20% of net self-employment income, after considering both the deduction for self-employment tax and the deduction for the SEP-IRA contribution, or $53,000.

Employers cannot make contributions conditional, or require that any part of the contribution be kept in the employee's account after the business has made its contributions.

44. The answer is C. An S corporation's accumulated adjustment account includes all items of income and expenses with the exception of tax-exempt income (and expenses related to tax-exempt income).

45. The answer is D. The transfer is not a qualified 351 exchange because Runway Corporation is an investment company. In a qualified section 351 exchange, no gain or loss is recognized provided:
- The transferor receives only stock in exchange for property (or money), and
- The transferor is in control of the corporation immediately after the exchange. This means at least 80% of the voting stock and at least 80% of all other classes of stock of the corporation.

However, section 351 does not apply when:
- The corporation is an investment company.
- The transferor transfers property during a bankruptcy in exchange for stock used to pay creditors.
- The stock received in exchange for the corporation's debt (other than a security) or for interest on the corporation's debt (including a security) that accrued while the transferor held the debt.

46. The answer is A. Neither a general partnership nor a sole proprietorship requires any type of formal agreement or state filing in order to be created. A corporation and an LLC each requires formal filing at the state level in order for the entity to be created.

47. The answer is C. A distribution that gives cash or other property to some shareholders and an increase in the percentage interest in the corporation's assets or earnings and profits to other shareholders would cause a stock dividend to be a taxable event. Generally, stock dividends and stock rights are not taxable. However, in the following cases, a stock dividend would be taxable:
- The distribution gives cash or other property to some shareholders and an increase in the percentage interest in the corporation's assets or earnings and profits to other shareholders.
- Shareholders are permitted to choose cash or other property instead of stock or stock rights.
- The distribution is in convertible preferred stock, or some shareholders receive preferred stock and others receive common stock.

If a stock dividend is deemed taxable, it would be included in the shareholder's income at its FMV at the time of distribution.

48. The answer is B. The partners share income and loss equally, and they are required to report their share of partnership income, regardless of whether it is distributed. Therefore, each partner will report $55,000 ($110,000 × 50%) of taxable income from the partnership. An individual partner must report his allocable share of partnership income on his own tax return, (Form 1040, Schedule E). The partner's allocable share of partnership income is reported to each individual partner on Schedule K-1.

49. The answer is B. If a taxpayer trades property and also pays money, the basis of the property received is the basis of the property given up, increased by any additional money paid. The answer is calculated as follows:

Cost of old equipment	$50,000
Subtract depreciation on old equipment	(26,000)
Adjusted basis of old equipment	24,000
Add cash paid for new equipment	12,000
Adjusted basis of new equipment	**$36,000**

50. The answer is D. A shareholder's basis in an S corporation will increase with:
- Additional contributions to capital, and
- The shareholder's share of corporate and exempt income.

51. The answer is D. Generally, the partnership's basis in contributed property is identical to the adjusted basis of the property in the hands of the contributing partner. Therefore, the partnership's tax basis in the contributed land is $10,000. The partnership's tax basis in the contributed equipment is $75,000. In addition, the partnership's holding period for the assets is the same as Kathryn's holding period, so if either asset is later sold, the partner's holding period is "tacked on" for purposes of determining the partnership's recognition of long-term or short-term gain or loss.

52. The answer is C. A fisherman or farmer who elects income averaging uses Schedule J, *Income Averaging for Farmers and Fishermen,* to figure his income tax. Certain farmers and fishermen may average all or some of their current year's farm income by allocating it to the three prior years. This may lower a farmer's current year tax if the current year taxable income is high and his taxable income from one or more of the three prior years was low.

53. The answer is D. The capital loss carryforward is $17,000. The net capital losses for 2015 are $50,000 ($100,000 - $50,000). Corporate capital losses are carried back three years and carried forward five years. The net capital losses cannot be carried back to 2012 because there were no capital gains that year, so the $24,000 in gains from 2013 must be offset first. This leaves $26,000 of capital losses. The $9,000 of capital gains from 2014 may also be offset, which leaves a carryforward of $17,000. This amount may be applied to any gains that are earned in the subsequent five tax years.

54. The answer is A. A partnership terminates when one of the following events takes place:
- All its operations are discontinued.
- At least 50% of the total interest in partnership capital and profits is sold or exchanged within a 12-month period, including a sale or exchange to another partner.

Answer B is incorrect because a corporation can legally own an interest in a partnership. Answer C is incorrect because the death of a partner will not necessarily dissolve a partnership if the partners have expressly agreed to continue the partnership. Answer D is incorrect because there must be a change of 50% in both capital and profits for the partnership to terminate. Therefore, a sale of a 40% interest in capital and a 60% interest in profits will not automatically terminate the partnership.

> **Note:** Unlike other partnerships, an "electing large partnership" does not terminate on the sale or exchange of 50% or more of the partnership interests within a 12-month period. An electing large partnership must have 100 partners or more and chooses electing large partnership (ELP) status by filing Form 1065-B instead of Form 1065. This election cannot be revoked without IRS permission.

55. The answer is D. Deductible losses related to business and income-producing property are reported on Form 4684, *Casualties and Thefts*, and on Form 4797, *Sales of Business Property*, and are deductible without regard to whether they exceed the $100 and 10% of AGI thresholds that apply for personal-use property.

56. The answer is D. A controlled group is a group of corporations that are related through common ownership, typically as either parent-subsidiary or brother-sister corporations. A parent-subsidiary controlled group involves a parent corporation that owns at least 80% of the voting power of at least one other corporation (with possible additional corporations that are at least 80% owned by either the common parent or one of the subsidiary entities). A brother-sister controlled group involves situations in which five or fewer individuals, estates, or trusts own 80% or more of the combined voting power for multiple corporations, and have identical common ownership within the individual corporations of at least 50%. Members of controlled groups are subject to rules regarding related party transactions that may require deferral of recognition for losses or expenses incurred by one party.

57. The answer is C. Even though no distributions were made during the year, Tara is required to report her share of the partnership's income. The income is allocated based on her partnership interest, so the answer is calculated as follows: (30% × $40,000 partnership income) = $12,000 of ordinary income to Tara, which increases her partnership basis. Since no distributions were made, her year-end basis is as follows: ($30,000 starting basis + $12,000 income) = $42,000.

58. The answer is C. The IRC defines a simple trust as a trust that:
- Distributes all of its income currently;
- Makes no distributions of principal; and
- Makes no distributions to charity.

Any trust that is not a simple trust is automatically a complex trust. A complex trust:
- Is allowed to accumulate income;
- Can make discretionary distributions of income;
- Can make mandatory (or discretionary) distributions of principal; and
- Can make distributions to charity.

59. The answer is B. A greenhouse is generally classified as section 1245 (rather than section 1250) property, because it is a single-purpose horticultural or agricultural structure. Section 1250 property generally consists of buildings (including their structural components), other inherently permanent structures, and land improvements of general use and purpose. Examples of section 1250 property include residential rental property, factory buildings, and office buildings. Since buildings are generally depreciated using the straight-line method, taxpayers usually get more favorable treatment of depreciation recapture for section 1250 property.

60. The answer is A. The distribution reduces Morris's E&P to zero. Leah must report dividend income of $210,000 and a capital gain of $10,000. The answer is calculated as follows:

Accumulated E&P	$120,000
Current year E&P	90,000
Current and accumulated E&P	**$210,000**

A distribution cannot create a deficit in a corporation's earnings and profits. Thus, the distribution to Leah reduces E&P to zero.

Gross distribution	$220,000
Subtract current and accumulated E&P	210,000
Capital gain to Leah	**$10,000**

Leah must recognize a dividend of $210,000 (the amount of the distribution from current and accumulated E&P), and the remaining $10,000 would either reduce her stock basis or produce a capital gain for her. Since the question stated that Leah's stock basis was already zero, the $10,000 would be reported as a capital gain.

61. The answer is D. The answer is calculated as follows:

Roger's starting basis	$16,000
Ordinary income (× 50%)	40,000
Exempt income (× 50%)	3,000
Year-end basis (before distribution)	**59,000**
Subtract distribution	(50,000)
Year-end basis (after distribution)	**$9,000**

62. The answer is C. A disregarded entity is a single-member limited liability company that is disregarded for federal tax purposes. A domestic LLC with one member as an individual will be treated as a sole proprietorship, or "disregarded" as being separate from its owner for income tax purposes (but still considered a separate entity for purposes of employment tax and certain excise taxes). An individual owner of a single-member LLC is subject to the tax on net earnings from self-employment in the same manner as a sole proprietorship.

63. The answer is B. Participant loans are not permitted with SIMPLE IRA accounts. Participants are always 100% vested in all of the funds in their SIMPLE IRA accounts. Withdrawals are permitted at any time, but they are subject to income taxes. If the employee is under age 59½, a 10% penalty tax may apply. An employee may also move assets from his SIMPLE IRA to another IRA or a qualified retirement plan, subject to certain restrictions.

64. The answer is C. One of the main advantages of a corporation is limited liability for directors, officers, shareholders, and employees. When forming a corporation, prospective shareholders provide money, property, or both in exchange for the issuance of the corporation's capital stock. A corporation is considered an entity separate from its shareholders and must elect a board of directors who are responsible for oversight of the company. In choosing between an S corporation and a C corporation, the latter structure will generally provide more flexibility for raising capital since it will not be subject to certain restrictions on the number and types of shareholders that apply to S corporations. A major drawback of the C corporation structure is double taxation. A C corporation's profits are taxed when earned and taxed again when distributed as shareholders' dividends.

65. The answer is C. Nicholas must report the $10,000 guaranteed payment as income. He is a 50% partner, so he must also report 50% of the partnership's income. The answer is calculated as follows: guaranteed payment $10,000 + $21,000 ($42,000 × 50%).

66. The answer is D. Freelance authors, photographers, and artists are exempt from the uniform capitalization (UNICAP) rules. Most businesses that create, purchase, and resell property or inventory are subject to UNICAP. Under UNICAP, a business must capitalize the direct costs and part of the indirect costs for production or resale activities. Smaller businesses such as the following are also exempt from the uniform capitalization rules:
- Resellers of personal property with average annual gross receipts of $10 million or less for the three prior tax years
- Businesses that produce inventory but have average annual gross receipts of $1 million or less

67. The answer is B. Before applying for tax exemption, the organization must be created using an organizing document. This document must limit the organization's purposes to those set forth in section 501(c)(3) and must specify that the entity's assets will be permanently dedicated to an exempt purpose. The organizing document should also contain a provision for distributing funds if it dissolves. In order to qualify for tax exemption under section 501(c)(3), an organization must generally request exemption from the IRS by the end of the fifteenth month after it was created, with a 12-month extension available.

68. The answer is C. Misty must report a taxable dividend of $160,000 ($260,000 FMV - $100,000 liability assumed). Her basis in the property is $260,000. When a corporation distributes property to a shareholder (rather than stock or cash), the amount distributed is based on the FMV of the property on the date of distribution. The amount distributed is reduced by any liabilities assumed by the shareholder. The basis of the property in the hands of the shareholder would be the FMV on the date of distribution.

69. The answer is A. Randy must report $10,000 of partnership income in 2015. After the distribution, his remaining partnership basis would be $500. Randy must report his share of partnership income in the year it is earned, regardless of the amounts actually distributed. The municipal bond interest is nontaxable interest, so it retains its character as nontaxable when it is distributed to Randy. However, the exempt income does increase Randy's basis in his partnership interest, so after the distribution he still has $500 in basis left. Since Randy had $10,000 of ordinary income from the partnership in 2015, he is required to report that amount in 2015, even if he did not receive it. The answer is calculated as follows:

Randy's starting partnership basis	$0
Ordinary income	10,000
Tax-exempt income	1,500
Basis at the end of 2015	**11,500**
Cash distribution in 2016	11,000
Basis after cash distribution	**$500**

70. The answer is C. A corporation whose S-election is revoked or terminated must generally wait five years before making an S-election again. There are exceptions that allow for entities to elect S-status earlier than the mandatory five-year waiting period, but only with IRS consent.

71. The answer is D. For the sale of livestock due to drought, flood, or other weather-related conditions in an area eligible for federal disaster assistance, the replacement period ends four years after the close of the first tax year in which the taxpayer realizes any part of his gain from the sale or exchange of livestock. The IRS may extend the replacement period on a regional basis if the weather-related conditions continue for longer than three years.

72. The answer is C. The maximum section 179 deduction the company can claim for 2015 is $355,000 ($100,000 for the equipment + $5,000 computer + $250,000 for the qualifying leasehold improvements). In 2015, there is a special rule that allows taxpayers to elect to deduct a maximum of $250,000 of qualified real property (QRP) under section 179. This provision applies only to certain industries and includes the following types of real property:
- Qualified leasehold improvement property
- Qualified restaurant property (such as a major renovation of a restaurant building)
- Qualified retail improvement property (such as a major interior upgrade of a retail clothing store)

A business is still eligible to deduct an additional $250,000 of other qualifying property to reach the total $500,000 section 179 limit for 2015.

73. The answer is D. The corporation's final return is due by October 15, 2015. It will cover the short period from January 1, 2015, through July 12, 2015. October 15 is the fifteenth day of the third month following the close of the corporation's tax year, which was a short year because the corporation dissolved.

74. The answer is A. Mark's partnership basis is increased to $71,000 ($46,000 + $25,000 [25% × $100,000]). The partnership has four partners, so each would increase the basis of his partnership interest by his share of the debt (25% × $100,000).

75. The answer is B. Section 280F places limits on the amount of depreciation that can be taken on passenger cars used in business. Although section 280F's caption refers to "luxury automobiles", the restrictions apply to most new passenger cars. There are also special limits placed on the depreciation of sport utility vehicles. Each year, the IRS releases guidance regarding the MACRS limitations for automobiles, indicating specified amounts, adjusted for inflation, for various makes and models of vehicles.

76. The answer is C. The corporation has an $80,000 dividends-received deduction and a $10,000 NOL. Its taxable income is $70,000 ($100,000 dividends earned - $30,000 business losses) before figuring the dividends-received deduction. If Apex Corporation claims the full dividends-received deduction of $80,000 ($100,000 × 80%) and combines it with its business loss of $30,000, it will have an NOL of $10,000. Therefore, the 80% of taxable income limit does not apply. The corporation can deduct the full $80,000.

77. The answer is A. A partnership does not pay income tax. However, a partnership can still be liable for other taxes, such as employment taxes (FUTA, Social Security, Medicare taxes) and excise taxes.

78. The answer is D. The differences in book and taxable income are reconciled on Schedule M-1 of Form 1120 by small corporations with less than $10 million of assets. Larger corporations with more than $50 million of assets use Schedule M-3. Schedule M-3 provides additional information and contains three main sections:
- Financial statement reconciliation
- Detail of income/loss items
- Detail of expenses/deductions

Starting in 2014, a new rule permits corporations that have at least $10 million but less than $50 million of total assets to file Schedule M-1 in place of Schedule M-3, Parts II and III, which reconcile net income or loss per the income statement and report expense and deduction items. However, Part I of Schedule M-3, *Financial Information and Net Income (Loss) Reconciliation*, is still required.

79. The answer is B. Because they used the car 70% for business, they can deduct 70% of the expenses as a business expense. The answer is calculated as follows:

$$([\$235 + \$20 + \$25] = \$280) \times 70\% = \$196$$
$$(\$5,500 \times 70\%) = \$3,850$$
Allowable expense: $4,046

80. The answer is A. In this case, Gabe is considered to constructively own 100% of the partnership, because the rules for constructive ownership consider the ownership of his family members, which includes brothers, sisters, spouses, ancestors, and lineal descendants. Therefore, his ownership is calculated as follows:

Gabe	20%
Gabe's son	20%
Gabe's brother	60%
Ownership	**100%**

81. The answer is D. A family farming corporation may use the cash method of accounting if its average annual gross receipts are $25 million or less. A tax shelter must always use the accrual method, regardless of its gross receipts. A corporation with long-term contracts must always use the accrual method. A C corporation with gross receipts exceeding $5 million must use the accrual method of accounting.

82. The answer is A. Gracie Development must recognize a taxable gain of $60,000. This transaction is treated as a sale. It is as if Gracie Development sold the building for $250,000 and used the profits from the sale to pay the debt. Gracie Development must realize a taxable gain as if the property had been sold at its fair market value and the proceeds were used to pay off the creditor.

83. The answer is A. Brett must report a capital gain of $6,000 on his tax return ($30,000 - $24,000 = $6,000). A shareholder's stock basis cannot go below zero. Therefore, if a nondividend distribution is made in excess of stock basis, the distribution is taxed as a capital gain on the shareholder's return.

84. The answer is B. The Disabled Access Credit is a nonrefundable credit for small businesses so they can provide access to persons with disabilities. An eligible small business is one that earned $1 million or less or had 30 or fewer full-time employees in the previous year.

85. The answer is D. The partnership must include the fair market value of the items it received in exchange for services. This is bartering income, and it is treated as if the partnership had received money. Therefore, the answer is $8,000 + $3,000 = $11,000.

86. The answer is C. The entire meal amount is a qualified expense, but subject to the 50% limitation on deductibility for meals and entertainment expenses. Janelle can deduct the full amount of the travel in the taxi cab. Therefore, the deductible portion of the expense is calculated as follows: ($250 × 50%) + $10 =$135.

87. The answer is D. The amount of a C corporation's earnings and profits determines the tax treatment of corporate distributions to shareholders. The starting point for determining corporate E&P is the corporation's taxable income. The following transactions increase the amount of E&P:
- Long-term contracts reported on the completed contract method
- Intangible drilling costs deducted currently
- Mine exploration and development costs deducted currently
- Dividends-received deduction

The following transactions reduce the amount of E&P:
- Corporate federal income taxes
- Life insurance policy premiums on a corporate officer
- Excess charitable contributions (over 10% limit)
- Expenses relating to tax-exempt income
- Excess of capital losses over capital gains
- Corporate dividends and other distributions

88. The answer is B. An office building is section 1250 property, which is generally depreciated using the straight-line method and is not subject to depreciation recapture. Ephraim has $1,667,948 of capital gain from the sale ($2,350,000 sale price - $682,052 adjusted basis).

89. The answer is B. An employer can provide $50,000 of term life insurance coverage tax-free to an employee. The value of any coverage over this amount must be included in wages and reported on an employee's Form W-2. The other benefits are usually not taxable to employees.

90. The answer is B. Chavez Corporation can take a deduction for the interest paid on the loan. However, the sales tax is not currently deductible. It must be added to the cost of the depreciable asset and depreciated over its useful life.

91. The answer is C. The normal due date for Form 1041 is the fifteenth day of the fourth month following the end of the entity's tax year (unless it falls on a weekend or holiday) For the 2015 tax year, the due date is April 18, 2016. It is subject to an automatic extension of five months if Form 7004 is filed. The tax year of an estate may be either a calendar or a fiscal year, subject to the election made at the time the first return is filed. An election will also be made on the first return as to method (cash, accrual, or other) to report an estate's income. Form 1041 must be filed for any domestic estate that has gross income for the tax year of $600 or more, or a beneficiary who is a nonresident alien (with any amount of income).

92. The answer is D. A business must file Form 8300, *Report of Cash Payments Over $10,000 Received in a Trade or Business,* when it receives a cash payment of more than $10,000 from one transaction or from two or more related transactions. The requirement also applies to certain monetary instruments, such as traveler's checks, bank drafts, cashier's checks, and money orders. The form requires the name, address, and Social Security number of the buyer. The reporting requirement is designed to combat money laundering.

93. The answer is B. The other answers are all prohibited under the section 1031 rules. Like-kind property does not include the exchange of property for personal use for property used for business or trade (as personal-use property is excluded altogether). In order for a like-kind exchange to be valid, both properties must be used in a business or held for investment. Most real property is considered like-kind property. For example, real property that is improved may be exchanged for vacant land. One exception for real estate is that property within the United States cannot be exchanged for property outside of the United States. Section 1031 also specifically excludes the following exchanges:
- Inventory
- Stocks, bonds, or notes
- Other securities or debt
- Partnership interests

A taxpayer reports a section 1031 exchange on Form 8824, *Like-Kind Exchanges*.

94. The answer is A. Partnerships are not subject to the passive loss limitation rules – they are only applied at the partner level. Taxpayers subject to the passive activity loss rules are:
- Individuals.
- Estates and Trusts.
- Closely-held C corporations. (Passive losses may offset active income, but not portfolio income.)
- Personal Service Corporations.

Partnerships and S corporations are not subject to the passive loss rules, but the individual partners and shareholders of these entities may be subject on their distributive share. In general, aggregate losses from passive activities are allowed only to the extent of aggregate income from passive activities. Suspended passive activity losses would become deductible in the year of disposal of the entire interest of the passive activity. For example, if an individual has suspended passive losses from an investment asset and then sells the investment (either at a loss or a gain), the suspended losses would be recognized upon the disposition of the asset.

95. The answer is D. The amount of current earnings and profits that is allocated to Valerie is $32,000 ($64,000 earnings × 50% stock ownership). Valerie must report dividend income of $32,000. The remaining amount of the distribution ($40,000 - $32,000 = $8,000) is treated as a return of capital and reduces Valerie's stock basis to $42,000 ($50,000 - $8,000). Corporate distributions are treated as dividends to the extent of the shareholder's share of corporate earnings and profits.

96. The answer is C. Assessments for local improvements are items that tend to increase the value of property, such as streets and sidewalks, and are added to the basis of a taxpayer's property. These items cannot be deducted as taxes. However, a business can deduct assessments for local benefits if they are for the maintenance, repairs, or interest charges related to the improvements.

97. The answer is D. Niven Corporation should first carry back the $8,000 of net capital losses up to three years, and carry forward any remaining amounts for up to five years. The treatment of capital losses for C corporations is very different than the treatment for individuals. There is no favorable tax rate treatment for long-term capital gains for corporations. Also, there is no $3,000 allowance for deductibility of capital losses against ordinary income, as is the case for individuals. A corporation can only offset capital losses with capital gains. Any capital losses that are not used within the carryback or carryforward periods are forfeited. A corporation also cannot choose the year to which losses are carried back. Losses must be carried back to the earliest year in which they can be used.

98. The answer is C. The original basis, which is $140,000 ($30,000 + $110,000), must be reduced by the depreciation. Therefore, Juan David's adjusted basis in the building before the sale is $118,000 ($140,000 - $22,000). The gain is then calculated as follows: ($205,000 - $118,000 basis) = $87,000 gain. Because the building is section 1250 property and Juan David has only taken straight-line depreciation, there is no depreciation recapture, and the entire amount of the gain is treated as long-term capital gain.

99. The answer is C. An S corporation cannot deduct charitable contributions. Only a C corporation can take a business deduction for charitable contributions of up to 10% of income. Charitable contributions made by an S corporation flow-through to the shareholders who may be able to deduct their share of the contributions on their own return. The two main reasons for electing S corporation status are:
- Avoiding double taxation on distributions
- Allowing corporate losses to pass through to shareholders

In addition, S corporations share the same liability protection benefits of C corporations.

100. The answer is C. Pioneer's cost of goods sold is calculated as follows:

Beginning inventory balance		$1,200,000
Manufacturing costs:		
	Raw materials purchases	5,200,000
	Freight charges	175,000
	Manufacturing wages and benefits	4,025,000
	Factory depreciation & section 179 deductions	200,000
	Other manufacturing costs	875,000
	Minus the ending inventory balance	(1,575,000)
COGS for 2015		**$10,100,000**

The other costs outlined earlier are not used in the manufacturing process, and therefore are not included in the calculation of cost of goods sold.

Answers to Exam #4: Businesses

1. The answer is D. A brother-sister controlled group involves a situation in which five or fewer individuals, estates, or trusts own 80% or more of the combined voting power for multiple corporations, and have identical common ownership within the individual corporations of at least 50%. In contrast, a parent-subsidiary controlled group involves a parent corporation that owns at least 80% of the voting power of at least one other corporation (with possible additional corporations that are at least 80% owned by either the common parent or one of the subsidiary entries).

2. The answer is A. Hadiya would report $35,000 of partnership losses and have a $6,000 loss carryforward. A partner can deduct partnership losses only to the extent of her adjusted basis in the partnership. Since Hadiya's distributive share of the loss exceeds her partnership basis, her basis is reduced to zero and the remaining loss is carried forward. The answer is calculated as follows:

Loss	$82,000
Hadiya's ownership percentage	x 50%
Hadiya's distributive share of loss	41,000
Minus her basis	(35,000)
Loss carried forward	**$6,000**

Partnership losses are never carried back.

3. The answer is C. Eugene must report the income on Form 4835. Form 4835 is used by landowners who rent their farmland, or receive a part of the crop as their rental payments (sharecropping), but who are not in the business of farming. A landowner is allowed to report on Form 4835 only if he does not materially participate in the farm business. If the landowner is actively involved in running the farm, he would report income and expenses on Schedule F.

4. The answer is A. A taxpayer must file Form 3115, *Application for Change in Accounting Method*, to request a change in either an overall accounting method or the accounting treatment for an individual item. With implementation of the final tangible property regulations for tax year 2014, many businesses are required to file Form 3115. A simplified procedure that waives the Form 3115 requirement is available for small businesses with assets totaling less than $10 million for the current year or average annual gross receipts totaling $10 million or less for the prior three tax years. IRS consent is also not required for the following:
- Making an adjustment in the useful life of a depreciable or amortizable asset (but a taxpayer cannot change the recovery period for MACRS or ACRS property)
- Correcting a math error or an error in figuring tax liability
- A change in accounting method when the change is required by tax law, such as when a business's average gross receipts exceed $5 million

Answer B is incorrect because Form 8832 is used by certain business entities to choose how they will be classified for tax purposes. Answer C is incorrect because Form 1065 is used to report partnership income. Answer D is incorrect because Form 8300 is used when a business receives a cash payment of more than $10,000 from one transaction or from two or more related transactions.

5. The answer is C. Saul may deduct Ingram's wages as a business expense. Ingram's wages are not subject to Social Security and Medicare taxes. Wages of a child under the age 18 who works for her parent in a business are not subject to Social Security and Medicare taxes if the trade or business is a sole proprietorship or a partnership in which each partner is a parent of the child. (Note: This rule does not apply to corporations.) Earned income, including wages that are paid to the taxpayer's own children, is not subject to the kiddie tax, regardless of the child's age. Payments for the services of a child of any age who works for his parent are generally not subject to backup withholding.

6. The answer is B. If liabilities assumed by the corporation exceed the basis of the assets transferred, the relief from liabilities in excess of basis is treated as boot. In the case of a section 351 exchange, a taxpayer will not recognize any gain or loss on the transfer, as long as the following conditions are met:
- The taxpayer receives only stock in exchange for the property, and
- The taxpayer has a controlling interest in the corporation immediately after the exchange. In order to qualify, the taxpayer must have at least 80% ownership in the corporate stock.

7. The answer is B. Cassandra cannot deduct the taxes as a current expense, since they are delinquent real estate taxes and the person who is legally liable for the debt is Alex. However, the taxes should be added to the property's basis and depreciated as part of the purchase price, since Cassandra intends to use the property as a rental. If a taxpayer agrees to pay the delinquent real estate taxes that the seller owes on real property, the buyer must treat those taxes as part of the asset's basis. The buyer cannot deduct them as taxes.

8. The answer is C. Shareholders in an S corporation must be U.S. citizens or residents. A nonresident alien cannot hold shares in an S corporation. All of the other taxpayers are permitted to be shareholders in an S corporation. Corporate shareholders (except for S corporation shareholders that meet the qualified subchapter S subsidiary rules) and partnerships are not eligible S corporation shareholders. However, certain trusts, estates, banks, and tax-exempt corporations, most notably 501(c)(3) corporations, are permitted to be shareholders.

9. The answer is B. Lisa must report $22,500 ($15,000 + $7,500), the sum of the required and discretionary distributions she received, rather than her entire share of DNI. The beneficiary of a trust that is required to distribute all its income currently must report her entire share of DNI, whether or not she actually received distributions for the full amount during her tax year. The beneficiary of a trust that is not required to distribute all its income currently must report all income that is required to be distributed to her currently (whether or not actually distributed), plus all other amounts paid, credited, or required to be distributed to her, up to her share of distributable net income. A portion of this income is related to the tax-exempt interest earned by the estate, and will therefore not be taxable income to Lisa.

10. The answer is A. Quicker Relay Corporation would recognize a gain of $430,000 ($620,000 liability - $190,000 basis). During a liquidation, a corporation will recognize gain or loss on distributions. In general, the gain or loss on a liquidating distribution is calculated by subtracting the basis of the property from the fair market value on the date of the distribution (FMV - basis = gain/loss). However, if the property is encumbered by a liability, the gain or loss is adjusted to reflect the assumption of the liability. If the liability is greater than the FMV of the property, the amount of the liability is treated as the FMV of the property.

11. The answer is A. Partnership tax returns are due on the fifteenth day of the fourth month after the end of the tax year, so the Sutter Partnership's return would be due January 15, 2016. However, most partnerships operate on a calendar year, so their due date is April 15. Partnerships may be granted an extra five months' extension of time to file, unlike individuals and corporations that have an extra six months.

12. The answer is A. The answer is $8,200. The amount is calculated as follows:

New computer system	$4,600
New multi-line phone system	3,600
Total qualifying section 179 purchases	**$8,200**

Section 179 applies only to certain asset purchases. The telephone bills would be a regular business expense, not a section 179 item. The bathroom renovation is not a qualifying section 179 expense. The cost of improvements to a building must be capitalized and depreciated using MACRS.

13. The answer is B. The answer is calculated as follows:

Starting basis	$95,000
Ordinary losses	(15,000)
Long-term capital gain	4,000
Short-term capital loss	(9,000)
Municipal bond interest income	2,000
Year-end basis	**$77,000**

In computing stock basis, a shareholder starts with his initial capital contribution to the S corporation (the same as a C corporation). Basis is then increased and/or decreased based on the flow-through amounts from the S corporation. An income item or a contribution will increase stock basis while a loss, deduction, or distribution will decrease stock basis.

14. The answer is A. Form 5498-SA, is used to report HSA contributions (when funds are added to the HSA). Form 1099-SA is used to report HSA *distributions* (when funds are withdrawn). A health savings account (HSA) is a medical savings account that offers tax-free distributions in order to pay for current medical expenses. HSAs allow taxpayers to save money for medical expenses on a tax-free basis. The HSA account is owned by the individual employee, but contributions to the HSA may be made by an employer or the employee.

15. The answer is C. For 2015, the standard mileage rate for business use of a vehicle is 57.5 cents per mile. Jetta cannot use the standard mileage rate because she operates five or more vehicles at the same time, which the IRS considers a fleet. A business may also not use the standard mileage rate if it:
- Claimed a depreciation deduction using any method other than straight-line, including MACRS
- Claimed a section 179 deduction on the car
- Claimed the special depreciation allowance on the car
- Claimed actual car expenses for a car that was leased

A taxpayer who uses the standard mileage rate can also deduct related parking and tolls.

16. The answer is C. In an otherwise nontaxable section 351 exchange, a shareholder might have to recognize gain if she receives money or property other than the corporation's stock. The gain is limited to the total of money and the FMV of the other property received. If the corporation assumes the shareholder's liabilities, the assumption generally is not treated as if the shareholder received money or other property, unless:
- The liabilities the corporation assumes are more than the shareholder's adjusted basis in the property transferred, in which case gain is recognized up to the difference. However, if the liabilities assumed give rise to a deduction when paid, such as a trade account payable or interest, no gain is recognized.
- There is no good business reason for the corporation to assume the liabilities, or if the main purpose in the exchange is to avoid federal income tax.

The shareholder's basis in her stock must be reduced by the amount of the liabilities assumed by the corporation. In this case, Rita has a gain of $16,000, equal to the $41,000 sum of property received ($20,000 stock + $15,000 cash + $6,000 of mortgage relief) minus her $25,000 adjusted basis in the property contributed. Since the $6,000 mortgage assumed was less than her $25,000 basis, and absent any indication the exchange was undertaken with the main purpose of avoiding federal income tax, the liability would not be considered in determining her recognized gain. The gain is therefore limited to the $15,000 of cash received.

17. The answer is C. All the costs must be added to the machine's basis ($5,500 + $125 + $250) = $5,875.

18. The answer is B. The IRS will automatically classify a domestic LLC that has at least two members and does not file a Form 8832 as a partnership for federal tax purposes.

19. The answer is C. The corporate charitable deduction for C corporations is limited to 10% of taxable income before figuring the dividends-received deduction. Therefore, the allowable charitable deduction is $12,500 = ($125,000 × 10%). The unused charitable contribution becomes a carryover to the following year and may be carried forward up to five years. After five years, any unused charitable deduction is lost.

20. The answer is D. The trust fund recovery penalty can be assessed upon anyone found to be responsible for collecting or remitting withheld income and employment taxes and who willfully fails to collect or remit them. The responsible person (or persons) must have either intentionally disregarded the law or been plainly indifferent to its requirements. The amount of the penalty is equal to the unpaid balance of the trust fund tax.

21. The answer is B. For businesses using the cash method, the general rule is that an expense paid in advance is deductible only in the year to which it applies. The expense for business insurance must be prorated because the payment does not qualify for the 12-month rule. Therefore, only $500 (6/36 × $3,000) is deductible in 2015; $1,000 (12/36 × $3,000) is deductible in 2016; $1,000 (12/36 × $3,000) is deductible in 2017; and the remaining $500 is deductible in 2018. Under the 12-month rule, the cash-basis taxpayer is not required to capitalize amounts paid that do not extend beyond the earlier of the following:
- 12 months after the benefit begins, or
- The end of the tax year after the tax year in which payment is made.

22. The answer is D. A personal service corporation always pays corporate tax at a flat rate of 35%. The answer is calculated as follows: ($68,000 - $22,000 NOL) × 35% = $16,100.

23. The answer is B. The ordinary income is calculated as follows ($50,000 - $20,000 = $30,000 of expenses). The tax-exempt interest and rental income is separately stated income, and the charitable contribution is also a separately stated item that is not used to figure an S corporation's income. The charitable contributions deduction is taken by the individual shareholder on her individual return (Schedule A, Form 1040). In this respect, the S corporation is similar to a partnership in its tax treatment of charitable contributions.

Note: Do not confuse this treatment with charitable contributions of a C corporation. A C corporation is allowed to deduct a limited amount of charitable contributions directly from its taxable income.

24. The answer is B. Crop insurance proceeds and government disaster payments are generally taxable in the year they are received. However, a farmer can elect to postpone reporting the income until the following year if she meets the following conditions:

- The farming business must use the cash method of accounting.
- Crop insurance proceeds were received in the same tax year the crops were damaged.
- Under normal business practices, the farming business would have reported income from the damaged crops in any tax year following the year the damage occurred.

25. The answer is A. Kristy will be forced to recognize $800 of imputed interest as dividend income. When a corporation makes an interest-free loan or a below-market loan to a shareholder, the imputed interest is deemed to be a taxable dividend. The corporation is not allowed to take a deduction for the imputed dividends that were paid. However, if the loan is made to an employee, the treatment of the imputed interest is different. When an employer makes an interest-free loan or a below-market loan to an employee, then the imputed interest is considered taxable compensation to the employee and is deductible by the employer.

26. The answer is B. In general, a partner's basis in distributed property is the same as the partnership's basis in the property immediately before the distribution. However, in this case, the distributed property had a basis that exceeded Tony's remaining basis in his partnership interest after the reduction in his basis in the partnership by the $15,000 cash portion of the distribution. A partner's basis in distributed property cannot exceed his basis in the partnership. Therefore, his partnership basis is reduced to zero, and his basis in the land is $50,000.

Starting basis	$65,000
Cash distribution	15,000
Remaining basis after cash distribution	$50,000

27. The answer is A. An unincorporated business jointly owned by a married couple is generally classified as a partnership for federal tax purposes. However, a married couple who operate a business together may choose to file as a qualified joint venture, filing on two separate Schedules C, as long as they file jointly. Unless a business meets the requirements of a qualified joint venture, a sole proprietorship must be solely owned by one spouse, although the other spouse may work in the business as an employee.

28. The answer is D. There is no gross receipts threshold for whether an entity must be taxed as a corporation. However, the following businesses formed after 1996 are automatically taxed as corporations:
- A business formed under a federal or state law that refers to it as a corporation
- A business formed under a state law that refers to it as a joint-stock company or joint-stock association
- Insurance companies, certain banks
- A business owned by a state or local government
- A business specifically required to be taxed as a corporation by the IRC (for example, certain publicly-traded partnerships)
- Certain foreign businesses
- Any other business that elects to be taxed as a corporation and files Form 8832, *Entity Classification Election*

29. The answer is B. Cheryl has a $20,000 taxable dividend and a $10,000 capital gain. A distribution is treated as a dividend to the extent that the corporation has earnings and profits. The amount distributed to Cheryl would come first from earnings and profits ($20,000) and be classified as a dividend. The remaining amount ($30,000 - $20,000) would be classified as a capital gain, because it exceeds Cheryl's stock basis, which is zero.

30. The answer is C. The calculation of book income is as follows:

Book net income	$380,000
Subtract: Municipal bond interest income	(60,000)
Add back: Federal income tax	120,000
Add back: Contribution carryover	4,300
Taxable income on Schedule M-1	**$444,300**

31. The answer is B. A business is allowed to deduct 50% of business-related entertainment expenses that are incurred for entertaining a current or prospective client, customer, vendor or employee, as long as certain conditions are met. It is not necessary to prove that the entertainment actually resulted in business income or another business benefit.

32. The answer is A. If a corporation cancels a shareholder's debt without repayment by the shareholder, the amount canceled is treated as a distribution to the shareholder. A corporate distribution to a shareholder is generally treated as a distribution of earnings and profits.

33. The answer is C. A beneficiary of a simple trust or an estate that is required to distribute all its income currently must generally report his share of the income required to be distributed currently, whether or not the distribution was received. If the income required to be distributed currently to all beneficiaries exceeds the trust or estate's DNI, each beneficiary must report his proportionate share of the DNI. The determination of whether trust income is required to be distributed currently depends on the terms of the trust instrument and applicable local law. A beneficiary of a complex trust or an estate that is not required to distribute all its income currently must report the sum of:

1. The amount of the income required to be distributed currently (whether or not actually distributed), or if the income required to be distributed currently to all beneficiaries exceeds DNI (without taking into account the charitable deduction), his proportionate share of DNI, and
2. All other amounts properly paid, credited, or required to be distributed, or if the sum of the income required to be distributed currently and other amounts properly paid, credited, or required to be distributed to all beneficiaries exceeds the DNI, his proportionate share of the excess of DNI over the income required to be distributed currently.

34. The answer is B. The answer is calculated as follows:

Gross receipts	$42,000
Supplies expense	(3,500)
Wages for part-time employee	(5,000)
Utility expenses	(800)
Business income	**$32,700**

The amounts for the section 1231 gain and the charitable contributions are not reported on Schedule C. Section 1231 gains and losses are netted against each other in the same manner as capital gains and losses (for example, the gains and losses from a stock sale), except that a section 1231 gain is considered a capital gain, while a section 1231 loss is treated as an ordinary loss. The charitable contributions would be reported on Schedule A if the taxpayer itemizes their deductions.

35. The answer is A. Mario's basis is the cash he contributed, and Juan's basis is his adjusted basis in the property. The FMV does not affect the basis of the partner's interest. The basis of a partnership interest is the money (cash) plus the adjusted basis of any property the partner contributed.

36. The answer is B. To establish and maintain a SIMPLE retirement plan, a business must have had 100 or fewer employees during the preceding year who received $5,000 or more in compensation during the preceding year. If the business has had a SIMPLE plan for more than a year and then exceeds the 100-worker limit, it can have a two-year grace period to establish a different retirement plan.

37. The answer is C. The first corporate tax return is due March 15 of the following year. This short period return covers the period from May 15 through December 31. Corporate tax returns are due on the fifteenth day two-and-a-half months after the end of the corporation's taxable year.

38. The answer is B. The corporation does not recognize any income or loss from this exchange. However, Manny (now the majority shareholder) must recognize ordinary income of $13,000 as payment for services he rendered to the corporation. If a taxpayer transfers property (or money) to a corporation in exchange for stock and immediately gains control of the corporation, the exchange is usually not taxable. This nonrecognition treatment does not apply when a person exchanges services for stock. In order to control a corporation, the taxpayer who transfers the property must own, immediately after the exchange, at least 80% of the stock.

39. The answer is C. A C corporation is taxed as a separate entity and does not have the characteristics of a pass-through entity. Income that is passed through to the shareholders does not retain its character, and it is taxed twice: first at the corporate level when initially earned by the corporation, and secondly at the shareholder level, generally through taxable dividend distributions to the shareholders. In contrast, partnerships, S corporations, and sole proprietorships are all pass-through entities. For example, a partnership is not a taxpaying entity. Each partner reports its distributive share of the partnership's income, gain, loss, deductions, and credits on its own income tax returns and these items generally retain the character that applied to them at the entity's level.

40. The answer is C. The partnership may choose to either deduct or amortize the amounts for legal fees and consulting expenses ($2,000 + $1,000 = $3,000) as organizational expenses. However, the amount paid in commissions to a broker to market partnership interests must be capitalized and cannot be amortized or deducted. The costs for marketing and issuing interests in the partnership such as brokerage, registration, legal fees, and printing costs are syndication costs that are not deductible or amortizable.

41. The answer is D. Ned must reduce the basis of his stock. A nondividend distribution is a distribution that is not paid out of the earnings and profits of a corporation. A nondividend distribution reduces the basis of the shareholder's stock. It is not taxed until the basis in the stock is fully recovered. When the basis of the stock has been reduced to zero, any additional nondividend distribution that is received must be reported as a capital gain.

42. The answer is B. The basis of Doreen's partnership interest is $480,000, calculated as follows:

Adjusted basis of contributed property	$800,000
Minus: Part of mortgage assumed by other partners (80% × $400,000)	320,000
Basis of Doreen's partnership interest	**$480,000**

If contributed property is encumbered by a liability, or if a partner's liabilities are assumed by the partnership, the basis of the contributing partner's interest is reduced (but not below zero) by the liability assumed by the other partners. Doreen must reduce her basis because the assumption of the liability is treated as a distribution of money to her. The assumption of the liability by the other partners is treated as contributions by them of money to the partnership.

43. The answer is B. Gains are recognized for distributions of appreciated property, but losses are not. The amount of gain is calculated as if the S corporation had sold the property to the shareholder at its fair market value. Even though both are pass-through entities, this is one instance in which an S corporation differs from a partnership. In the case of a partnership, gains from appreciated property distributed to a shareholder are generally deferred. With an S corporation, however, the gains must be recognized upon distribution.

44. The answer is B. The video recorder, laptop, and digital camera are all considered listed property. Cellular telephones are no longer considered listed property.

Video recorder	$195
Laptop	450
Digital camera	123
Total	**$768**

Special rules apply to listed property, which includes cars and other vehicles used for transportation; property used for entertainment, recreation, or amusement, such as photographic or video-recording equipment; and certain computers. If an item is used for both business and personal purposes, deductions for depreciation and section 179 are based on the percentage of business use. Further, if business use is not more than 50%, section 179 deductions and bonus depreciation allowances are not allowed, and depreciation must be calculated using the straight-line method.

45. The answer is C. A gain of $70,000 ($160,000 − $90,000) must be recognized, because only $80,000 of the $160,000 condemnation award was reinvested. If property is condemned (or disposed of under the threat of condemnation), gain or loss is figured by comparing the adjusted basis of the condemned property with the net condemnation award. Gain is recognizable to the extent of the lesser of the amount above or the portion of the award that was not reinvested by the time-frame requirements for involuntary conversions.

46. The answer is A. Depletion is the using up of natural resources by mining, quarrying, drilling, or felling. The depletion deduction allows an owner to account for the reduction of a product's physical reserves. Industries that qualify for the depletion deduction are:
- Mining
- Timber
- Oil and gas
- Geothermal energy producers
- Other similar industries

A patent does not qualify for a depletion deduction because it is not a resource that gets used up physically. Instead, patents are amortized.

47. The answer is D. Renee must reduce her basis in the partnership interest to zero. She will have a $32,000 basis in the land. A partner cannot have a negative partnership basis. She does not recognize any income from this transaction and will defer any gain on the land until she sells it. If Renee had received cash instead of property, she would have been forced to recognize the gain.

48. The answer is B. In order to apply for recognition of exempt status under section 501(c)(3) of the Internal Revenue Code, entities use Form 1023, *Application for Recognition of Exemption*. In 2014, a new streamlined Form 1023-EZ was introduced for small tax-exempt organizations. The application is three pages long, compared to 26 pages for the traditional Form 1023. To qualify for the shorter form, an organization must have:
- Gross receipts of $50,000 or less in the prior three years,
- Projected gross receipts of $50,000 or less in the following three years, and
- Assets with a fair market value of $250,000 or less.

Organizations that do not qualify for exemption under section 501(c)(3) may qualify for tax-exempt status by filing Form 1024, *Application for Recognition of Exemption Under 501(a)*.

49. The answer is B. Software development in the United States qualifies for the domestic production activities deduction (DPAD), which is authorized by section 199 and applies to activities related to installing, developing, improving, or creating goods that are "manufactured, produced, or grown within the United States." This deduction also applies to the construction of real property in the United States, domestic software development, and any qualified domestic film production (except for pornographic films.) The following types of business are specifically excluded from claiming the DPAD:

- Construction services that are cosmetic in nature, such as drywall and painting
- Leasing or licensing items to a related party
- Selling food or beverages prepared at restaurants or dining establishments
- The transmission or distribution of electricity, natural gas, or water
- Any advertising, product placement, customer service businesses, and other telecommunications services
- Most service-type businesses

The DPAD is equal to 9% of the lesser of the business's qualified production activities income or taxable income determined without regard to the DPAD.

50. The answer is C. Unlike most tax-exempt entities that are required to file Form 990, religious organizations (churches, synagogues, mosques, etc.) are generally not required to file an information return to report their income and loss. Churches are also exempt from payment of federal income tax and therefore they are not required to file an application for exemption with the IRS, but many churches still seek a formal exemption. Federal law imposes several reporting requirements on exempt organizations, but the main reporting requirements for churches have to do with employment taxes (if they pay employees) and unrelated business income tax, or UBIT. An exempt organization that has $1,000 or more of gross income from an unrelated business must file Form 990–T. Since First Community Church does not have $1,000 of unrelated business income, it is not required to file Form 990-T, but it is still required to file employment tax returns (the Form 941 series), because it pays employee wages.

51. The answer is C. The two partnerships are considered related parties, so the loss is not allowed. Losses will instead be suspended until the property is eventually disposed of in a non-related party transaction. The basis of each partner's interest in the partnership is decreased (but not below zero) by the partner's share of the disallowed loss. If the purchaser later sells the property, only the gain realized that is greater than the loss not allowed will be taxable. If any gain from the sale of the property is not recognized because of this rule, the basis of each partner's interest in the partnership is increased by the partner's share of that gain.

52. The answer is D. An accrual-based C corporation is allowed to deduct charitable contributions authorized during the taxable year by the board of directors and paid by the fifteenth day of the third month following the close of the taxable year.

53. The answer is C. Angie must include $27,000 (30% × $90,000) in her gross income for the year, in spite of having only received a $23,000 distribution. A partner pays tax on income that is earned by the partnership, even if it is not distributed. A general partner's share of partnership trade or business income is considered income from self-employment and is subject to self-employment tax.

54. The answer is D. Prepayment penalties on a mortgage are deductible as interest expense. The other items listed cannot be claimed as business expenses. Any type of political contribution, kickback, or bribe is not deductible. In addition, lobbying expenses that are incurred to try to influence federal or state legislation are not deductible as a business expense. Repairs to equipment that add value to an asset or increase its useful life are considered improvements and must be capitalized and depreciated.

55. The answer is C. Since Benevolent Corporation operates on the accrual basis, it must meet the all events test and economic performance must have occurred before deducting and/or accruing the expense. Benevolent is not required to pay the expense first. Under the accrual method of accounting, transactions are accrued as they occur, regardless of when the cash (or other form of payment) is received.

56. The answer is B. Distributions from an S corporation with no accumulated earnings and profits are generally treated as a nontaxable return of capital, up to the amount of the shareholder's adjusted stock basis. However, if an S corporation distributes appreciated property, the distribution is treated as a sale to the shareholder. To the extent the FMV of the property exceeds the corporation's basis, the corporation would recognize gain. The gain passes through to the shareholders and increases the basis of their stock. Gain is determined when the final year-end reconciliations are made and the shareholder has adjusted his stock basis for any increases, but before any decreases attributable to the current year are deducted. The gain is reported as a capital gain on the shareholder's Schedule D. In this case, Lydia must report $15,000 of capital gain on her tax return. This includes the gain of $13,000 recognized by Pascal and passed through to her. In addition, since the distribution reduces the basis of her stock to zero, the amount exceeding her basis ($2,000) is also treated as capital gain.
The answer is calculated as follows:

Adjusted basis before distribution	$60,000
Capital gain related to distribution	13,000
Adjusted basis of stock	73,000
Distributions of property (FMV)	(75,000)
Excess over basis - capital gain	**$2,000**

57. The answer is B. The answer is calculated as follows: $120,000 × 80% = $96,000 dividends-received deduction. A corporation can deduct a percentage of certain dividends received during its tax year. The dividends-received deduction is a tax deduction for corporations on the dividends paid to it by other corporations in which it has an ownership stake. If the corporation receiving the dividend owns 20% of the dividend-paying corporation, the deduction is 80%.

58. The answer is C. In general, a partner's basis in distributed property will be the same as the partnership's basis in the property immediately before the distribution. However, in this case, the distributed property had a basis that exceeded Justine's remaining partnership interest after the cash distribution. Therefore, her partnership basis is reduced to zero, and the basis of the property is $29,000.

Starting basis	$60,000
Cash distribution	31,000
Remaining basis after cash distribution	**$29,000**

59. The answer is C. An S-election may be revoked if shareholders holding more than 50% of the stock agree to the termination. Since Charlotte and Thomas own more than 50% of the outstanding stock, they can elect to revoke the S-election.

60. The answer is A. The IRS may reclassify the excess $1,500 per month of rental payments as a constructive dividend, and the corporation would lose that amount as a deduction. If a corporation rents property from a shareholder and the rent is unreasonably more than the shareholder would charge an unrelated person to rent the same property, the excessive part of the rent may be treated as a distribution to the shareholder.

61. The answer is C. Lynden Corporation must include the $12,000 on each employee's Form W-2 because it is taxable as wages. The amounts are subject to income tax withholding, as well as to Social Security and Medicare tax. The car allowance is treated as part of a nonaccountable plan.

62. The answer is C. A personal service corporation is not required to use the accrual method of accounting, regardless of the amount of its gross receipts. In general, the following entities are required to use the accrual method:
- A corporation (other than an S corporation) with average annual gross receipts for the prior three tax years exceeding $5 million
- A partnership with a corporate partner (other than an S corporation) with average annual gross receipts for the prior three tax years exceeding $5 million
- Any business that carries, produces, or sells inventory, unless the business has average annual gross receipts of $1 million or less
- Any tax shelter, regardless of its size
- Any corporation with long-term contracts

63. The answer is A. In a liquidating distribution of cash for a partner's entire interest in a partnership usually results in capital gain or loss for the partner. The gain or loss is the difference between the amount realized and the adjusted basis of the partner's interest in the partnership. Therefore, Carl has an $8,000 capital gain upon the disposition of his partnership interest ($20,000 - $12,000 = $8,000).

64. The answer is B. A corporation's treatment of distributions is different during a complete liquidation. In a liquidation, a corporation recognizes gain on appreciated assets and losses on depreciated property. Shareholders may also recognize gain or loss on a corporation's distribution of assets during a liquidation based on the fair market value of the assets distributed versus their basis in the shares of the corporation. In this case, Gordon's gain would be calculated as follows:
- $10,000 + $12,000 = $22,000 distribution
- $22,000 - $17,000 stock basis = $5,000 gain

65. The answer is C. Section 1250 property generally consists of buildings (including their structural components), most other permanent structures, and land improvements of general use and purpose. Examples of section 1250 property include residential rental property, factory buildings, and office buildings. Since buildings are generally depreciated using the straight-line method, taxpayers usually receive more favorable treatment of depreciation recapture for section 1250 property versus 1245 property.

66. The answer is A. State incorporation fees are considered qualifying organizational costs. However, the following items are capital expenses that cannot be amortized:

- Costs for issuing and selling stock or securities, such as commissions and printing costs
- Costs associated with the transfer of assets to the corporation

A business can potentially take an immediate deduction of up to $5,000 of qualifying organizational costs and $5,000 of qualifying start-up costs in the year it commences business.

67. The answer is C. Leisure Crafts Corporation will not recognize gain or loss on the sale of the asset. There is no loss recognized in this transaction because this is a sale to a related party. A loss on the sale of an asset to a related party is not allowed unless the distribution is done in a complete liquidation. In this case, related parties include members of a family, including siblings, spouse, ancestors (parents, grandparents), and lineal descendants (children, grandchildren). This list is not exhaustive, and related parties can also be entities. IRC section 267 not only applies to family members, but also includes related businesses, trusts, fiduciaries, and a host of other transactions.

68. The answer is A. If a business has at least 50 full-time employees, (including full-time equivalent employees), on average during the prior year, the employer is a considered an ALE for the current calendar year. ALEs are subject to the employer shared responsibility provisions and the employer information reporting provisions of the ACA. The Employer Shared Responsibility provisions became effective January 1, 2015.

69. The answer is C. The corporation treats this $6,000 as a short-term loss that may be carried back for up to three years and carried forward for up to five years. When a corporation carries a net capital loss to another tax year, it is treated as a short-term loss. It does not retain its original identity as long-term or short-term. A corporation can deduct capital losses only up to the amount of its capital gains. In other words, if a corporation has an excess capital loss, it cannot deduct the loss in the current tax year. A capital loss is carried to other years in the following order:
- Three years prior to the loss year
- Two years prior to the loss year
- One year prior to the loss year. Any loss remaining is carried forward for up to five years.

70. The answer is D. All of the costs must be added to the basis of the land. The original basis of an asset includes:
- The purchase price, including any borrowed money to pay for the property
- Expenses of making the purchase, such as legal fees or realtor fees
- Any existing liabilities that the seller assumes (such as delinquent property taxes)

Costs incurred to demolish a building are added to the basis of the land on which the demolished building was located. The costs cannot be claimed as a current deduction.

71. The answer is A. A partner cannot have a negative basis. A partner generally recognizes gain on a partnership distribution only to the extent any money (and marketable securities treated as money) included in the distribution exceeds the adjusted basis of the partner's interest in the partnership. Any gain recognized is generally treated as capital gain from the sale of the partnership interest on the date of the distribution. Since Jacob received a $10,000 cash distribution when his basis was only $7,000, he must recognize gain of $3,000 and reduce his partnership basis to zero. If partnership property (other than marketable securities treated as money) is distributed to a partner, he generally does not recognize any gain until the sale or other disposition of the property. Unless there is a complete liquidation of a partner's interest, the basis of property (other than money) distributed to the partner by a partnership is its adjusted basis to the partnership immediately before the distribution. However, the basis of the property to the partner cannot be more than the adjusted basis of his interest in the partnership reduced by any money received in the same transaction. In this case, because Jacob's basis in the partnership has already been reduced to zero, his basis in the distributed property is also zero.

72. The answer is D. An exempt entity may file a request for exemption within 15 months of initial organization. Retroactive exemption is still available within that time period.

73. The answer is D. In general, a business can deduct only 50% of business-related meal and entertainment expenses. However, there are some circumstances in which meals are not subject to this limit. The following meals are not subject to the 50% limit:
- Meals that are included in employees' wages as taxable compensation
- Meals that qualify as a de minimis fringe benefit, such as occasional coffee and doughnuts
- Meals furnished to employees when the employer operates a restaurant or catering service
- Meals furnished to employees as part of a teambuilding activity, such as a company picnic
- Meals that are required by federal law to be furnished to crew members of certain commercial vessels
- Meals furnished on an oil or gas platform or drilling rig located offshore or in Alaska

These meals are 100% deductible by the employer.

74. The answer is B. Hudson River Corporation would report a $110,000 gain ($200,000 FMV - $90,000 basis). Samuel would report a $200,000 dividend (the fair market value of the property). All distributions of appreciated property would trigger gain recognition for the corporation. The distribution to the shareholder is treated as a sale, and gain is reported on the transaction. However, a corporation would not recognize a loss on the distribution of property.

75. The answer is D. Since Nicoletta is an accrual-basis corporation, the wages are deductible as they are accrued. The full amount of the bonus and other wages to employees is deductible in 2015.

76. The answer is B. A business that otherwise qualifies for the DPAD may use one of two simplified calculation methods if it meets certain tests. First, it can use the small business simplified overall method to apportion cost of goods sold and other deductions, expenses, and losses between DPGR and non-DPGR if it meets any of the following tests:
- It is engaged in a farming business and is not required to use the accrual method.
- Its average annual gross receipts are $5 million or less in the prior three years.
- It is a qualifying small business taxpayer that is eligible to use the cash method.

Estates, trusts, certain oil and gas partnerships, and certain partnerships owned by expanded affiliated groups cannot use this method. Under the small business simplified overall method, the total cost of goods sold and other deductions, expenses, and losses are ratably apportioned between DPGR and non-DPGR based on relative gross receipts. Alternatively, a business generally can use the simplified deduction method to apportion other deductions, expenses, and losses (but not cost of goods sold) between DPGR and non-DPGR if it meets either of the following tests.

- Its total trade or business assets at the end of the tax year are $10 million or less.
- Its average annual gross receipts (defined above) are $100 million or less.

The use of certain of these methods is limited to small businesses that meet specified parameters.

77. The answer is D. There is no such thing as a casualty loss limitation. There are three shareholder loss limitations:

- Stock and debt basis limitations
- At risk limitations
- Passive activity loss limitations

The fact that a shareholder receives a Schedule K-1 reflecting a loss does not mean that the shareholder is automatically entitled to claim it. If a shareholder of an S corporation is allocated an item of loss or deduction, the shareholder must have adequate stock and/or debt basis to claim the loss. Even if a shareholder has adequate stock and/or debt basis to claim an S corporation loss, he must also consider the at-risk and passive activity loss limitations and therefore still may not be able to claim the loss.

78. The answer is B. Because the cash received does not exceed the basis of her partnership interest, Fernanda does not recognize any gain on the distribution. Any gain on the land will be recognized when she later sells or disposes of it. The distribution decreases the adjusted basis of her partnership interest to $57,000 ($165,000 − [$80,000 + $28,000]).

79. The answer is D. Generally, transferring property into a corporation in exchange for stock is a taxable event. Since Jacobo is not "in control" of the corporation after the exchange, he must treat the exchange as a sale. For Section 351 purposes, "control" means ownership of at least 80% of the total stock. Since this transaction does not qualify for Section 351 nonrecognition treatment, Jacobo must recognize a gain. The gain is $340,000 ($700,000 FMV -$360,000 basis). Jacobo's basis in his stock is $700,000 after the exchange.

80. The answer is D. An LLC with at least two members can choose to be taxed as a partnership (its default status) or, upon election, a corporation (either a C corporation or, if eligible, an S corporation).

81. The answer is B. The expenses incurred during a complete liquidation of a corporation can be deducted on the final corporate return.

82. The answer is A. Qualset's basis in the new plane is $70,000 (the $30,000 basis of the old plane plus the $40,000 paid). The FMV of the new plane has no bearing on the basis in a section 1031 exchange. If a business trades property in a qualified like-kind exchange and also pays money, the basis of the property received is the basis of the property given up, increased by the additional money paid.

83. The answer is B. The amount of a partnership's loss that a partner is allowed to deduct on her tax return is dependent on the partner's basis in the partnership. In general, a partner cannot deduct losses that exceed her partnership basis. Losses disallowed due to insufficient basis are carried forward until the partner can deduct them in a later year. Robin's share of the partnership liabilities increases her basis to $101,000 ($1,000 cash investment + $100,000 share of the partnership's loan balance [$500,000 × 20%]). Robin can deduct her entire $20,000 share of the loss ($100,000 × 20%) because it does not exceed her debt basis, but her basis is reduced to $81,000.

84. The answer is D. For a business expense to be deductible, it must be both *ordinary* and *necessary*. An ordinary expense is one that is common and accepted in the taxpayer's industry. A necessary expense is one that is helpful and appropriate for the particular trade or business. In addition, even if a business expense is both ordinary and necessary, it must be *reasonable* in amount. However, an expense does not have to be required to be deductible.

85. The answer is D. A complex trust is allowed to accumulate income, unlike a simple trust that is required to distribute all of its income each year. If a trust fails to make distributions, it becomes a complex trust by default.

86. The answer is C. In addition to an NOL due to casualty or theft, exceptions to the two-year NOL carryback rule include the following:

- An NOL due to a farming loss may be carried back for five years.
- Certain qualified small businesses may carry back a loss for three years.
- Product liability losses may be carried back for ten years.

87. The answer is C. A private foundation is required to file an annual information return every year, regardless of income. Private foundations file Form 990-PF.

88. The answer is A. Amara's basis is calculated as follows:

Initial Contribution	$75,000
Increases from pass-through of income	
Ordinary Income	52,000
Tax-exempt interest	5,000
Distributions	(20,000)
Decreases from pass-through of expenses	
Short-term capital loss	(4,000)
Charitable contributions	(5,000)
Section 179 deduction	(20,000)
Adjusted basis at December 31, 2015	**$83,000**

89. The answer is C. Small corporations are exempt from the corporate AMT and are not required to file Form 4626. A small corporation is defined as one with average annual gross receipts for the prior three years that did not exceed $7.5 million (or $5 million for its first three-year period).

90. The answer is A. Chris realizes $25,000 from the sale of his partnership interest ($10,000 cash payment + $15,000 liability relief). He reports $4,000 ($25,000 realized − $21,000 basis) as a capital gain. The sale of a partner's interest in a partnership usually results in capital gain or loss. The gain (or loss) is the difference between the amount realized and the adjusted basis of the partner's interest in the partnership. If the selling partner is relieved of any partnership liabilities, that partner must include the liability relief as part of the amount realized.

91. The answer is D. This is income in respect of a decedent (IRD) and must be included in Mateo's gross income, (not on his mother's final tax return). IRD is any taxable income that was *earned* but not *received* by the decedent at the time of their death. IRD is not taxed on the final return of the deceased taxpayer. IRD is reported on the tax return of the person (or entity) that receives the income. IRD retains the same tax character that would have applied if the deceased taxpayer were still alive. So the rental income would be taxed as rental income, and the wages would be taxed as ordinary income. IRD can come from various sources, including:
- Unpaid salary, wages, or bonuses
- Distributions from traditional IRAs and employer-provided retirement plans
- Deferred compensation benefits
- Accrued but unpaid interest, dividends, and rent
- Accounts receivable of a sole proprietor

92. The answer is C. Form 990-T is used by tax-exempt organizations to report and pay the tax on unrelated business income. Any domestic or foreign tax-exempt organization must file Form 990-T, *Exempt Organization Business Income Tax Return*, if it has gross income from an unrelated trade or business of $1,000 or more.

93. The answer is A. Inventory is not eligible for the section 179 deduction. The other assets listed all qualify for accelerated depreciation (section 179).

94. The answer is B. With the exception of the rental income, the proceeds from the used machinery sale, and the SEP-IRA contribution, all of the items listed above are reportable on Schedule F, resulting in a net farm profit of $750,000. Gross income from farming activity includes income from sales of farm products, including livestock raised for sale or purchased for resale. Rent received for the use of farmland is generally rental income, not farm income, and is reported on Form 4835, *Farm Rental Income and Expenses*. Sales of land, depreciable machinery and equipment, and livestock held for draft, breeding, sport, or dairy purposes are reported on Form 4797, *Sales of Business Property*. In the case of a sole proprietorship or partnership, if the owners of the business contribute to their own retirement accounts, they must take the deduction as an adjustment to income on Form 1040.

95. The answer is A. $3,865. The standard mileage rate in 2015 is $0.575, so driving expenses are equal to $0.575 X 1,200 = $690. The total amount of business expenses is $3,175 + $690, or $3,865.

96. The answer is A. Telecast has a $4,000 gain from the conversion. The adjusted basis of the property was $20,000, and Telecast received an insurance reimbursement of $45,000. Since Telecast only used $41,000 of the insurance reimbursement on qualifying replacement property, the company would recognize a gain of $4,000 ($45,000 - $41,000), the amount that was not reinvested.

97. The answer is B. When calculating the alternative minimum tax, a corporation calculates the alternative tax net operating loss (ATNOL), which is the excess of the deductions allowed for figuring alternative minimum taxable income (AMTI), excluding the ATNOL deduction, over the income included in AMTI. The amount of the ATNOL that can be deducted when calculating AMTI generally cannot exceed 90% of AMTI. If the ATNOL exceeds this limit, it can be carried back two years or forward up to 20 years.

98. The answer is A. Partnerships and C corporations cannot own stock in an S corporation. Estates, certain trusts, individuals, and some exempt entities are permitted to own stock in an S corporation. An S corporation can have up to 100 shareholders, and it can have both voting and nonvoting stock, as long as there is only one class of stock.

99. The answer is B. In a two-partner partnership, when a partner dies and the surviving partner becomes the sole owner of the business, the partnership is no longer in existence and a final partnership tax return must be filed. The partnership's tax year ended on the date of termination, September 18, 2015. When a partnership is terminated before the end of its regular tax year, Form 1065 must be filed for the short tax year from the beginning of the tax year through the date of termination. The return is due on the fifteenth day of the fourth month following the date of termination, or January 15, 2016, in this case.

100. The answer is C. When property is distributed in a complete liquidation, the transaction is treated as if the corporation sold the assets to a buyer at fair market value. The corporation recognizes gain or loss on the liquidation in an amount equal to the difference between the FMV and the adjusted basis of the assets distributed. Amounts received by the shareholder in complete liquidation of a corporation are treated as full payment in exchange for the shareholder's stock. A liquidating distribution is considered a return of capital and is not taxable to the shareholder until the shareholder recovers all of his basis in the stock.

After the basis of the stock has been reduced to zero, the shareholder must report any additional amounts received as a capital gain. If a dissolving corporation distributes property that is subject to a liability, the gain or loss is adjusted to reflect assumption of the liability. If the liability is greater than the FMV of the property, the amount of the liability is treated as the FMV of the property. In this case, because the remaining loan amount is more than the FMV of the truck, the amount of the liability is treated as the truck's FMV. The corporation must recognize a $48,000 gain on the distribution ($60,000 loan - $12,000 basis). Because Jackson personally assumed the $60,000 loan on the truck, the amount of the distribution for the truck is reduced by the $60,000 loan assumption, resulting in a $0 distribution to Jackson. Although the $60,000 liability is treated as the FMV of the truck for calculating gain for the corporation, on the shareholder side, IRC Sect. 301(b)(2) reduces the amount of the distribution (but not below zero) to the shareholder by the amount of the liability assumed by the shareholder.

Answers to Exam #5: Representation

1. The answer is D. In 2015, Congress passed the *Fixing America's Surface Transportation Act*. A provision in this law gives power to the Internal Revenue Service to authorize the US State Department to suspend or deny delinquent taxpayers' passport privileges. Taxpayers owing more than $50,000 to the IRS will receive notice of the revocation. The U.S. State Department also will not issue a passport to anyone who currently owes more than $50,000. The IRS must first file a lien. The $50,000 threshold includes penalties and interest.

2. The answer is C. A lien is a legal claim to the property of the taxpayer as security for a tax debt. Generally, a federal tax lien will continue until the liability is satisfied, it becomes unenforceable by lapse of time (the collection statute expires), or a bond is accepted in the amount of the liability.

3. The answer is A. A practitioner cannot take into consideration the chances that a tax return may or may not be audited, or that a particular matter may or may not be raised on audit. Alexander is playing "audit lottery", which is a type of practitioner advice that is specifically prohibited by the IRS in Circular 230.

4. The answer is A. A practitioner must, at the request of a client, promptly return any and all original records that the client needs to comply with his federal tax obligations. This requirement does not include any forms or schedules the practitioner prepared because she is withholding these documents pending the client's payment. The practitioner may retain copies of the records returned to a client.

5. The answer is D. The IRS *Collection Financial Standards* are used to evaluate a taxpayer's ability to pay a delinquent tax liability. These standards help determine allowable living expenses that are necessary to provide for a taxpayer's (and his family's) health and welfare and/or production of income while his tax debt is being repaid. Allowances for housing, utilities, and transportation vary by location, while standard amounts are allowed nationwide for food, clothing, out-of-pocket health care expenses, and other items. Consideration is also given to the taxpayer's income, his bank and retirement accounts, real estate and other assets, and his outstanding debts. Further consideration may need to be given to the taxpayer's obligations for court-ordered payments, such as child support and alimony.

6. The answer is D. Under IRC section 6673, Max could face a penalty of up to $25,000 for making frivolous arguments before the United States Tax Court.

7. The answer is B. Tax evasion is an illegal practice in which individuals or businesses intentionally avoid paying their true tax liabilities. Those caught evading taxes are subject to criminal charges and substantial penalties. Tax avoidance, though not specifically defined by the IRS, is commonly used to describe the legal reduction of taxable income, such as through deductions and credits. Taxpayers with offshore bank accounts and foreign trusts have additional reporting requirements to the federal government, but the accounts are not illegal.

8. The answer is C. If an enrolled agent or other practitioner withdraws from representation of a client, he must write "WITHDRAW" across the top of the first page of Form 2848, *Power of Attorney and Declaration of Representative*, with his signature and the date below it. It must be either mailed or faxed to the IRS. The form must clearly indicate the applicable tax matters and periods. If a taxpayer is revoking the power of attorney, he must write "REVOKE" across the top of the form with his signature and the date below it. If a taxpayer or representative does not have a copy of the power of attorney, a statement of revocation or withdrawal must be sent to the IRS.

9. The answer is C. A durable power of attorney is terminated upon a taxpayer's death. A durable power of attorney is not subject to a time limit and will continue in force after the incapacitation or incompetency of the individual. An ordinary power of attorney is automatically revoked if the person who made it is found to be incompetent, but a durable power of attorney can only be revoked by the person who made it, and while that person is mentally competent.

10. The answer is A. The IRS Office of Appeals provides taxpayers an alternative to going to court to fight disagreements about the application of tax law. The role of Appeals is to resolve disputes on a fair and impartial basis that does not favor either the government or the taxpayer. Appeals officers are directed to give serious consideration to settlement offers by taxpayers or their representatives. New policies instituted in 2014 change the way the office handles appeals of examination and other compliance determinations. Under the new approach, Appeals will not attempt to do its own fact-finding investigations or raise new issues that were not addressed during the tax compliance process. Rather, Appeals will attempt to settle a case after the collection or examination division has made a determination that a taxpayer disagrees with.

11. The answer is B. Both taxpayers are *jointly and severally liable* for the tax and penalties on a joint return even if they later divorce. Joint and several liability means that each taxpayer is legally responsible for the entire liability. Thus, both spouses are generally held responsible for all the tax due, even if one spouse earned all the income or claimed improper deductions or credits. This is also true even if a divorce decree states that a former spouse will be responsible for any amounts due on previously filed joint returns.

12. The answer is D. The practice of enrolled actuaries is limited to certain Internal Revenue Code sections that relate to their area of expertise, principally those sections governing employee retirement plans.

13. The answer is B. If an individual loses eligibility to practice, the IRS will not recognize a power of attorney that names the individual as a representative. Individuals who have been disbarred as a result of certain actions cannot practice before the IRS.

14. The answer is A. Under IRC section 7525, communications relating to tax advice between an enrolled agent and a taxpayer are confidential to the same extent that the communications would be privileged if they were between a taxpayer and an attorney, and the advice relates to:
- Noncriminal tax matters before the IRS, or
- Noncriminal tax proceedings brought in federal court by or against the United States.

This confidentiality privilege does not extend to:
- Communications regarding tax shelters
- Communications in furtherance of a crime or fraud
- Any criminal matter before the IRS
- The preparation of tax returns

15. The answer is C. Best practices, according to Circular 230, include:
- Clearly communicating with a client regarding the terms of engagement
- Establishing relevant facts, evaluating the reasonableness of assumptions or representations, relating the applicable law to the relevant facts, and arriving at a conclusion supported by the law and the facts (not by the client's information)
- Advising the client regarding any potential penalties
- Acting fairly and with integrity in practice before the IRS

16. The answer is B. Under IRC section 6531 (periods of limitation on criminal prosecutions), there is a six-year statute of limitations for the criminal offense of willfully attempting to evade or defeat any tax. Do not confuse this criminal provision with the collection statute on a fraudulent return. There is no statute of limitations *for collection* when a fraudulent return is filed, but this is a civil matter, not a criminal one.

17. The answer is C. Failure to timely file tax returns or to pay taxes may be grounds for denying an application for enrollment. The Return Preparer Office will review all of the facts and circumstances to determine whether a denial of enrollment is warranted. Answer A is incorrect because an enrolled agent is not required to have a Social Security number. Answer B is incorrect because U.S. citizenship is not required to practice before the IRS. Answer D is incorrect because insolvency and bankruptcy are not grounds to deny enrollment.

18. The answer is A. Generally, when a taxpayer files bankruptcy, the 10-year collection statute is suspended by the length of time the taxpayer is in bankruptcy, plus an additional 6 months (IRM, Section 5; *Collection Statutes*).

19. The answer is A. The IRS is restricted from issuing a levy while an installment agreement is pending, for 30 days after rejection or termination and during any appeal. The statute of limitations on collection is also suspended during this time (IRC 6331(k)(2)(A) through (D)).

20. The answer is B. The Statutory Notice of Deficiency is often called the "90-day letter." It gives the taxpayer 90 days from the date of the notice to file a petition in the U.S. Tax Court challenging the proposed deficiency. A taxpayer has 150 days if his address is outside of the country on the day the notice of deficiency is mailed.

21. The answer is B. A disbarred practitioner can seek reinstatement from the Office of Professional Responsibility five years after disbarment.

22. The answer is A. U.S. Citizens and Resident aliens with a valid SSN can claim EITC. The SSN must be valid for work purposes. A taxpayer cannot claim EITC using an Individual Taxpayer Identification Number (ITIN) or Adoption Taxpayer Identification Number (ATIN).

23. The answer is C. Only licensed attorneys are allowed to practice before the U.S. Tax Court without passing a qualifying test. EAs and CPAs must take a separate exam that gives them the right to practice before the Tax Court.

24. The answer is A. Esther must respond to the summons. A summons legally compels a person, taxpayer, or third party to meet with the IRS and provide information, documents, or testimony. An individual has the right to contest a summons based on various technical, procedural, or Constitutional grounds. However, if a taxpayer or other witness fails to respond to a summons within the prescribed period, the IRS may seek judicial enforcement through U.S. district court. When a tax return preparer is served a summons (or court order or subpoena), she is not bound to disclosure requirements under IRC section 7216 that require written consent from a client before any disclosure of personal information is allowed. The required information must be clearly identified in the summons or other document.

25. The answer is D. The trust fund recovery penalty (TFRP) may be assessed against any person who is responsible for collecting or paying income and employment taxes withheld, and who willfully fails to pay them. A *responsible person* is any person who has the duty to perform and the power to direct the collecting, accounting, and paying of trust fund taxes. This person may be:
- An officer or an employee of a corporation
- A member or employee of a partnership
- A corporate director or shareholder
- A member of a board of trustees of a nonprofit organization
- Another person with authority and control over funds to direct their disbursement
- Another corporation or third party payer

26. The answer is B. Under IRC section 6694(a), if there is an understatement due to an unreasonable position, the penalty is the greater of $1,000 or 50% of the income derived by the tax return preparer related to the return or claim for refund.

27. The answer is C. Under Circular 230, preparers are required to keep copies of all returns they have prepared or to retain a list of clients and tax returns prepared. At a minimum, the list must contain the taxpayer's name and taxpayer identification number, the tax year, and the type of return prepared. The copies or the list may be stored either electronically or as hard copies. The copies of tax returns or the lists must be retained for at least three years after the close of the return period. The close of the return period is defined as June 30, meaning the three-year period to retain records begins July 1.

28. The answer is D. Once a tax liability is assessed, the statute of limitations for collection begins to run. In general, the date of assessment is the date on which the IRS receives a taxpayer's return with a tax owed. If a taxpayer does not file a return, the assessment date is the date on which the IRS assesses any additional tax owed. There is no statute of limitations for instances where a return is not filed or a fraudulent return was filed.

29. The answer is C. Section 10.35 is a new provision of the revised Circular 230. It states that a practitioner must be competent to engage in practice before the IRS. Competence is defined as having the appropriate level of knowledge, skill, thoroughness, and preparation for the specific matter or matters related to a client's engagement. Circular 230 says a practitioner can become competent in various ways, including consulting with experts in the relevant area or studying the relevant law. Section 10.35 replaces the complex rules that previously governed covered opinions.

30. The answer is A. Form 872-A, *Special Consent to Extend the Time to Assess Tax*, is used by taxpayers to voluntarily extend the statute of limitations. A taxpayer always has the right to refuse to extend the period of limitations or limit this extension to a mutually agreed-upon issue or mutually agreed-upon period of time (See Publication 1035, *Extending the Tax Assessment Period*).

31. The answer is C. Taxpayers and preparers cannot rely on guidance issued by IRS publications to avoid accuracy-related penalties. Although the information in IRS publications is drawn from the Internal Revenue Code, Treasury regulations, and other primary sources of authority, the publications are not considered to have substantial authority. Substantial authority means the authority to serve as the basis for interpretation of current tax law and to establish precedents for the future.

32. The answer is A. Revenue rulings are written determinations released by the IRS that interpret the tax laws as applied to specific factual situations. A private letter ruling applies only to the individual taxpayer who requests the ruling. Technical advice memoranda provide nonbinding written advice in response to questions that arise from examinations. Information letters are issued in response to requests for general information by taxpayers. They are advisory only and have no binding effect on the IRS.

33. The answer is D. A third party authorization is not sufficient to designate a preparer to receive a tax refund check. A signed Form 2848, *Power of Attorney and Declaration of Representative*, must be used. Form 2848 is also used to authorize an individual to represent a taxpayer or an entity before the IRS. A third party authorization will automatically end no later than the due date (without extensions) for filing the next year's return.

34. The answer is A. A taxpayer must appeal a rejected offer in compromise within 30 days.

35. The answer is C. When a recognized representative has unreasonably delayed or hindered an examination, collection, or investigation, an Internal Revenue Service employee may request the permission of his immediate supervisor to contact the taxpayer directly for information. Answer D is incorrect because a representative does not necessarily have to be a practitioner for his power of attorney to be valid (for example, a father who is representing a son or an executor representing an estate).

36. The answer is C. Zena is allowed to represent Thiago during the examination of his joint return, provided Thiago signs a valid power of attorney (Form 2848). In the case of a joint return, both taxpayers decide independently whether or not they want to be represented by a recognized representative (either by the same representative or by different representatives), or not represented at all. Each taxpayer must execute their own separate Form 2848 if they want to be represented.

37. The answer is B. There is an automatic stay of all IRS assessment and collection of tax when a taxpayer files in bankruptcy court. The stay remains in effect until the bankruptcy court lifts it or discharges liabilities, meaning they are eliminated or no longer legally enforceable.

38. The answer is A. Enrolled agents cannot use the term "certified" when describing their professional designation. The other choices would be allowable representations.

39. The answer is C. The IRS will grant an installment agreement only if it provides for full payment of the tax due. A taxpayer cannot negotiate for a lower tax liability using an installment agreement.

40. The answer is D. A tax preparer cannot make disclosures to solicit additional business from an existing client for business unrelated to the IRS (for example, disclosures to sell or solicit insurance, stocks, or other financial services). In this case, the preparer would need written consent from the client. IRC section 7216 provides rules and sanctions for inappropriate disclosure of client information. Each violation of section 7216 could mean a fine of up to $1,000, a prison term of up to one year, or both. There is also a separate civil penalty of $250 for improper disclosure or use of taxpayer information, as outlined in IRC section 6713. However, unlike section 7216, this code section does not require that the disclosure be "knowing or reckless".

41. The answer is C. A preparer is not required to authenticate a taxpayer's Social Security number with the federal government in determining eligibility for the EITC. However, a preparer does have significant due diligence requirements, including filing Form 8867, *Paid Preparer's Earned Income Credit Checklist,* with a taxpayer's return; conducting a thorough interview with the taxpayer every year and documenting his answers to questions; and completing the EITC worksheet. The IRS also suggests that a preparer confirm identities and taxpayer identification numbers of taxpayers, their spouses, and dependents on returns he prepares. However, actually inspecting a client's Social Security card is not required.

42. The answer is C. If a practitioner becomes aware that a client is being investigated for criminal fraud, the preparer should end representation immediately. Generally, only criminal tax attorneys would have the appropriate legal expertise needed in such cases. In addition, a tax preparer may be considered a witness in the criminal investigation, since the section 7525 practitioner-client confidentiality privilege does not cover criminal matters. Communications in the context of a civil proceeding that later becomes a criminal case are likewise not covered.

43. The answer is C. An official complaint against a practitioner from the OPR is not required to disclose the identity of the employee who drafted the complaint. The complaint must include the nature of the complaint, a demand for an answer to the charges, instructions on how to respond to the complaint, the specific charges against the practitioner, and the sanctions recommended.

44. The answer is C. Solicitation by mail of a former client is not disreputable conduct. It is disallowed only if the client or former client has communicated that he does not want to be solicited. The OPR can censure, suspend, or disbar a practitioner from practice before the IRS for incompetence or for disreputable conduct, such as giving false or misleading information, or participating in any business or accepting assistance from a disbarred practitioner. Disreputable conduct also includes:
- Willfully failing to e-file returns electronically when subject to the e-filing mandate, and
- Failing to include a valid PTIN on tax returns.

45. The answer is A. Cora is allowed to destroy the records related to her continuing professional education four years following the date of the EA renewal for which the CPE is credited.

46. The answer is C. Form 2848 now provides space for the information and signatures of up to four authorized representatives.

47. The answer is C. An enrolled agent's practice rights do not extend to representation before the courts – except for the United States Tax Court, and only if they pass a special U.S. Tax Court exam and meet other U.S. Tax Court practice requirements. An enrolled agent cannot represent a client in U.S. district court.

48. The answer is A. An enrolled agent is required to complete a minimum of 16 hours of continuing professional education each year. Two of these hours must be an approved ethics course.

49. The answer is C. The preparer must take reasonable steps to inform the taxpayer within 24 hours of the rejection. In addition, the preparer is required to disclose the reasons for rejection.

50. The answer is B. An owner of a firm that employs preparers will not be subject to the preparer penalty if any of the following apply:
- There was substantial authority for the position taken on the return.
- There was a reasonable basis for the position, and the position was adequately disclosed.
- There was reasonable cause for the underpayment and the preparer acted in good faith.

The determination of whether there was reasonable cause and/or a preparer acted in good faith is made on a case-by-case basis, taking into account all pertinent facts and circumstances. To meet the reasonable basis standard, a tax return preparer may rely in good faith, without verification, on information furnished by a taxpayer, advisor, another preparer, or other party.

However, under a rewritten section 10.36 in the revised Circular 230, new compliance measures are specified for a practitioner in charge of a firm's tax practice. A practitioner (or practitioners, if the duty is shared) who oversees a firm's practice must ensure adequate procedures are in place for every member, associate, or employee to comply with the requirements specified in Circular 230. If a firm has not identified an individual with principal authority over the practice, the IRS may identify one or more practitioners who will be considered responsible for the section 10.36 compliance requirements. A practitioner(s) who does not take reasonable steps to ensure the firm has adequate procedures in place to comply with Circular 230 requirements may face disciplinary action. He may also be subject to sanctions if he knows of other members of the firm who are engaging in a pattern of noncompliance, and he fails to take prompt action to correct the noncompliance.

51. The answer is B. An unenrolled practitioner cannot represent a client before the IRS without the taxpayer present (Publication 947, *Practice Before the IRS*).

52. The answer is B. Under section 10.21 of Circular 230, a practitioner is required to promptly notify a client of an error or omission and advise him of the consequences of not correcting the error or omission. A practitioner, however, is not required to amend prior year returns, nor is she required to notify the IRS about a client's errors.

53. The answer is A. Due to the Affordable Care Act, a taxpayer must either have qualifying health insurance coverage throughout the year, qualify for an exemption from coverage, or make a "shared responsibility payment" when they file their federal tax return. If a tax debt is incurred because of an individual shared responsibility payment as a result of the Affordable Care Act, the amount owed is not subject to penalties, levies or the filing of a Notice of Federal Tax Lien. However, interest will continue to accrue and the IRS may offset future federal tax refunds until the balance is paid in full (Publication 594, *The IRS Collection Process*).

54. The answer is D. Disbarred individuals are prohibited from practice before the IRS. However, a disbarred individual is still allowed to perform duties in certain capacities before the IRS. A suspended or disbarred individual may:
- Represent himself with respect to any matter
- Appear before the IRS as a trustee, receiver, guardian, administrator, executor, or other fiduciary if duly qualified/authorized under the law of the relevant jurisdiction
- Appear as a witness for the taxpayer
- Furnish information at the request of the IRS or any of its officers
- Receive information concerning a taxpayer from the IRS pursuant to a valid tax information authorization

55. The answer is B. Direct deposit of a taxpayer's refund can be designated only to an account in the taxpayer's name. It would be both illegal and unethical for a paid preparer to specify her own bank account as the designated account to receive a taxpayer's refund.

56. The answer is C. A power of attorney is not required to be submitted by an attorney of record in a case that is docketed in the Tax Court. The Tax Court has its own rules of practice and procedure and its own rules regarding admission to practice before it. Accordingly, the rules of practice in Circular 230 differ from the rules of practice for the Tax Court.

57. The answer is B. A request for an offer in compromise will not release a tax lien. The IRS will release a lien:
- When the tax debt is fully paid.
- When payment of the debt is guaranteed by a bond.
- When the statute period for collection has ended. (In this case, the release is automatic.)

58. The answer is B. Certified financial planners are not classified as "enrolled practitioners" under Circular 230 and cannot practice before the IRS.

59. The answer is D. The IRS does not recommend that all client information be stored electronically. The IRS requires tax preparers and other businesses to take appropriate steps to safeguard taxpayers' private information. The IRS makes the following specific recommendations:
- Take responsibility or assign an individual or individuals to be responsible for safeguards
- Assess the risks to taxpayer information in the office, including operations, physical environment, computer systems, and employees
- Make a list of all the locations where taxpayer information is kept (computers, filing cabinets, bags, and boxes, etc.)
- Make a written plan on how the business will safeguard taxpayer information
- Put appropriate safeguards in place

- Use only service providers who have policies in place to maintain an adequate level of information protection
- Monitor, evaluate, and adjust the security program as the tax preparer's business or circumstances change

If a taxpayer has been the victim of identity theft (such as another person fraudulently using his Social Security number to file a tax return), he should notify the IRS immediately. He will need to submit Form 14039, *Identity Theft Affidavit*, along with documentation to verify his identity.

60. The answer is D. The new online directory includes enrolled practitioners as well as AFSP participants. The Annual Filing Season Program is the IRS's new voluntary program to replace the registered tax return preparer program. Those who pass the program's education and testing requirements receive an AFSP Record of Completion for the year. Participants will be included in a public, searchable database of tax return preparers on the IRS website. The *Directory of Federal Tax Return Preparers with Credentials and Select Qualifications* includes the name, city, state, zip code, and credentials of all attorneys, CPAs, EAs, ERPAs, and enrolled actuaries with a valid PTIN, as well as all AFSP Record of Completion holders. An individual may opt out of being listed in the directory. Unenrolled preparers with current PTINs who are not Record of Completion holders are not listed in the directory.

61. The answer is C. Targeted direct mail solicitations are permitted under Circular 230. Practitioners must retain a copy of all solicitations for a period of at least 36 months from the date of the last transmission or use.

62. The answer is B. If required to file at least 250 returns of any type during the calendar year, a corporation (either an S corporation or C corporation) must file Form 1120S, *U.S. Income Tax Return for an S Corporation*, or Form 1120, *U.S. Corporate Income Tax Return* (as appropriate), on magnetic media. The term *magnetic media* means magnetic tape, tape cartridge, and diskette, as well as other media, such as electronic filing, which are specifically permitted by IRS regulations.

63. The answer is C. A practitioner can recommend or advise a client on a position, as long as the position is not incorrect, inconsistent, or incomplete; is not frivolous; and is adequately disclosed.

64. The answer is D. If a taxpayer fails to file a return and the failure to file is due to fraud, the penalty is 15% for each month or part of a month that the return is late, up to a maximum of 75%.

65. The answer is C. There is no requirement that an authorized e-file provider have a permanent business location outside his home. In fact, many e-file providers work exclusively from home offices. An authorized IRS e-file provider is a business authorized by the IRS to participate in IRS e-file. The business may be a sole proprietorship, partnership, or corporation. The provider applicant must:
- Be a United States citizen or a legal U.S. alien lawfully admitted for permanent residence;
- Be at least 18 years old as of the date of application; and
- Meet applicable state and local licensing and/or bonding requirements for the preparation and collection of tax returns.

66. The answer is B. Forms W-7, *Application for IRS Individual Taxpayer Identification Number*, must include original or certified copies of documentation such as passports and birth certificates. Notarized copies of documentation are no longer accepted.

67. The answer is B. Fraud, as distinguished from negligence, is always intentional. One of the elements of fraud is the intent to evade tax. Some badges of fraud that the IRS looks for include:
- False explanations regarding understated or omitted income
- Large discrepancies between actual and reported deductions from income
- Concealment of income sources
- Numerous errors in the taxpayer's favor
- Fictitious records or other deceptions
- Large omissions of personal service income, specific items of income, gambling winnings, or illegal income
- False deductions, exemptions, or credits
- Failure to keep or furnish records
- Incomplete information given to the return preparer regarding a fraudulent scheme
- Large and/or frequent cash dealings that may or may not be common to the taxpayer's business
- Verbal misrepresentations of the facts and circumstances

Generally, the presence of only one indication of fraud is not sufficient to determine fraud has actually taken place (e.g., unreported income alone does not necessarily prove fraud).

68. The answer is C. The signing tax return preparer should be the preparer who has primary responsibility for the accuracy of the return. The requirement that all preparers obtain a PTIN did not change the rules regarding who should be the signing tax return preparer.

69. The answer is B. Under Circular 230 section 10.34, a practitioner must advise the client of the penalties that are reasonably likely to apply regarding a position on a tax return, if he advised her regarding the position or if he prepared the tax return. The practitioner must also advise the client of how to avoid these penalties through disclosure (or by not taking the position). However, the practitioner is prohibited from taking into consideration the chances that a tax return may or may not be audited, or that a particular matter may or may not be raised on audit.

70. The answer is D. IRC section 6695 lists the penalties that may be assessed in connection with the preparation of tax returns for other persons. The penalty is $50 for each violation of the following types:
- Failure to furnish a copy of a return or claim to a taxpayer
- Failure to sign a return or claim for refund
- Failure to furnish an identifying number (PTIN) on a return
- Failure to retain a copy or list of a return or claim
- Failure to file correct information returns

71. The answer is D. Censure is a public reprimand, with the practitioner's name published in the Internal Revenue Bulletin. The facts of the case that triggered the censure are not published. Unlike disbarment or suspension, censure generally does not prevent a practitioner from filing tax returns or representing taxpayers before the IRS.

However, in certain situations, a censure may place conditions on a practitioner's future representations in order to promote high standards of conduct.

72. The answer is C. Although a tax return preparer may rely in good faith, without verification, on information furnished by a taxpayer, Sarina would not be exercising due diligence under section 10.22 if she accepted such a statement from a client without further information. In such a situation, the OPR says a practitioner must make reasonable inquiries of the client, including, for example, the following:
- Does the client have another automobile for personal use?
- Did the client commute to work?
- Did the client keep records of the business mileage?

73. The answer is B. A preparer is in compliance if all tax returns that are due have been filed and all taxes that are due have been paid (or acceptable payment arrangements have been established).

74. The answer is C. The IRS may accept an offer in compromise from Bruno based on doubt as to collectability. There is no dispute that he owes the tax, but it is doubtful that he could ever pay the full amount of tax liability owed within the remainder of the statutory period for collection.

75. The answer is B. The EITC will be disallowed, and the taxpayer will have a balance due, including penalties and interest. In addition, the taxpayer may be disallowed from claiming the EITC in future years.

76. The answer is B. IRC section 6662 sets forth various accuracy-related penalties for understatement of tax. Shelby would be subject to a substantial overvaluation misstatement penalty of 20%. This penalty applies when a taxpayer incorrectly reports an asset's value or its adjusted basis on a tax return, resulting in an underpayment of tax. A substantial overvaluation misstatement exists if the value claimed on a tax return for any property is 150% or more of the amount determined to be the correct value. The penalty increases to 40% of the net understatement of tax if the taxpayer claims a value for property on a tax return that is 200% or more of the correct amount. This is known as a *gross valuation misstatement*. IRC section 6662 penalties for substantial understatement, substantial overvaluation, and negligence or disregard of rules or regulations are each calculated as a flat 20% of the net understatement of tax.

77. The answer is A. Preparers who acquire an existing IRS e-file business by purchase, transfer, or gift must submit a new IRS e-file application and receive a new electronic filing identification number (EFIN). Agnes is required to submit an e-file application and request a new EFIN.

78. The answer is A. Tax preparers are required to retain a complete copy of each return they have prepared, or a list of taxpayers' names and TINs, and the tax years for which returns were prepared. The copies or list must be retained for a minimum of three years after the close of the return period. The close of the return period is defined as June 30, meaning the three-year period to retain records begins July 1.

79. The answer is A. A misdemeanor conviction alone is unlikely to cause a practitioner to face disciplinary action from the OPR. There are four broad categories of preparer misconduct, all of which may result in disciplinary action:
- Misconduct while representing a taxpayer
- Misconduct related to the practitioner's own return
- Giving a false opinion, knowingly, recklessly, or through gross incompetence
- Misconduct not directly involving IRS representation, such as a felony conviction

80. The answer is D. IRC section 7206 is a felony charge that applies to a tax preparer convicted of fraud and false statements in the preparation of fraudulent income tax returns. A preparer could face a fine of up $100,000, imprisonment for up to three years, or both.

81. The answer is D. Tax returns with valid adoption taxpayer identification numbers (ATIN) may be e-filed in most cases. In addition, individual tax returns can be e-filed for the two tax years preceding the current tax year.

82. The answer is D. Taxpayers have a right to be represented during the examination process. They also have a right to appeal if they disagree with the examination report. However, taxpayers do not have a right to ignore or decline an IRS summons, although they can request representation during the summons process.

83. The answer is A. The ethics requirement for the enrolled agent license renewal is a minimum of two hours of ethics per year, so Sebastian has not fulfilled his ethics requirement. Circular 230 specifies a minimum of 16 hours of continuing education credit per year, with at least two hours devoted to ethics. If a preparer takes more than two hours of ethics in a single year, the extra ethics hours can count toward the overall minimum requirement for the enrollment cycle.

84. The answer is D. The CAP program is generally quicker than a collection due process (CDP) hearing and is available for a broader range of collection actions. However, the taxpayer cannot appeal to the U.S. Tax Court or any other court if he disagrees with a CAP decision. The decision by Appeals is binding on both the taxpayer and the IRS. Also, under CAP, the taxpayer cannot contest the underlying tax liability.

85. The answer is B. Under Circular 230 section 10.28, a practitioner must promptly return any and all records a client needs to comply with his federal tax obligations. This includes any documents or records the client had before he hired the practitioner to prepare his return, such as materials prepared by a third party. However, Circular 230 does not require a practitioner to give the client a tax return that the practitioner prepared, or any other work product that he prepared, if the client refuses to pay his fee.

86. The answer is C. There are two sections of the Internal Revenue Code that prohibit the unauthorized disclosure or use of taxpayer information in connection with the preparation of tax returns. IRC section 6713 is a civil penalty of $250 for each unauthorized disclosure of information in connection with the preparation of a return. The maximum penalty cannot exceed $10,000 in a calendar year. This is in contrast to IRC section 7216, which is a criminal provision that prohibits tax return preparers from disclosing or using tax return information. Under section 7216, a disclosure must be "knowing or reckless" for penalties to apply. Section 7216 imposes a fine of up to $1,000, imprisonment for up to a year, or both, along with the costs of prosecution. Depending on the specific facts and circumstances of Russell's case, either code may apply.

87. The answer is B. Beatrice is not a preparer under Circular 230 rules, so she is not required to obtain a PTIN. If an employee of a business prepares the business's tax returns as part of her job responsibilities, the employee is not required to sign as a paid preparer. Accordingly, unless the employee prepares other federal tax returns for compensation, she would not be required to obtain a PTIN.

88. The answer is A. Form 2848 is a power of attorney form that is a taxpayer's written authorization for an eligible individual to act on the taxpayer's behalf in tax matters. Any practitioner (generally, enrolled agents, CPAs, and tax attorneys) can be designated as a representative on Form 2848 and can receive confidential tax information and perform other actions specified on the form, such as representing a taxpayer at an IRS appeals conference. In contrast, Form 8821, *Tax Information Authorization*, does not confer any representation rights. It simply authorizes an individual, corporation, firm, organization, or partnership to inspect or receive confidential information for the type of tax and periods listed.

89. The answer is D. Under the new Circular 230 section 10.82, the OPR may move quicker to sanction practitioners by using expedited procedures in certain circumstances, including when a practitioner has been convicted of a crime involving dishonesty or breach of trust. The procedures are also allowed when a practitioner has demonstrated a pattern of "willful disreputable conduct" involving the following:
- Failing to file his federal income tax returns in four of the five previous tax years
- Failing to file a return required more frequently than annually (such as an employment tax return) during five of the seven previous tax periods

In addition, the expedited suspension procedures are allowed when an attorney or CPA has already had his license revoked for cause by any state licensing agency or board.

90. The answer is C. After a taxpayer has a closing conference with an IRS examiner, he will receive a "30-day letter". This letter includes a notice explaining the taxpayer's right to appeal the proposed changes; a copy of the revenue agent report that explains the examiner's proposed changes; an agreement or waiver form; and a copy of Publication 5, *Your Appeals Rights and How to Prepare a Protest If You Don't Agree.* The notice is known as the 30-day letter because the taxpayer has 30 days from the date of the notice to accept or appeal the proposed changes.

91. The answer is A. Circular 230, which is found in Title 31 of the Code of Federal Regulations, governs practice before the Internal Revenue Service. For reference, the Internal Revenue Code is found in Title 26 of the U.S. Code.

92. The answer is C. For cash donations of $250 or more, the taxpayer must have a receipt or written acknowledgement from the charitable organization that includes:
- The amount of cash the taxpayer contributed
- The date of the contribution
- Whether the qualified organization gave any goods or services as a result of the contribution
- If applicable, a description and a good faith estimate of the value of goods or services provided by the organization as a result of the contribution

As part of their due diligence, tax preparers should ask their clients about the type of substantiation they have for charitable contributions. A taxpayer is expected to be able to substantiate any item on his tax return, whether it be for donations or for business expenses on Schedule C. A taxpayer cannot deduct amounts that are estimates. A written record, including one prepared on a computer, generally is required to be considered adequate.

93. The answer is D. All of the situations reflect potential conflicts of interest for a practitioner. A practitioner is allowed to represent parties who have a conflict of interest, as long as the practitioner receives written consent from each party after full disclosure has been made. A practitioner may represent a client when a conflict of interest exists if:
- The practitioner reasonably believes that he will be able to provide competent and diligent representation to each affected client;
- The representation is not prohibited by law; and
- Each affected client waives the conflict of interest and gives informed consent, confirmed in writing.

If there is a potential conflict of interest, the practitioner must disclose the conflict and be given the opportunity to disclose all material facts. The written consent must be retained for at least 36 months from the date representation ends. At minimum, the consent should adequately describe the nature of the conflict and the parties the practitioner represents.

94. The answer is C. The IRS created Direct Pay in 2014. Direct Pay is a secure IRS service that allows individual taxpayers to pay their estimated taxes or individual tax bill online. Direct Pay cannot be used by business taxpayers, it is for individuals only.

95. The answer is C. An enrolled agent who is appealing an official censure may still use the designation of enrolled agent, as long as he is not disbarred, suspended, or placed on inactive status. A person who has passed the exam but has not completed the application process may not use the designation of enrolled agent to describe his status. An enrolled agent who is on inactive status or who has not renewed his license may not use the designation.

96. The answer is C. In cases involving both criminal and civil fraud in the U.S. court system, the burden of proof rests with the government. The taxpayer's explanations, or lack of explanations, may help distinguish between civil and criminal fraud. A criminal conviction for tax evasion (under section 7201) usually establishes liability for the civil fraud penalty. The civil fraud penalty can be imposed even when the taxpayer is acquitted in a criminal fraud prosecution. However, when it comes to an examination of a taxpayer's return, the taxpayer has the burden of proof to substantiate expenses in order to deduct them. A taxpayer can usually meet this burden of proof by having receipts for the expenses.

97. The answer is C. Katherine is allowed to sign on behalf of her husband whether or not she has a signed power of attorney. A spouse can sign a joint return for a spouse who cannot sign because he is serving in a combat zone, even without a power of attorney.

98. The answer is A. A late payment on an installment agreement will usually result in the generation of a 30-day notice that the agreement will be terminated, which allows the IRS time to make changes to the installment agreement. The IRS typically charges a fee for reinstating an installment agreement that has gone into default.

99. The answer is C. Any tax preparer who files 11 or more Forms 1040, 1040A, 1040EZ, and 1041 during a calendar year must use IRS e-file. However, clients may choose not to e-file their returns. In these cases, a preparer should attach Form 8948, *Preparer Explanation for Not Filing Electronically*, to her client's paper return. The taxpayer must mail the return himself and include a hand-signed and dated statement documenting his choice to file on paper.

100. The answer is D. Circular 230 Section 10.37 has a new paragraph that allows a practitioner to rely on the advice of another person, as long as the advice is reasonable and the reliance is in good faith. However, a practitioner cannot rely on advice if he knows or reasonably should know that:
- The advice is not reliable: for instance, if he has not provided all of the relevant facts to the other practitioner.
- The person giving the advice is not competent or qualified. For instance, if the practitioner giving the advice has limited knowledge of tax law, he would not be competent.
- The person giving the advice has a conflict of interest that violates Circular 230.

Answers to Exam #6: Representation

1. The answer is A. Enrolled agents must renew their enrollment status every three years. As part of the application process, the IRS checks the candidate's filing history to verify that he has filed his federal returns and paid applicable taxes.

2. The answer is B. Under section 6060, an employer of other tax preparers must keep a record of those employed and make it available for IRS inspection upon request. The records must include the name, taxpayer identification number, and place of work for each tax return preparer employed. Records must be retained for at least three years following the close of the return period.

3. The answer is D. Generally, confidential taxpayer information can only be disclosed upon a taxpayer's written authorization. However, a tax return preparer is not required to obtain disclosure consent from a client if the disclosure is made for any of the following reasons:
- A court order or subpoena issued by any court of record whether at the federal, state, or local level. The required information must be clearly identified in the document (subpoena or court order) in order for a preparer to disclose information.
- An administrative order, demand, summons, or subpoena issued by any federal agency (such as the IRS), state agency, or commission charged under the laws of the state with licensing, registration, or regulation of tax return preparers.
- To report a crime to proper authorities. Even if the preparer is mistaken and no crime has occurred, he will not be subject to sanctions if he makes the disclosure in good faith.
- For purposes of peer reviews.
- Finally, a preparer may disclose private client information to his attorney, or to an employee of the IRS, in connection with an IRS investigation of the preparer.

4. The answer is C. A financial account or prepaid debit card can have a maximum of three refunds direct deposited into it per tax year. Any additional deposits for the year for which an electronic refund is requested will be converted to a paper refund check and mailed to the taxpayer. The IRS is limiting the number to try to prevent criminals from easily obtaining multiple refunds.

5. The answer is C. Interest owed by a taxpayer will be abated or waived in the following instances:
- When it is excessive, barred by statute, or erroneously or illegally assessed
- When it is assessed on an erroneous refund
- When it was incurred while the taxpayer was in a combat zone or in a declared disaster area

Further, the IRS will waive interest that is the result of certain errors or delays caused by an IRS employee, which are known as managerial acts and ministerial acts. However, in contrast to abatement of penalties, reasonable cause is not allowed as the basis for abatement of interest.

6. The answer is D. Stacy must inform each client of the potential for conflict of interest and then obtain written waivers of the conflict from both clients. Circular 230 requires a practitioner to notify each client of the conflict and have each client provide informed consent, confirmed in writing. The consent must be signed no later than 30 days after the conflict is known by the practitioner and it must be retained for 36 months. When a conflict of interest exists, a practitioner must reasonably believe that she will be able to provide competent and diligent presentation to each client. The representation cannot be prohibited by law.

7. The answer is A. In determining whether a taxpayer has the ability to pay a tax liability, the IRS will consider a taxpayer's expenses and whether he has any degree of control over their amounts. If child support has been ordered by a court, it is a mandated expense that the taxpayer must legally pay. A taxpayer's Collection Information Statement will provide the IRS detailed financial information about the taxpayer's income, his bank and retirement accounts, real estate and other assets, and his outstanding debts. The statement may include information concerning the taxpayer's obligations for court-ordered payments, such as child support and alimony, since the taxpayer will generally have little flexibility regarding these obligations.

8. The answer is B. All the acts of the taxpayer, when seen as a whole, indicate fraud. Fraud, as distinguished from negligence, is always intentional. One of the elements of fraud is the intent to evade tax. The existence of several "badges of fraud" will usually indicate fraud, rather than negligence.

9. The answer is A. Practitioners generally may not use official IRS insignia in their advertising. However, a practitioner may use the IRS e-file logo.

The IRS e-file logo cannot be combined with the IRS eagle symbol, the word "federal", or with other words or symbols that suggest a special relationship between the IRS and the practitioner. Advertising materials must not carry the FMS (IRS Financial Management Service), IRS, or other Treasury seals.

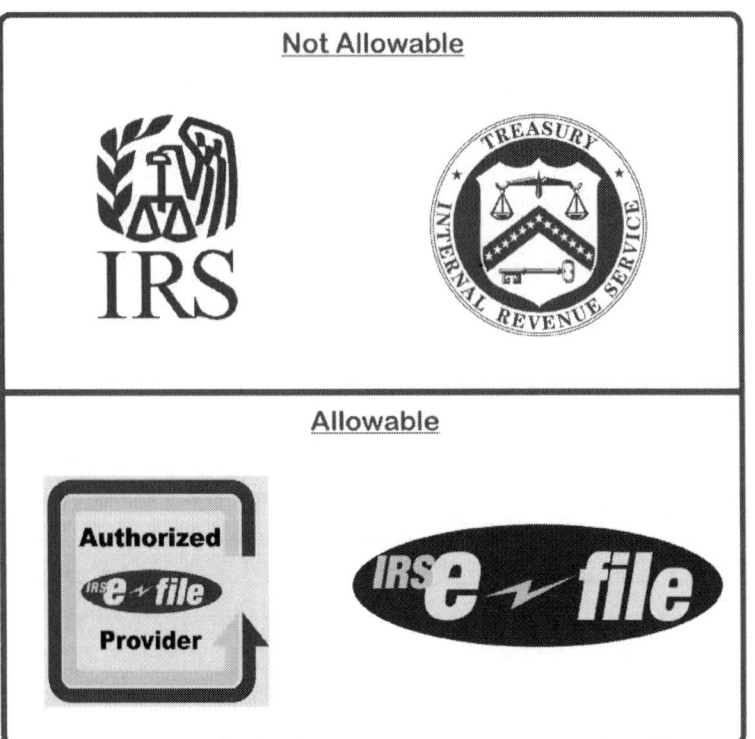

10. The answer is D. A levy does not apply to the taxpayer's clothing and undelivered mail. Property exempt from levy also includes, among other assets, the following:
- Fuel, provisions (food), furniture, personal effects in the taxpayer's household, arms for personal use, or livestock, up to $9,080 in total value for 2015 and $9,120 for 2016.
- Books and tools necessary for the trade, business, or profession of the taxpayer, up to $4,540 in total value for 2015 and $4,560 for 2016.
- Unemployment benefits and amounts payable under the Job Training Partnership Act.
- Worker's compensation, including amounts payable to dependents.
- Certain annuity or pension payments, but only if payable by the Army, Navy, Air Force, Coast Guard, or under the Railroad Retirement Act or Railroad Unemployment Insurance Act. Traditional or Roth IRAs are not exempt from levy.
- Judgments for the support of minor children (child support).
- Certain public assistance and welfare payments, and amounts payable for Supplemental Security Income for the aged, blind, and disabled under the Social Security Act. Regular Social Security payments are not exempt from levy.
- The taxpayer's principal residence (usually).

After 1998, the seizure of a personal residence by the IRS is prohibited for any liability under $5,000. For all liabilities of $5,000 or more, the IRS must obtain approval from a U.S. District Court judge or magistrate prior to seizing a personal residence.

11. The answer is B. An IRS interview must be suspended when the taxpayer clearly requests to consult with a representative. Throughout the examination process, the taxpayer can act on his own behalf or have someone represent him. The taxpayer is not required to be present if the representative is a federally authorized practitioner (generally, an enrolled agent, CPA, or attorney). The taxpayer is also not required to be present if the representative is one of the other qualified individuals listed in Circular 230, such as a family member or an employee representing an employer.

12. The answer is C. A practitioner who has been disciplined cannot represent clients before the IRS. However, if a taxpayer wants the disciplined practitioner to accompany him to a conference or meeting with the IRS, the practitioner may do so. In that case, he may only respond to questions and provide facts and/or documents. The practitioner may not advocate for the taxpayer or argue the merits of any issue raised.

13. The answer is A. To claim the Earned Income Tax Credit, the taxpayer (and spouse, if filing a joint return) must have a valid Social Security number. The SSN must also be valid for employment purposes. Any qualifying child listed on Schedule EIC also must have a valid SSN as well, unless the child was born and died in the same year.

14. The answer is D. The IRS has broad legal authority to issue a summons when a taxpayer or other witness refuses to comply with requests for IRS records or other information. IRC section 7602 authorizes the IRS to issue summonses for the following purposes:
- To ascertain the correctness of any return;
- To prepare a return where none has been made;
- To determine the liability of a person for internal revenue tax;

- To determine the liability at law or in equity of a transferee or fiduciary of a person in respect to any internal revenue tax;
- To collect any internal revenue tax liability; or
- To inquire into any civil or criminal offense connected with the administration or enforcement of the internal revenue law.

A summons should require only that the witness appear on a given date to provide testimony or produce existing books, paper, and records that "may be relevant or material". A summons cannot require a witness to prepare or create documents, including tax returns, which do not exist. A summons also cannot be issued solely to harass a taxpayer or to pressure him into settling a dispute.

15. The answer is D. All of the above would disqualify the taxpayer from claiming the Earned Income Tax Credit. Taxpayers whose investment income is more than $3,400 in 2015 cannot claim the EITC. Taxpayers who file MFS cannot claim the credit. A taxpayer must have a valid Social Security Number that is valid for employment purposes in order to qualify for EITC. A taxpayer cannot claim EITC using an Individual Taxpayer Identification Number (ITIN) or Adoption Taxpayer Identification Number (ATIN).

16. The answer is B. The IRC section 7525 confidentiality privilege does not extend to the preparation of income tax returns. Therefore, any discussions surrounding the preparation of a tax return are not privileged.

17. The answer is D. Receipt of taxpayer refund checks is allowed, but the tax practitioner must have a power of attorney in order to do so. A practitioner may never cash (or endorse) a taxpayer refund check. A power of attorney is not required in some situations when dealing with the IRS. The following situations do not require a power of attorney:
- Providing information to the IRS
- Disclosure of tax return information based on authorization through Form 8821
- Allowing the IRS to discuss return information with a third party designee
- Allowing the IRS to discuss return information with a fiduciary
- Representing a taxpayer through a non-written consent

18. The answer is C. In an effort to cut down on identity theft, the IRS has instituted new measures for tax preparers who accept electronic signatures to authenticate the identity of taxpayers. The procedures vary depending on whether the tax preparer's interaction with the taxpayer is in-person or remote. For remote interactions, the preparer must verify that the name, Social Security number, address, date of birth, and other personal information provided by the taxpayer are consistent with information obtained through record checks with applicable agencies or institutions, or through credit bureaus or similar databases. For in-person interactions, the preparer must inspect a valid government-issued picture ID, compare the picture to the applicant, and record the name, Social Security number, address, and date of birth, unless the preparer has identified the same client in the past using these procedures while originating the client's tax return. A credit check or other identity verification is optional.

19. The answer is D. The IRS may accept an offer in compromise based on three grounds: (a) doubt as to collectability, (b) effective tax administration, or (c) doubt as to liability.

20. The answer is C. In 2015, the IRS instituted stricter procedures for obtaining an ITIN. A provision of the PATH Act of 2015 requires that taxpayers who were issued ITINs before 2013 renew their ITINs on a staggered schedule between 2017 and 2020. ITINs will automatically expire after three years of non-use.

21. The answer is C. Lloyd must notify Kelly of the error and tell her the consequences of not correcting it. He is not required to amend prior year tax returns to correct the error. A practitioner is required by Circular 230 to advise the taxpayer when he becomes aware that the client has not complied with the revenue laws of the United States. However, the practitioner is not responsible for fixing the noncompliance issue once he has notified the client of the issue. The practitioner is also not responsible for notifying the IRS of noncompliance.

22. The answer is A. Enrolled agents, like attorneys and certified public accountants (CPAs), have unlimited practice rights before the IRS. This means they are unrestricted as to which taxpayers they can represent, what types of tax matters they can handle, and the IRS offices they can practice before. They do not have rights before the U.S. Tax Court (unless having passed a special exam and meeting other U.S. Tax Court requirements), or other U.S. courts.

23. The answer is C. Erin may qualify for injured spouse relief by filing to receive her share of the refund that was applied toward her husband's debt. Injured spouse relief may also apply when a spouse has past due income tax, child support, or other obligations that are applied toward a tax refund.
Note: An injured spouse is not to be confused with an innocent spouse, which is a different legal situation. If certain conditions are met, an innocent spouse may apply for relief from additional tax if a spouse or former spouse failed to report income or claimed improper deductions on a jointly filed tax return.

24. The answer is A. A practitioner may not charge a separate fee for direct deposit. Charging a flat fee for e-filing is allowed. Contingent fees for e-filing are not permitted. A practitioner may charge fees based on the following:
- Fixed fees for specific routine services
- Hourly fee rates
- Range of fees for particular services
- Fee charged for an initial consultation

25. The answer is A. The Internal Revenue Code defines substantial authority as an "objective standard involving an analysis of the law and application of the law to relevant facts". The weight given an authority depends on its "relevance and persuasiveness" and the type of document providing the authority. For example, a revenue ruling is accorded greater weight than a private letter ruling addressing the same issue for all taxpayers except for whom the private letter ruling was specifically drafted. More recent documents also carry greater weight than older ones. Under IRC section 6662, sources of substantial authority include the following: provisions of the Internal Revenue Code, temporary and final regulations, court cases, administrative pronouncements, tax treaties, and Congressional intent as reflected in committee reports. The list was later expanded to include proposed regulations, private letter rulings, technical advice memoranda, IRS information or press releases, notices, and any other similar documents published by the IRS in the Internal Revenue Bulletin.

26. The answer is C. Any individual who is paid a fee to prepare a return must sign it and fill out the preparer area of the return. This is true even when the paying client is a family member. However, an employee working for an employer may not have to sign the return if the employer or another employee has the ultimate liability for the return's accuracy.

27. The answer is A. A "reportable transaction" is a transaction of a type that the IRS has determined as having the potential for abusive tax avoidance or evasion. If a reportable transaction is not disclosed and results in an understatement of tax, a higher penalty in the amount of 30% of the understatement of tax attributable to the reportable transaction may be assessed. Reportable transactions must be reported on Form 8886, *Reportable Transaction Disclosure Statement.*

28. The answer is B. If a CPA is suspended from practice by a state board of accountancy, he will also be disbarred from practice before the IRS, regardless of whether the suspension was due to a non-tax matter.

29. The answer is C. When applying to become an authorized IRS e-services provider, an individual who is certified or licensed (such as an attorney, CPA, or enrolled agent) must enter current professional status information. All other individuals, including unenrolled tax return preparers, must be fingerprinted as part of the application process. After the application is submitted, the IRS will conduct a suitability check on the firm and on each person listed on the application as either a principal or responsible official. Suitability checks may include the following:
- A criminal background check
- A credit history check
- A tax compliance check to ensure that the applicant's personal returns are filed and paid
- A check for prior noncompliance with IRS e-file requirements

30. The answer is D. A taxpayer is not required to have filed for divorce or legal separation when innocent spouse relief is requested. A taxpayer must meet all of the following conditions to qualify for innocent spouse relief:

- The taxpayer filed a joint return that has an understatement of tax (deficiency) solely attributable to a spouse's erroneous item. An erroneous item includes income received by the other spouse but omitted from the joint return. Deductions, credits, and property basis may also be erroneous items if they are incorrectly reported on the return.
- When the taxpayer signed the joint return, he or she did not know, and had no reason to know, that there was an understatement of tax on the return.
- Taking into account all the facts and circumstances, it would be unfair to hold the taxpayer liable for the understatement of tax.

31. The answer is B. A formal complaint against a practitioner may be served in the following ways: certified mail; first-class mail, if previously returned undelivered by certified mail; private delivery service; in person; or by leaving the complaint at the office of the practitioner. Electronic delivery, such as e-mail, is not a valid means of serving a complaint.

32. The answer is D. To meet the reasonable basis standard, a tax return preparer may rely in good faith, without verification, on information furnished by a taxpayer, advisor, another preparer, or other party. While limited, there is a potential exception to the imposition of a preparer penalty where the understatement of tax was due to an unreasonable position taken on the return if it is shown that there is reasonable cause for the understatement and the preparer acted in good faith.

33. The answer is D. Under Internal Revenue Code §6695, a tax preparer who violates EITC due diligence requirements faces $505 penalty for each violation in 2015. Starting in 2015, IRC§§6695(h) allows a cost-of-living adjustment, and the penalty will be adjusted for inflation each year.

34. The answer is B. In most cases, tax returns are audited for up to three years after filing. However, the IRS may audit for up to six years if there is substantial unreported income (25% or more of income is unreported).

35. The answer is D. A power of attorney is valid until revoked. It may be revoked by the taxpayer or withdrawn by the representative, or it may be superseded by the filing of a new power of attorney for the same tax and tax period.

36. The answer is B. When an individual strikes out the jurat on a return, it becomes a frivolous return. The jurat is an affidavit in which the taxpayer and/or preparer attests to the truth of the information contained in the return and attached return information. Civil penalties for frivolous returns include the following:
- A $500 penalty imposed under section 6702;
- Additional penalties for failure to file a return, failure to pay tax owed, and fraudulent failure to file a return; and
- A penalty of up to $25,000 under section 6673 if the taxpayer makes frivolous arguments before the United States Tax Court.

37. The answer is C. A practitioner is not allowed to charge an "unconscionable fee" for his services. However, Circular 230 does not define what constitutes "unconscionable." The other choices are acceptable fee practices.

38. The answer is A. Taxpayers must sign their returns under penalty of perjury. This means that the taxpayer must make a declaration that the return is true, correct, and complete to the best of the knowledge and belief of the taxpayer.

39. The answer is D. Under the EITC due diligence requirements, a preparer must not know (or have reason to know) that the information used to determine eligibility or to compute the amount of the Earned Income Credit is incorrect. A preparer must ask his client additional questions if the information furnished seems incorrect or incomplete.

40. The answer is D. An enrolled agent becomes official on the date the Return Preparer Office issues his enrollment card. Form 23 is the application for enrollment. An applicant must undergo a background check prior to enrollment. It can take up to 60 days or more for the IRS to process an application.

41. The answer is B. Preparers who anticipate filing 11 or more Forms 1040, 1040A, 1040EZ, and Forms 1041 (fiduciary returns) during the year must use IRS e-file. The requirement also applies to tax preparation firms, which must compute the number of returns prepared by their members in the aggregate. Business tax returns, such as Form 1120 or Form 1065, are not subject to the current e-file mandate (although some large corporate and partnership returns are subject to separate electronic filing requirements).

42. The answer is C. Performance as a notary is not considered disreputable conduct. A practitioner may perform duties as a notary public. However, a practitioner who is a notary public and is engaged in a matter before the IRS (or who has a material interest in the matter) cannot engage in any notary activities related to that matter. All of the other acts listed are considered disreputable conduct. The definition of "disreputable conduct" includes:
- Willfully failing to e-file returns electronically if they fall under the e-filing mandate, and
- Failing to include a valid PTIN on tax returns.

43. The answer is A. Form 8275, *Disclosure Statement*, is filed to disclose a tax position on a tax return.

44. The answer is D. A tax preparer must not endorse or otherwise cash any refund check issued to the taxpayer. A preparer cannot withhold a taxpayer's refund check because of a fee dispute. However, a preparer is not required to file a client's tax return without first obtaining payment.

45. The answer is A. Simply preparing a tax return, furnishing information at the request of the IRS, or appearing as a witness for the taxpayer is not practice before the IRS. These acts can be performed by anyone. Practice before the IRS covers all matters relating to the following:

- Communicating with the IRS on behalf of a taxpayer regarding the taxpayer's rights, privileges, or liabilities under laws and regulations administered by the IRS.
- Representing a taxpayer at conferences, hearings, or meetings with the IRS.
- Preparing and filing documents with the IRS for a taxpayer.
- Corresponding and communicating on behalf of a taxpayer.

46. The answer is C. A hard (paper) copy is not required. The preparer must provide a complete copy of the return to the taxpayer. Preparers may provide this copy using any media, including electronic, that is acceptable to both the taxpayer and the preparer. The copy does not need to include the Social Security number of the paid preparer, but it must include his PTIN. A complete copy of a taxpayer's return includes Form 8453, U.S. Individual Income Tax Transmittal for an IRS e-file Return, and any documents the preparer cannot electronically transmit, if applicable, as well as the electronic portion of the return.

47. The answer is C. A private letter ruling (PLR) is a written communication from the Internal Revenue Service in response to a taxpayer's written request for guidance on a particular tax issue. PLRs become public record once issued, but all of the taxpayer's personal information is removed.

48. The answer is D. IRC section 10.34 states that a practitioner may not willfully sign a tax return or claim for refund that the practitioner knows (or reasonably should know) contains a position that:
- Lacks a reasonable basis.
- Is an unreasonable position as described in IRC section 6694 (a)(2).
- Is a willful attempt by the practitioner to understate the liability for tax, or a reckless or intentional disregard of rules or regulations.

In determining potential penalties, the IRS will take into account a pattern of conduct to assess whether a practitioner acted willfully, recklessly, or through gross incompetence. Reasonable basis is defined as follows: "Reasonable basis is a relatively high standard of tax reporting that is significantly higher than not frivolous or not patently improper. The reasonable basis standard is not satisfied by a return position that is merely arguable." The precise likelihood that a reasonable basis position will be upheld on its merits is not defined in Circular 230. For purposes of avoiding section 6694 penalties, the reasonable basis standard applies only if the relevant tax position is disclosed on the return or document so that the IRS is aware of a potential issue.

49. The answer is A. In tax disputes involving $50,000 or less, taxpayers may choose to use the Tax Court small tax case procedure.

50. The answer is C. There are three types of Treasury regulations: legislative, interpretive, and procedural. There is no such thing as a "Congressional regulation" issued by the Treasury Department.

51. The answer is C. Most paid preparers need both a PTIN and an EFIN. Each tax preparer needs to have his own PTIN, which is issued to individuals. An electronic filing identification number (EFIN) is a number issued by the IRS to individuals or firms that have been approved as authorized IRS e-file providers. All preparers in a firm may be covered by a single EFIN.

52. The answer is C. Section 10.24 of Circular 230 does not prohibit the employer of other tax practitioners from hiring or accepting assistance from a practitioner who has received a reprimand from the IRS. A reprimand is the lightest sanction the IRS gives out. It is a private letter from the director of the OPR, stating the practitioner has committed some kind of misconduct under Circular 230. Although the issuance of a reprimand is kept private, it stays on a practitioner's record.

53. The answer is B. The IRS will generally not waive a penalty that is incurred when a taxpayer relied on advice from a tax advisor about a common Form 1040 tax issue. Typically, this relief is limited to tax issues that are considered highly technical and complicated. This type of penalty relief only relates to accuracy-related penalties. For penalty relief provided due to reasonable cause, a taxpayer must establish that he exercised ordinary business care and prudence, but was assessed a penalty due to circumstances beyond his control.

54. The answer is D. A disbarred practitioner may not practice before the IRS, except to represent himself. He may not represent a client. Practitioners who are disbarred in a disciplinary proceeding are not allowed to practice before the IRS. If a disbarred practitioner seeks reinstatement, he may not practice before the IRS until the Office of Professional Responsibility authorizes reinstatement.

55. The answer is B. A third party designee may respond to IRS notices about math errors, offsets, and return preparation. The taxpayer completes the Third Party Designee Authorization directly on the tax return, entering the designee's name and phone number and a self-selected five-digit PIN, which the designee will have to confirm when requesting information from the IRS. A third party designee may:
- Exchange information concerning the return with the IRS;
- Call the IRS for information about the processing of the return or the status of refund or payments;
- Request and receive written tax return information relating to the tax return, including copies of notices, correspondence, and account transcripts; and
- Respond to certain IRS notices about math errors, offsets, and return preparation.

The taxpayer is not authorizing the designee to receive any refund check, bind the taxpayer to any IRS contract or agreement (including additional tax liability), or otherwise represent the taxpayer before the IRS.

56. The answer is B. If Javier amends his 2012 return on or before April 18, 2016, it will be within the three-year statute of limitations and the return will be accepted. But if his amended 2012 return is postmarked after April 18, 2016, it will fall outside the three-year period and he will not receive a refund.

57. The answer is C. Circular 230's definition of practice before the IRS is broad, stating it "comprehends all matters connected with a presentation to the Internal Revenue Service or any of its officers or employees relating to a taxpayer's rights, privileges, or liabilities under laws or regulations administered" by the IRS. However, section 10.32 states "nothing in the regulations in this part may be construed as authorizing persons not members of the bar to practice law". This is included in Circular 230 to clarify that the provisions of Circular 230 do not allow non-attorneys to practice law. While not explicitly stated, rendering legal advice on a tax issue may be considered practice before the IRS.

58. The answer is D. The centralized authorization file (CAF) is the IRS's computer database that contains information regarding the authorizations that taxpayers have given representatives for their accounts. When either a Form 2848, *Power of Attorney or Declaration of Representation*, or Form 8821, *Tax Information Authorization*, is submitted to the IRS, it is processed for inclusion in the CAF and a CAF number is assigned to the tax practitioner or other authorized individual.

59. The answer is A. IRS examiners are instructed to work out times, dates, and locations that are convenient for the taxpayer. A taxpayer may request a change of venue as a matter of convenience (for example, if the taxpayer moved from California to New Jersey and his tax preparer was in California). However, the IRS has the right to make all final decisions regarding the timing and location of an audit.

60. The answer is B. A large and unexpected tax liability is not a sufficient reason to receive help from the Taxpayer Advocate Service (TAS). The TAS is a free and confidential service within the IRS whose goal is to help taxpayers resolve problems with other IRS divisions. It is independent of other divisions of the IRS. Other factors or situations affecting whether the TAS may offer assistance include the following:
- The taxpayer will suffer significant costs if relief is not granted;
- The taxpayer has experienced a delay of more than 30 days to resolve a tax issue;
- The taxpayer did not receive a response or resolution to his problem or inquiry by the date promised;

- A system or procedure has either failed to operate as intended, or failed to resolve the taxpayer's problem or dispute within the IRS; or
- The manner in which the tax laws are being administered raises considerations of equity, or it has impaired or will impair the taxpayer's rights.

61. The answer is C. A preparer does not have to actually submit the EITC worksheet, which computes the credit, to the IRS. He must keep it as part of his records. The records a preparer must retain are as follows:
- Form 8867, Paid Preparer's Earned Income Credit Checklist
- EITC worksheet(s) or his own worksheet
- Copies of any taxpayer documents he relied on to determine eligibility for or amount of EITC
- A record of how, when, and from whom the information used to prepare the form and worksheet(s) was obtained
- A record of any additional questions the preparer asked and his client's answers

All records should be kept for at least three years in either paper or electronic format, and they must be produced if the IRS asks for them.

62. The answer is D. The taxpayer cannot designate refunds for direct deposit to credit card accounts. Taxpayers often elect the direct deposit option because it is the fastest way of receiving refunds. Providers must accept a direct deposit election to any eligible financial institution designated by the taxpayer. The taxpayer may designate refunds to savings, checking, share draft, or consumer asset accounts (for example, IRA or money market accounts).

63. The answer is C. Under the regulations pertaining to IRC section 6662, sources of "substantial authority" of federal tax law include the following: provisions of the Internal Revenue Code, temporary and final regulations, court cases, administrative pronouncements, tax treaties, and Congressional intent as reflected in committee reports. This list was later expanded to include proposed regulations, private letter rulings, technical advice memoranda, IRS information or press releases, notices, and any other similar documents published by the IRS in the Internal Revenue Bulletin. The information in IRS publications is drawn from the Internal Revenue Code, Treasury regulations, and other primary sources of authority, but IRS publications themselves are not considered to have substantial authority. The same is true for IRS tax forms and instructions. The Internal Revenue Manual is essentially a policy and operations manual for IRS employees. It is an official compilation of policies, delegated authorities, procedures, instructions, and guidelines relating to the organization, functions, administration, and operations of the IRS, but it does not itself have substantial authority.

64. The answer is A. Rejected electronic individual income tax return data can be corrected and retransmitted without new signatures or authorizations if changes do not differ from the amounts of "total income", or "AGI", on the original electronic return by more than $50, or from the amounts of "total tax", "federal income tax withheld", "refund" or "amount you owe" by more than $14. However, the preparer must give a taxpayer a copy of the corrected tax return.

65. The answer is A. A family member can represent members of her immediate family. Immediate family means a spouse, child, parent, grandparent, grandchild, brother, or sister of the individual. Step-parents, step-children, step-brothers and step-sisters are also considered immediately family as well. Because of their special relationship, immediate family members can represent a taxpayer and practice before the IRS, provided they present satisfactory identification and proof of authority to do so. In this case, Cherie would need a signed Form 2848 with Abby's signature.

66. The answer is D. Natalie does not have to complete the full 72 hours of CPE required during this enrollment cycle since she was only an enrolled agent for two years. For renewal purposes, the annual CPE requirements only apply for the years during which someone was an enrolled agent. An EA who receives initial enrollment during an enrollment cycle must complete two CPE hours for each month enrolled during the enrollment cycle. Enrollment for any part of a month is considered enrollment for the entire month. In addition, an EA who receives their initial enrollment during an enrollment cycle must complete two CPE hours of ethics or professional conduct for each year enrolled during the enrollment cycle. Enrollment for any part of a year is considered enrollment for the entire year.

67. The answer is B. If an IRS examiner determines a section 6694 penalty applies:
- A detailed report is prepared
- The preparer is provided with a copy
- The preparer then has 30 days to request an appeal before the penalty is assessed.

68. The answer is C. Taxpayers have a number of options related to their tax refunds. They may:
- Apply a refund to next year's estimated tax.
- Receive the refund as a direct deposit.
- Receive the refund as a paper check.
- Split the refund, with a portion applied to next year's estimated tax and the remainder received as direct deposit or a paper check.
- Use the refund (or part of it) to purchase U.S. Series I Savings Bonds. Taxpayers can purchase up to $5,000 in bonds for themselves or others.

A tax refund cannot be used to purchase municipal bonds directly (only U.S. Savings Bonds).

69. The answer is C. The jurisdiction of the Tax Court does not include employment and certain excise taxes. The jurisdiction of the Tax Court includes:
- Income tax, estate tax, and gift tax
- Worker classification
- Innocent spouse claims
- Liens and levies
- Awards of administrative costs
- Enforcement of overpayments
- Redetermination of interest
- Modification of estate tax decisions
- Litigation costs awards
- Abatement of interest

70. The answer is D. The date of filing is not required. However, it is necessary to state the year or periods involved, such as "2014-2015 tax years". An IRS power of attorney must contain:
- The type of tax and the tax years covered
- The name and address of the representative
- The name and taxpayer identification (number of the taxpayer)
- The signatures of the representative and the taxpayer

The IRS will not accept a power of attorney if it does not contain all the information listed above.

71. The answer is C. In most cases, tax returns can be audited for up to three years after filing. However, the IRS may audit for up to six years if there is substantial unreported gross income.

72. The answer is D. The IRS must give a taxpayer reasonable notice before contacting other persons about his tax issues. This provision does not apply:
- To any pending criminal investigation
- When providing notice would jeopardize collection of any tax liability
- When providing notice may result in reprisal against any person
- When the taxpayer authorized the contact

73. The answer is B. If a practitioner uses direct mail, e-mail, fax communications, or other distribution methods to advertise, the provider must retain a copy of the advertisement, as well as a list or other description of the firms, organizations, or individuals to whom the communication was sent until the end of the calendar year following the last transmission or use. He must provide a copy to the IRS upon request.

74. The answer is D. The OPR can issue a notice for judicial proceedings for censure, suspension, or disbarment. It can also send a letter of reprimand to a preparer. Criminal penalties may be imposed on a tax preparer for fraudulent activity, but the OPR refers criminal activity to the IRS's own criminal division or to the Department of Justice for prosecution.

75. The answer is B. A taxpayer who files a tax return that is considered "frivolous" faces a penalty of $5,000, in addition to any other penalty provided by law. This penalty may be doubled on a joint return. A taxpayer will be subject to this penalty if he files a tax return based simply on the desire to interfere with the administration of tax law. The penalty for making frivolous arguments before the U.S. Tax Court is even steeper at $25,000.

76. The answer is A. Penny may appeal the termination of her installment agreement. If she appeals within a 30-day period after the termination, the IRS will be prohibited from levying her assets until her appeal is completed.

77. The answer is A. Tax protester positions are not the same as willful understatements of liability. If a preparer willfully understates a client's tax liability, he is subject to penalties. Under IRS regulations, understatement of liability means:
- Understating net tax payable
- Overstating the net amount creditable or refundable

78. The answer is A. A taxpayer is allowed to record the examination interview. The request to record the interview should be made in writing. The taxpayer or representative must notify the examiner ten days in advance and bring his own recording equipment. The IRS may also record an interview.

79. The answer is D. An individual who provides only typing, reproduction, or other mechanical assistance in the preparation of a return is not a tax return preparer and is not under the jurisdiction of Circular 230. Because she is not a paid preparer, she also would not be required to obtain a PTIN. The following are subject to Circular 230 jurisdiction, and thus to disciplinary oversight by the Office of Professional Responsibility:
- State licensed attorneys and CPAs who interact with federal tax administration at any level and capacity.
- Enrolled agents, enrolled retirement plan agents, and enrolled actuaries.
- Persons providing appraisals used in connection with tax matters (such as valuing estate and gift assets).
- Unlicensed individuals who represent taxpayers before the IRS examination division, IRS customer service, and Taxpayer Advocate Service in connection with returns they prepared and signed.
- Licensed and unlicensed individuals who give written advice that has the potential for tax avoidance or evasion.
- Any person submitting a power of attorney in connection with limited representation or special authorization to practice before the IRS in a specific matter before the agency.

80. The answer is B. Under Circular 230, a practitioner may not notarize documents for the clients he represents before the IRS. If the practitioner is a notary public and is employed as counsel, attorney, or agent in a matter before the IRS or has a material interest in the matter, he cannot engage in any notary activities relative to that matter. A practitioner is allowed to charge contingent fees in certain cases, but never for preparation of an original return. A practitioner may represent clients with a conflict of interest as long as it is disclosed in writing to all affected parties and all parties agree in writing. A practitioner may discuss and recommend tax shelters to a client, but the disclosure and ethics rules regarding tax shelters and tax shelter opinions are very strict.

81. The answer is B. A paid preparer is required by law to sign a tax return and fill in the preparer areas of the form. The preparer must also include his PTIN on the return, but is not required to include his Social Security number. Although the preparer signs the return, the client is ultimately responsible for the accuracy of every item on it.

82. The answer is C. An administrative law judge has 180 days to make a decision in a disciplinary case against a practitioner. The practitioner may appeal the decision to the Treasury Appellate Authority within 30 days after the decision. The OPR may also appeal the judge's decision, if a decision was reached in favor of the practitioner. In either case, the Treasury Appellate Authority will receive briefs and render what is known as the "Final Agency Decision". For the OPR, this decision is final, but the practitioner may contest the Final Agency Decision in a U.S. district court. The judge will review the findings from the administrative law hearing, but will only set aside the decision if it is considered arbitrary or capricious, contrary to law, or an abuse of discretion.

83. The answer is B. A Notice of Deficiency (90-day letter) must be issued before a taxpayer can go to the Tax Court. A taxpayer has 90 days from the date of the notice to respond and file a petition with the court. If a taxpayer fails to respond to the notice, she must pay the tax deficiency first and then sue the IRS for a refund in a U.S. district court or Court of Federal Claims.

84. The answer is D. A practitioner cannot prepare or sign a tax return if he lacks sufficient competence. Competence requires the appropriate level of knowledge, skill, thoroughness, and preparation. Circular 230 states that competence can be achieved by consulting with experts in the relevant area or by studying the relevant law.

85. The answer is B. Taxpayers may rely on revenue rulings as official IRS guidance on an issue. A taxpayer may use a revenue ruling as guidance in order to make a decision regarding taxable income, deductions, and how to avoid certain accuracy-related IRS penalties. However, revenue rulings may be challenged in court. Revenue rulings are official IRS interpretations and the IRS is bound by them, but the courts are not.

86. The answer is B. If a taxpayer does not pay his taxes by the due date, he will be subject to a failure-to-pay penalty of ½ of 1% (0.5%) of unpaid taxes for each month or part of a month after the due date that the taxes are not paid. This penalty can be as much as 25% of a taxpayer's unpaid taxes.

87. The answer is A. Under Circular 230, the definition of a tax return includes the following: an original return, an amended return, and a claim for a refund.

88. The answer is D. A PTIN cannot be shared. A PTIN is an individual preparer's number, so each preparer must obtain his own PTIN. A paid preparer who fails to include his PTIN on a return he has prepared for compensation faces a $50 fine per failure, up to a maximum of $25,000 per year.

89. The answer is D. Communications about the promotion of a tax shelter are not covered by the confidentiality privilege under section 7525. A tax shelter is any plan where the significant purpose of the plan is for the evasion or avoidance of tax.

90. The answer is D. The IRS may withhold an IRS record that falls under one of the FOIA's nine statutory exemptions, or one of three exclusions under the Act. The exemptions protect against the disclosure of information that would harm the following: national security, the privacy of individuals, the proprietary interests of business, the functioning of the government, and other important recognized interests.

91. The answer is A. Rajeev must first create an IRS e-Services account. He will need to supply personal information, including his Social Security number or other taxpayer identification number and his address where the IRS will mail confirmation of the account. This part of the application process can take up to 45 days. After the IRS approves his e-Services account, Rajeev will undergo a thorough IRS suitability check that may include a review of his criminal background, credit history, and tax compliance history. Only then will he be accepted as an authorized IRS e-file provider, an umbrella term for anyone authorized to participate in e-file, from software developers to transmitters. Preparers who want to e-file for clients must be approved as electronic return originators (ERO). The application to become an authorized e-file provider must also identify a firm's principals and at least one responsible official.

92. The answer is C. Form 8821 is not sufficient for representation work. Form 8821, *Tax Information Authorization*, is an information request form that only authorizes the disclosure of tax information. Form 2848 (or an alternative non-IRS power of attorney form) is required to represent a taxpayer before the IRS.

93. The answer is B. A practitioner may publish and advertise a fee schedule. A practitioner must adhere to the published fee schedule for at least 30 calendar days after it is published.

94. The answer is D. Currently not collectible status means the IRS has determined that a taxpayer has no ability to pay his tax debts and that other options, such as an installment agreement or offer in compromise, are not feasible. While a taxpayer is in status 53, all collection activities will be halted for at least one year, or until his income increases. Penalties and interest will continue to be added to the tax debt during this period.

95. The answer is A. Omar is in violation of section 10.23 of Circular 230, which states that a practitioner must not unreasonably delay the prompt disposition of any matter before the IRS. Omar's advice is an example of making a submission to delay or impede tax administration, because the IRS will not consider resolution of a collection action when a taxpayer is not in compliance.

96. The answer is A. Since Conner has principal authority for overseeing the firm's tax practice, he must take reasonable steps to ensure that adequate procedures are in place and are followed to comply with Circular 230. Under section 10.36, Conner could be subject to discipline if the violation is a result of willfulness, recklessness, or gross incompetence, and is part of a practice or pattern of failure to comply. Steps to demonstrate compliance with the oversight requirements of section 10.36 may include:
- Circular 230 training for all members of the department
- Requirements that other preparers' work is reviewed
- Periodic monitoring of compliance
- Written quality control procedures

97. The answer is B. Only a practitioner (generally, an enrolled agent, CPA, or tax attorney) with a signed power of attorney may represent a taxpayer at an IRS appeals conference. An unenrolled tax preparer may be a witness for a taxpayer at an appeals conference, but may not serve as a representative for the taxpayer. An unenrolled tax preparer may represent a taxpayer before IRS revenue agents, but not before revenue officers or appeals officers. For returns prepared after December 31, 2015, only unenrolled return preparers participating in the Annual Filing Season Record of Completion (AFSP) program may represent a taxpayer, and only with respect to returns prepared and signed by the preparer.

98. The answer is D. Anyone who receives compensation for preparing all (or substantially all) of a federal tax return (or claim for refund), including attorneys and certified public accountants, is required to obtain a PTIN. CPAs and attorneys who do not receive compensation for preparing tax returns, such as a CPA who only does audit work or an attorney who only does criminal defense, do not need to obtain a PTIN. However, all Enrolled Agents are required to have a PTIN, even if they do not prepare any tax returns.

99. The answer is B. The enrollment cycle refers to the three successive enrollment years preceding the effective date of renewal.

100. The answer is B. Most paid preparers are under a mandate to e-file tax returns. If a paid preparer is required to e-file a return, an additional form must be mailed along with the return. Tax returns prepared by a paid preparer but filed on paper must be submitted with Form 8948, *Preparer Explanation for Not Filing Electronically*. A reason must be provided for each return that is not e-filed. A taxpayer may decline to e-file.

About the Authors

Richard Gramkow, EA, MST

Richard Gramkow is an Enrolled Agent with more than eighteen years of experience in various areas of taxation. He holds a master's degree in taxation from Rutgers University and is currently a tax manager for a publicly held Fortune 500 company in the New York metropolitan area.

Christy Pinheiro, EA, ABA®

Christy Pinheiro is an Enrolled Agent and an Accredited Business Accountant. Christy was an accountant for two private CPA firms and for the State of California before going into private practice. She is a member of the California Society of Enrolled Agents and CalCPA.

Kolleen Wells, EA

Kolleen Wells is an Enrolled Agent and a Certified Bookkeeper who specializes in tax preparation for individuals and small businesses. She has worked in the accounting field for many years, including positions at a CPA office and at the county assessor's office.

Joel Busch, CPA, JD

Joel Busch is a professor of tax law at San Jose State University, where he teaches courses at both the graduate and undergraduate levels. Previously he was in charge of tax audits, research and planning for one of the largest civil construction and mining companies in the United States.

Made in the USA
San Bernardino, CA
14 January 2017